SORRY WORKS! 2.0

Disclosure, Apology, and Relationships
Prevent Medical Malpractice Claims

Doug Wojcieszak, James W. Saxton, and Maggie M. Finkelstein

Doug Wojcieszak

James W. Saxton, Esq.

Maggie M. Finkelstein, Esq.

Sally Saxton, Illustrator

authorHOUSE®

AuthorHouse™
1663 Liberty Drive
Bloomington, IN 47403
www.authorhouse.com
Phone: 1-800-839-8640

First published by AuthorHouse 2/27/2010

ISBN: 978-1-4389-6973-2 (sc)

Printed in the United States of America
Bloomington, Indiana

This book is printed on acid-free paper.

James W. Saxton has represented physicians and hospitals in state and federal courts for over 25 years. He is presently the Chairman of Stevens & Lee's Health Care Litigation Group and Co-Chair of the firm's Health Care Department. His practice includes litigation, risk reduction and representation of healthcare organizations and insurers.

Mr. Saxton uses his extensive experience as a litigator to advise health care providers throughout the United States in connection with understanding and reducing their professional liability risk by promoting excellence in patient satisfaction and incorporating certain loss control protocols. He develops risk reduction strategies for professional liability insurers nationwide and has created tools and educational programs to support them. Recently, this has extended to merging clinical and professional liability risk reduction strategies in high risk areas such as bariatric surgery and obstetrics. Mr. Saxton has also created a risk reduction tool for incorporation of the Electronic Medical Record. This also includes the creation of education and training on disclosure and apology that covers legal and insurance issues and cultural and ethical concerns.

Mr. Saxton has published more than 200 articles, several handbooks and seven textbooks. His recent work includes <u>Sorry Works! Disclosure, Apology and Relationships Prevent Medical Malpractice Claims</u>. Other works include, <u>The Satisfied Patient, Second Edition: A Guide to Preventing Malpractice Claims by Providing Excellent Customer Service</u>; <u>Five-Star Customer Service: A Step-by-Step Guide for Physician Practices</u>; and <u>15 Policies and Procedures to Reduce Liability for Physician Practices</u>, published by HCPro, Inc.

Mr. Saxton lectures frequently and is an invited speaker across the country on health care issues, including liability reduction and risk management and disclosure and apology, and presents to prominent health care organizations such as the American College of Surgeons, the American Society for Metabolic and Bariatric Surgery, American Health Lawyers Association The American Society for Healthcare Risk Management, and The American Association of Physician Insurers. Mr. Saxton is a fellow of the College of Physicians of Philadelphia, the oldest professional medical organization in the country, and is on the Board of Directors and Executive Committee for the Surgical Review Corporation and Surgical Excellence, LLC.

Mr. Saxton is the past chair of the American Health Lawyers Association's Healthcare Liability and Litigation Practice Group and a member of numerous professional associations. He received a J.D. from Duquesne University (1982) and a B.A. from Shippensburg State University (1979).

Maggie M. Finkelstein is a shareholder with Stevens & Lee's healthcare litigation and risk management group. She concentrates her practice in health law with a focus on loss control, event management, and disclosure for physicians, hospitals, staff, and long-term care communities. She has developed risk reduction opportunities in the health care industry and has evaluated various specialty-specific liability risk issues including the risk associated with bariatric surgery, obstetrics, and gastroenterology. Ms. Finkelstein works with captive professional liability insurers in controlling risk. She has also been involved in the creation of new insurance vehicles and companies geared to liability risk reduction. She has defended physicians, hospitals, and long-term care communities in both federal and state courts.

Ms. Finkelstein is a member of the American Health Lawyers Association and regularly publishes on loss control and risk management topics, including disclosure after an adverse event, liability risk reduction, patient accountability, and patient satisfaction. Publications have included books, handbooks, and book chapters. She is the co-author of Sorry Works! Disclosure, Apology and Relationships Prevent Medical Malpractice Claims; Five-Star Customer Service: A Step-by-Step Guide for Physician Practices; 15 Policies and Procedures to Reduce Liability for Physician Practices; *"Bariatric Surgery: A Comprehensive Bariatric Program Can Act to Reduce Liability Risks and to Promote Patient Safety"*; *"The New Universal Protocol: Can Adhesive Labels Prevent Wrong Site Surgery and Reduce Liability Risks?"*; and Minimizing Endoscopic Complications: Gastrointestinal Endoscopy Clinics of North America.

Prior to joining Stevens & Lee, she was a law clerk for the Honorable William W. Caldwell in the U.S. District Court for the Middle District of Pennsylvania and worked as a chemistry technician and microbiologist at Johnston Laboratories. Ms. Finkelstein is also a registered patent attorney with the U.S. Patent and Trademark Office.

Ms. Finkelstein graduated *summa cum laude* from Widener University School of Law (2000) and received a B.S. in Biology from Pennsylvania State University (1992).

**Doug Wojcieszak** is a disclosure training consultant who has had several personal and professional experiences with tort reform and medical malpractice issues. He lost his oldest brother to medical errors in 1998, and his family successfully sued the hospital and doctors, with the case settling in 2000. The hospital attorneys apologized to Wojcieszak's family, but only after the case was settled and money exchanged hands, and they never admitted fault for the incident.

Around the same time his brother's case was concluding, Wojcieszak left his employment with the Illinois House Republicans and accepted the position of executive director of Illinois Lawsuit Abuse Watch (I-LAW), a grassroots, pro-tort reform group. He was able to place over 200 positive stories about lawsuit abuse and capping lawsuit damages with TV, radio, and print media throughout Illinois. During his time with I-LAW, Wojcieszak also first read and studied full-disclosure methods for medical errors as a way to lower malpractice lawsuits and liability costs as well as reduce medical errors.

Wojcieszak left I-LAW in 2001 and returned to the Illinois House Republicans for a brief stint, after which he founded a public relations consulting firm: Tactical Consulting. The firm has had several clients, including a pro-plaintiffs group, Victims and Families United (VAFU). Wojcieszak served as the group's spokesperson in 2004 and touted traditional plaintiffs/anti-tort reform messages such as insurance reform and increased doctor discipline. However, while representing VAFU, Wojcieszak revisited full-disclosure methods and created a marketing term — "Sorry Works!" — to successfully promote apologies for medical errors as the solution to the medical malpractice crisis.

Wojcieszak was able to place over 50 stories about Sorry Works! during 2004 with numerous media outlets, including the *Chicago Tribune, St. Louis Post-Dispatch,* and CNBC, and a worldwide story through the Associated Press. He noticed that Sorry Works! while agreeable to many trial lawyers, also attracted the interest and support of many doctors and insurers. These observations led Wojcieszak to create a new, separate group — The Sorry Works! Coalition — in February 2005 solely dedicated to promoting Sorry Works! and full-disclosure methods as a middle-ground solution to the malpractice crisis. He currently serves as the group's spokesperson.

The Sorry Works! Coalition has grown quickly to nearly 4,000 members nationwide, the website has received over four million hits, and the group has been publicized in countless popular and trade publications, including *Time Magazine, National Review, National Law Journal,* and *American Medical Association News.*

Sorry Works! has become the nation's leading organization advocating full-disclosure as a middle-ground solution to the medical malpractice crisis, and the group's website has become the site for information and updates on the full-disclosure movement.

In his speeches on Sorry Works! Wojcieszak teaches healthcare, insurance, and legal professionals what patients and families want most after adverse events and bad outcomes: honesty, accountability, communication, and a real commitment to fix problems. Wojcieszak has given his talks to prominent medical, healthcare, and insurance organizations throughout the United States.

Sorry Works! 2.0

Disclosure, Apology, and Relationships Prevent Medical Malpractice Claims
by Doug Wojcieszak, James W. Saxton, Esq., and Maggie M. Finkelstein, Esq.

ACKNOWLEDGEMENT

The authors wish to personally thank each reader for their interest in this important topic. It is our hope that the information and strategies in this book will allow physicians, nurses, all clinicians, hospitals, long-term care facilities, healthcare organizations, insurers, and attorneys to embrace enhanced communication and disclosure after an adverse event. The benefit will inure not only to all of these healthcare individuals and facilities, but also to your patients, residents, and their families.

Special thanks are extended to Stevens & Lee, who has truly made a commitment to not only represent healthcare professionals, but also to understanding how important topics like safety and communication can impact their practice and business. Thanks to members and friends of The Sorry Works! Coalition for their strong support of this endeavor and their consistent efforts to further the disclosure and apology movement. To the many individuals who provided assistance, particularly Cynthia Burry, Amy Matthias, and Gynith Shaeffer of Stevens & Lee, we extend our thanks.

Many thanks are also extended to Press Ganey, particularly Matt Mulherin and Dr. Melvin Hall; Neil Hutcher, M.D.; Pat Sedlak, Sr. Vice President - Marsh USA ; Sheila Warren, CPHQ; F. Dean Griffen, M.D.; and Flip Corboy, Esq., for their contributions and reviews of the book. They are not only highly respected colleagues, but also friends, and we express our gratitude to each of them. A special thanks to Dr. David Dillman for his insights into improving the readability of the text.

We thank our very talented artist, Sally Saxton, who created the book illustrations, capturing many of the critical moments in time. As they say, a picture paints a thousand words. Use them as reminders of this important topic.

Ms. Finkelstein personally thanks her husband for his strong support and interest as well as her parents and siblings for their support throughout the years.

Mr. Wojcieszak personally thanks Dr. Steve Kraman for his guidance, honest opinions, and friendship over the last four years. Mr. Wojcieszak also thanks his wife, brother, and business partner for all of their support, and a special to thank you to Mom and Dad for always teaching that good can come out of bad.

FOREWORD

by James W. Saxton, Esq.
Chairman, Health Care Litigation Group
Co-Chair, Health Care Group
Stevens & Lee

E-mail: jws@stevenslee.com

Sorry Works! . . . works, but don't think about it as a name, but rather as a concept. It really does work. Concern about the concept most likely stems from confusing the concept of showing empathy and compassion versus an apology where one accepts responsibility. Both are important, but very different concepts. Many lawyers, risk managers, and insurance professionals thought that "sorry" meant one was somehow admitting liability or that they had done something "wrong," perhaps accepting responsibility. This concern was enough to make many pause . . . some from even interacting with patients and family after an unfortunate outcome. Laws had to be passed so doctors could say, "I'm sorry," without being somehow made to also have admitted fault!

We're making it too hard. Sorry Works! works when there is an adverse outcome. Everyone is sorry, as they should be. Everyone wants to show empathy, which is a basic human response and need. It is a little sad that this concept has become at all controversial. Admittedly, with the phrase, "I'm sorry," there is room for misinterpretation, all the way around and probably in good faith. A doctor could misinterpret the concept, thinking this means he or she is accepting responsibility for a known complication of a procedure or for failing to meet patient expectations. That is not the case. Patients may think "I'm sorry" means that someone did something wrong. Insurance companies may think it means that they will be required to make a payment. These conclusions underscore the importance of education and institution of a process and a program.

To be clear, "sorry," or showing empathy, *works* by making a difficult situation a little better nearly 100% of the time. It does not mean the pain, discomfort, and expenses that go along with an adverse outcome will go away. Of course not. It does not mean 100% of the time the patient will not go to a lawyer or not consider a lawsuit. However, it does make these very difficult situations a little better almost 100% of the time. "Sorry" works.

At times, an apology and literally accepting responsibility for an error needs to happen. An apology that includes acceptance and ownership is powerful and important and far better than the alternative of years of contentious public litigation in many situations. However, it is admittedly more complex. Sometimes it is hard to quickly determine fault (meaning responsibility). In America and other similar countries where there is not a "no-fault system," we need to be thoughtful about the method. Further, once we accept responsibility, sometimes it is difficult to determine value. Determining value for inherently subjective damages is challenging, but can be accomplished. Do lawyers help? Maybe, but not all the time. Some would argue that the transactional cost of a settlement with a lawyer and full blown litigation has climbed rather high. If we had the 50% transactional costs and expenses and settled with a family three years earlier, we could certainly do a lot of good. However, sometimes lawyers do help, a lot.

Think of Sorry Works! first as a concept...the act of kindness, caring, and reaching out to the patient and family after an adverse event. Part of that process will be expressing sorrow: *"I'm so sorry your mother suffered from this complication."* We will show you how this can be done appropriately without admitting fault prematurely. We will show you how it actually makes the entire situation better for the providers even if the event moves forward to litigation. We will also explain when it is appropriate to apologize and accept responsibility, and how to do so.

Let's not get bogged down with why it may not work, but instead discuss how we can thoughtfully make it happen. Doug Wojcieszak knows firsthand, and the hard way, how badly Sorry Works! is needed. He and his family went through it. In chapter one, he will share with you his story.

Our team of healthcare litigators, along with risk managers, jury consultants, psychologists, and physicians, in collaboration with insurers and hospitals across the country, has dealt with this issue time and time again. The Sorry Works! Coalition and Stevens & Lee have collaborated to put forth this straightforward book on this concept often referred to as disclosure, and a concept we feel is really a subset of "enhanced communication post-adverse event." We will go through what Sorry Works! is and what it is not - why it works and most importantly how it works. We have done so only after seeing it work for many, many doctors, hospitals, insurers, and, critically important, patients. We have talked to the "naysayers" and worked through the concept with them as well. Many have found out how important this concept is the hard way — in court. You need not.

We can tell you that since the release of the first edition of Sorry Works! this sub-group has shrunk in size considerably. We have rolled out this concept to hospitals, health systems, physician practices, state medical associations, and on behalf of many professional liability insurers. The response has been overwhelmingly positive! It is taking hold!

However, there is more work to be done with post adverse event communication by not only doctors, insurers, hospitals, but…patients. This is going to be more of a focus in 2010 (see Chapter 8). There is clearly a job for patients here. We must get patients on the same side of the table as our doctors post-adverse event. It really works better when, at least initially, patients go to their doctors first. Also, it is important to understand that Sorry Works! or disclosure and apology does not just happen. Like so many things in life, there needs to be a process, a method, a plan, and execution steps. That is where this book has and can continue to help.

If you ever sat through a meeting with a doctor and a patient after heartfelt empathy is exchanged with everyone in the room crying and yet everyone in the room feeling better, you would understand that "sorry" works for everyone. Let's get started.

James W. Saxton

"After walking through the storm together, there is a strong sense of relief as the clouds lift."

PREFACE

This book is, in part, adapted from speeches I have given to medical, insurance, and legal organizations across the United States and in Australia and Canada over the last several years. Liability exposure has been a major issue for healthcare and insurance professionals for a long time, and they are looking for new solutions to an old problem. More and more doctors, nurses, risk managers, hospital administrators, and insurance executives are turning to Sorry Works! for answers. I thought it was time to put Sorry Works! in a book that was concise and to the point. Along the way I met and had the pleasure of working with James Saxton and his team at the law firm of Stevens & Lee. It was fascinating to me how as lawyers and health law consultants they were spreading the same message. To make sure this message was well grounded in law and risk management principles, we collaborated, and this book is part of that partnership. This book adequately covers the topic of disclosure and apology but has intentionally been kept short so even the busiest professional could read it on a plane ride or over a weekend.

Though Sorry Works! has its roots in medicine, it is my hope that this book finds a wider audience in corporations, the small business community, and other sectors of our society that are concerned about litigation. I also hope the book appears in college and medical and law school course syllabi so future doctors, lawyers, and business people can read, discuss, and debate it. Indeed, if Sorry Works! can *work* in medical malpractice (often thought to be one of the most contentious and expensive litigation arenas) imagine what it can do elsewhere! Moreover, though Sorry Works! is a process and program, it also a way of life universal to all people. Indeed, Sorry Works! returns us to our parents' lessons about apology and fixing mistakes.

People can actually live with mistakes, but they do not accept or tolerate cover-ups. Sorry Works! taps into this psyche and, in doing so, provides a simple yet devastatingly effective way to reduce litigation and associated expenses while improving outcomes and safety, which further decreases litigation exposure. The keys are honesty, candor, and a real commitment to fix problems when something goes wrong. All three elements must be present to prevent conflict, and Sorry Works! shows you how to do it.

I hope you find this book useful as well as enjoyable and welcome your feedback at doug@sorryworks.net or by calling 618-559-8168. Thank you!

Doug Wojcieszak
Founder/Spokesperson
The Sorry Works! Coalition
www.sorryworks.net

CHAPTER 1

SORRY WORKS! WHEN IT ALL STARTED

On May 5, 1998, my oldest brother, Jim Wojcieszak, walked into a Cincinnati, Ohio hospital at two in the morning complaining of chest, shoulder, neck, and stomach pains. Jim was a big, burly man…the kind of guy who was asked to play football in high school, so he shouldered pain extremely well. For Jim to show up in an emergency room at 2:00 a.m. with no prodding from Mom and Dad meant he was in *excruciating* pain.

Jim told the attending physician he was either having the worst case of indigestion he had ever had or he was suffering a heart attack. Jim had a temperature of 101.4° F, and the physician detected a "slight" heart murmur. Jim told the physician he had no history of heart murmurs. The physician told my brother that at age 39 he was too young to be having a heart attack, and he must be suffering from indigestion or stomach flu. However, the physician never drew blood to rule out a heart attack — he just assumed because of my brother's age and physical appearance that nothing was amiss. How we wish he had been right.

The doctor started an IV for the pain and also administered an ulcer cocktail. Jim's pain persisted, but they released him anyway at 5:45 a.m. A few hours later, Jim called my parents complaining that he could not sleep. He could not lay on his back or his side; the pain was simply too great. Furthermore, he was coughing and spitting up blood. Mom and Dad quickly picked up Jim and took him to their family physician.

Our family physician became excited quickly. He said the emergency room "dropped the ball." Jim didn't have a "slight" heart murmur — he had a significant heart murmur. Moreover, the oxygen levels in Jim's blood were dangerously low. Our doctor said that Jim would probably be in the ICU by that evening, and he sent Jim and my parents back to the same hospital.

Back to the hospital they went. My father dropped Jim and Mom off at the emergency room and parked the car in a lot far from the hospital. Jim and Mom walked into the emergency room, but there was no one there to greet them or help them. Mom told Jim to sit down in the waiting room, and she walked quickly down a long hall to the main entrance of the hospital to get help, but no one was at the hospital's main reception desk either. So, she went back down the long hall to the emergency room waiting area, where she bumped into two nurses who were bringing in coffee. Around this time, Dad finally arrived from the parking lot, and both he and Mom noticed that Jim had fallen asleep in the waiting room because his oxygen levels were so low. My parents were shocked and upset at how there was a total lack of urgency in the emergency room.

Jim was eventually admitted, and this time the hospital staff drew Jim's blood, and, sure enough, the enzyme was present in the blood showing the heart was in distress. When quizzed by my dad why blood was not drawn when Jim was in the emergency room at 2 a.m., an ER resident quipped, *"Remember, this is the art of medicine, and Jim is a young man."*

The doctors told my parents that Jim had a bacterial infection of the heart that was attacking his mitral valve. They had begun administering a broad spectrum of antibiotics, and surgery may be needed in several weeks to repair damage, but only after the bacterial infection had cleared. Jim was admitted to the ICU.

The ICU was the site of a second, serious mistake. The computer monitor over Jim's bed read *"Ray Wojcieszak."* Who's Ray? That's my dad. This was a critical fact because Dad had a heart stress test performed in the same hospital a few months prior to Jim being admitted, and even though Dad was in his sixties at the time, the cardiologist said he had the heart of a 30-year-old man. No blockage. Low cholesterol. Excellent cardiac health.

So, there was my dad arguing with the attending physician about who was who — the attending physician was convinced that Ray was in the bed — and having to produce driver's licenses to prove he was indeed Ray and the man in the bed was Jim. The staff changed the name on the computer monitor to read *"Jim Wojcieszak,"* but we believe they were still probably looking at Dad's charts showing no blockage, low cholesterol, and excellent cardiac health. In short, they used Dad's charts to form their diagnosis of a bacterial infection of Jim's heart.

Later that evening, the physicians prescribed nitroglycerin for the pain in Jim's chest and back, but the pain persisted. In fact, Jim could not lie down in a bed. Laying on his side or back was excruciatingly painful. So, they propped him up in a special chair, but the pain still continued. They said the antibiotics needed time to clear the bacterial infection and the pain would decrease over time.

The next morning, the attending physician and a cardiac specialist visited and informed Jim and my parents that a valve would need to be replaced in his heart once the bacterial infection cleared. However, they assured our family that a valve replacement was a "*straightforward*" operation and not to worry. Shortly after the physicians left, the nurse told Jim he would soon receive lunch, which made him happy because he was very hungry. Two hours later lunch had still not arrived. When my parents called the nurse to inquire about lunch, she told them it had been forgotten.

After eating lunch, Jim needed to use the bathroom for a bowel movement. He beeped the nurse, and she came down to his room — but she was not the regular nurse. The substitute nurse helped Jim out of bed and had him walk across the room to the bathroom, and then she helped him walk back to his chair after using the bathroom. Shortly after she left, Jim started coughing and spitting up blood. When the oxygen sensor was put back on his finger, alarms went off and his regular nurse increased his oxygen levels, but Jim still had trouble breathing.

Later that afternoon, Jim tried to use the bathroom again, this time to urinate, and his regular nurses caught him and gave him a tongue lashing for walking in his room. She informed him that ICU patients in his condition do not get out of bed. So, why did the substitute nurse allow him to walk?

Around 7:00 p.m., two physicians who neither Jim nor my parents had seen before entered Jim's room and examined him. They learned that Jim was a smoker, and one of the physicians said that Jim looked like *"shit,"* which upset my mother greatly. They reconfirmed the diagnosis of a bacterial infection and said that Jim's condition was unchanged from the day before, even though oxygen alarms were sounding and he was spitting up blood.

Through the evening, the oxygen alarms kept sounding every so often, and Jim continued to cough up blood. At 2 a.m., my mother called the hospital to see how Jim was doing, and the nurse informed her Jim was not doing well. When my mother asked what else could be done, the nurse abruptly terminated the conversion.

The next afternoon — the last day of Jim's life — his face was puffy and swollen. He was exhausted because he had not slept for three days. And he was scared. Around mid-afternoon, tests were ordered to run a probe up his groin to see if anything had been missed around the heart. A nurse told my parents, *"We're finally going to do something for this young man! We're going to take action!"* My parents were shocked and thought to themselves, *"What do you mean you're going to finally do something? What have you people been doing for the last two days?"*

The test showed one major artery blocked 95% or better and three other arteries blocked 60% or better. Furthermore, one of his heart valves was completely destroyed. Three physicians told my parents that surgery would be needed in the next day or so, but not to worry. The lead physician patted my mother's hand and said, *"Mother, don't worry, Jim will have a normal and healthy life . . . we fix people."*

However, a few minutes later, the three doctors rushed back to my parents and with hurried, excited voices informed them that Jim was crashing. The nurses were putting him on a ventilator and preparing him for surgery, and the doctors hustled my parents to see Jim. Mom and Dad saw Jim for a brief moment, during which Jim screamed not to let them put him on a machine. Those were his last words.

An hour later, the surgeon arrived at the hospital and spoke with my parents. To my parents' disbelief, the surgeon said he did not think Jim would make it off the operating table. He left to scrub in, and nurses escorted my parents to a waiting room. The nurses kept using the word "*grave*" to describe Jim's condition, and they insisted that Mom eat some high-calorie food so she could endure the "*long, terrible night ahead.*"

A few hours later, the ER resident who had quipped about the "*art of medicine*" and had been part of the original team of physicians that diagnosed Jim with a bacterial infection informed my parents that Jim's ear lobes and fingertips were blue by the time he was put on the heart-lung machine. Unbelievably, the resident had a smile on his face when he delivered this news to them! He then abruptly halted the conversation, saying he had to run home to his three children. Unbelievable.

My parents were in a waiting room with their pastor and close friends. The nurses kept coming in every half hour or so to say the situation was very, very grave. My mother knew Jim was going to die. She felt very hot and flush and kept visiting the woman's bathroom to splash cold water on her face and lean against a cold wall; then she would return to the waiting room. On one return trip to the waiting room she bumped into the cardiologist who had diagnosed Jim with a bacterial infection of the heart. When the cardiologist saw my mother, his eyes widened and he immediately turned around and began walking quickly in the other direction and darted down another hall. My mother, who raised three boys and knows how to catch men, tracked him down. She demanded to know what had happened. The cardiologist began stumbling around, picking at his hands, and mumbling that the bacterial infection prevented surgery from happening sooner. But then why were they operating now if Jim still had a bacterial infection? The nervous, distraught doctor made no sense and only angered my mother further.

Less than two hours later, Jim was dead.

The surgeon, who had not been involved in Jim's care prior to the surgery, walked out of the operating room in surgical garb and told my father the following in a very angry tone: "*If the jerks at this hospital had done their job and gotten your son to me two days ago when they should have I could have saved him — no problem. We do bypass surgeries all the time, and your son would be on his way to recovery, but he is dead. I'm sorry.*"

My father and the surgeon spoke extensively about the diagnosis of a bacterial infection, and the surgeon said the heart tissue had no signs of bacterial infection or his stitches would not have held. Furthermore, the surgeon was shocked by the treatment Jim had received. The surgeon suggested an autopsy.

The autopsy was performed, and no sign of bacterial infection was found. Official cause of death: Heart attack.

The same day the autopsy results arrived, we also received a sympathy card from the hospital addressed to Mrs. Jim Wojcieszak. Jim was not married.

After the funeral and all the relatives and friends went home, my parents went back to the hospital seeking answers, especially my father, the Ph.D. engineer. *"What happened? Why did it happen? Can the processes be improved so it never happens again?"* These were all questions my parents — especially my dad — had. But the door was unceremoniously slammed in their face. Meetings were promised, but did not transpire. Even the surgeon who was so honest the night Jim died told my parents: *"Look, our legal counsel has instructed me not speak with you any further. You will have to leave."*

Here was my father, who made a living asking countless questions and improving processes so aircraft engines and nuclear-powered naval vessels would be safe, being not-so-politely told to butt out of his own son's death. *"None of your business — get lost."* Maddening.

This deny-and-defend, circle-the-wagons routine made my parents extremely angry. It made litigation, which should have been the last recourse, the only option available to us. It made money, which should have been the third or fourth concern, the only issue worth fighting over. So, we filed a lawsuit.

I remember receiving calls from my parents any time our plaintiff attorney called them. Getting a call from the lawyer's office was good — somebody was taking them seriously. Somebody cared. Somebody wanted to do something.

However, the defense depositions of my parents were a nightmare. At one point, my mother was crying so hard our attorney stopped the deposition, at which time one defense attorney turned to one of his colleagues and started chatting about his kid's soccer team. My father was furious at this callous behavior.

My parents described the overall litigation experience as a hellish episode of reliving their son's death every day for a year and a half. They thought the process was going to cause them to have heart attacks! Indeed, filing a lawsuit was not a "lottery ticket" or a game. They simply wanted answers, justice, and for the medical system to improve so the mistakes would not be repeated.

After a year and a half of litigation in Cincinnati (not a "judicial hellhole" by any stretch of the imagination), the judge literally turned to the hospital, doctors, and their attorneys and proclaimed they were wasting the court's time, malpractice was clear, and they should settle with our family.

At that point, the lawyers and insurers came up with the brilliant idea of offering our family a few thousand dollars, which angered the judge, and he demanded they make a good faith effort to settle the case before wasting any more of his time.

We received a sizeable settlement, which is sealed. After money exchanged hands and my parents signed the liability waiver, the *attorneys* — not the physicians — "apologized," but no one ever admitted fault. Furthermore, no one ever took ownership of the mistakes, nor did they tell us how the hospital and doctors were going to improve their processes so the same mistakes would never be repeated.

Despite the fact our family received money — what tort reformers consider the holy grail of medical malpractice — we still have not found peace more than a decade after Jim's death. We are still angry with the doctors who have never sought us out and apologized, even though they have no further liability in our case (we cannot sue them anymore). Furthermore, we believe the errors that killed Jim are injuring and killing other patients today. In short, my family never received closure, but I also believe the doctors, nurses, and hospital executives who were involved in Jim's care didn't receive closure either. They probably are good people who made a series of terrible mistakes…mistakes that will haunt them for the rest of their lives because they never apologized. Indeed, *maddening*.

That's my personal story that led to the development of Sorry Works! However, the creation of Sorry Works! also includes my professional life. I am a public relations and political consultant. I started my career working in the Illinois legislature on the Republican side of the aisle as a staff member. I worked on tort reform issues, and around the time my brother's case was being litigated, I was offered a job as the state-wide director of a pro-tort reform group aptly named "Illinois Lawsuit Abuse Watch." When I was interviewing for the job, I told the people on the other side of the table about Jim's case, and they universally replied, "*Oh, we believe in legitimate litigation, but it's the frivolous, wacky lawsuits that delay justice for good people like you and your family.*" They offered the job, and I accepted.

I started working for Illinois Lawsuit Abuse Watch – or I-LAW – in November 1999, and a month later the first scholarly paper on the benefits of disclosure and apology was published by Dr. Steve Kraman and Ginny Hamm, JD of the Lexington, Kentucky, Veterans Affairs (VA) Hospital.[1] In short, the paper said that the litigation experience at their hospital appeared to improve by disclosing, apologizing, and compensating patients and families after legitimate medical errors. That paper really spoke to me. It was common sense. So, I took the paper to my boss in the Illinois tort reform movement. I was convinced that this idea of disclosure could benefit the doctors, healthcare organizations, and insurers that funneled so much money into the tort reform movement — as well as patients and families.

My boss responded, "*Doug, we should never tell a doctor that he or she is wrong.*"

I was flabbergasted. "*You know my story…you know what happened to my brother,*" I rebutted. "*Of course doctors make mistakes…the question*

---

1   Kraman, S., MD, and Hamm, G., JD. "Risk Management: Extreme Honesty May Be the Best Policy." *Annals of Internal Medicine.* 1999:131(12); 963-967.

is are those mistakes going to be litigated or is there a better way? I believe this paper shows us a better way…it makes a lot of sense to me."

To which my boss replied, *"Well, Doug, you can take a trip down to the AMA or Illinois State Medical Society, but I can't guarantee you'll have a job when you get back."*

I was 29 years old and living in Chicago with bills to pay, so I dropped the idea and got back to the tort reform hymnal of capping damages and beating up the plaintiff's bar. However, my eyes had been opened to the realities of medical malpractice politics.

I worked for I-LAW for a year and then went back to the Illinois legislature for a short stint, after which time I formed my own public relations firm. The plaintiff's bar in Illinois knew that I could talk about litigation issues, and they asked if I could tell their side of story in the Illinois medical malpractice debate. I said *"sure"* because they did have a story to tell. Through my PR firm, we talked about typical plaintiff concerns of increasing doctor discipline and reforming insurance companies; however, I revisited the disclosure issue. This time I had a chance to talk with Dr. Steve Kraman at the VA and other people involved in disclosure. My firm developed the term "Sorry Works!" to describe the process of apology and disclosure after medical errors, and we began attracting media coverage in Illinois. Some funny things started to happen.

Trial lawyers said Sorry Works! fit with how they were trained in law school to get justice for their clients. My clients told me that despite all the bad things said in the media about trial lawyers being greedy ambulance chasers, they were trained as advocates to always seek four things for patients and families: Answers, accountability, fixes, and swift justice. To them, Sorry Works! delivered in all four areas, and they encouraged our firm to continue forward.

However, we also started receiving calls from healthcare and insurance professionals, and the conversation on the other end of the line was always a little strained and awkward: *"Hey, Benedict Arnold, I mean, Doug, we know you traded us in for the trial lawyers, but this Sorry Works! stuff is really interesting. Where can we get some more information?"*

As a political professional I knew we were on to something. Sorry Works! is truly a middle-ground solution to the medical malpractice crisis. It is rare to find solutions to highly polarized debates that provide all sides what they want most, but this is exactly what Sorry Works! appeared to be able to do: Fewer lawsuits and better control over liability exposure for healthcare and insurance professionals; swift justice with no constitutional limits for patients, families, and their attorneys; and safer healthcare, which benefits everyone.

> **"Sorry Works! is truly a middle-ground solution to the medical malpractice crisis... Fewer lawsuits and better control over liability exposure for healthcare and insurance professionals; swift justice with no constitutional limits for patients, families, and their attorneys; and safer healthcare, which benefits everyone."**

So, in February 2005, my PR firm helped organize The Sorry Works! Coalition as a nationwide group of healthcare, insurance, and legal professionals as well as patients, families, and consumers. I currently serve as the group's spokesperson.

As a reader you may say, *"Well, Wojcieszak, you have quite a story. I'm sorry to hear about your brother...don't like to hear about such tragic cases. And you certainly do have an interesting professional background having worked for both tort reformers* **and** *the trial bar, but nowhere in the last few pages did I read that you're a physician, lawyer, or insurance professional. You've never treated anyone, you've never defended a doctor or hospital against a lawsuit, nor have you had to write a claims check. So, if you've never walked in our shoes, how you can write anything in the pages to follow that is going to have any credibility or relevance to me? We in healthcare usually only take advice from our colleagues."*

Here's my perspective...I'm the patient...I'm the family member...I'm the *customer*, and the *customer* perspective is a critical issue in the medical malpractice crisis. Several major hospitals and insurers have figured out this simple fact, and by instituting a disclosure program they have significantly reduced lawsuits and litigation expenses. For example, the University of Michigan Health System (the largest hospital system in Michigan) has cut lawsuits in half, reduced litigation expenses by two-thirds (or $2 million annually), and reduced their insurance reserves from $72 million in 2001 to less than $20 million in 2007.[2] Similar positive figures about disclosure and apology programs are being reported by the University of Illinois Medical Center, Catholic Healthcare West, Kaiser Hospitals, the VA Hospitals, COPIC Insurance, and others. The Sorry Works! Coalition was created in 2005 to share these success stories and to encourage more hospitals, insurance companies, and providers to embrace disclosure and apology.

Further, in 2006, I made the connection with James Saxton of the law firm of Stevens & Lee. Jim is a trial lawyer by training and has spent over 25 years defending doctors and hospitals in the courtroom. He and the firm of Stevens & Lee have been at the forefront of helping to create insurance companies and advise physicians and hospitals on disclosure issues. I was surprised but pleased to hear Jim at a national program say that doctors must begin to move up the five-star curve and that enhanced communication post-disclosure was critical. It was clear to me that collaboration was key. Since then, we have spoken at the same programs and work together on cutting-edge programs and tools to make Sorry Works! work. In fact, this book is one of those collaborations. We understand that disclosure is only a part of a larger picture – effective communication, patient safety and patient rights are also critical components.

Healthcare professionals need to understand — and this book will teach — that people can actually live with mistakes, even serious mistakes, if the offending party is honest, candid, and quick to offer

---

2   Boothman, R. Presentation to the New Jersey Council of Teaching Hospitals, October 2006.

reasonable solutions. However, people cannot live with, accept, or tolerate cover-ups. This intolerance of cover-ups is amplified when it involves our health or the well-being of a loved one we entrusted to a medical professional.

"That doctor won't return my phone calls... the nurses won't look me in the eye... no one will give me answers or level with me... just what the hell is going on here?"

It is precisely this anger that pushes *customers* to call a lawyer. Remember, most folks do not like lawyers, so a *customer* has to be extremely angry to pick up the phone and call a lawyer. Also, remember this one simple truism: The most successful trial lawyer is powerless without an angry *customer* calling them.

Review Points:

- ◆ Anger and the need for information causes patients and families to call a plaintiff's lawyer.
- ◆ An apology and disclosure program can benefit healthcare professionals, patients and families.
- ◆ Disclosure is part of an effective patient safety program.

CHAPTER 2

WHAT "I'M SORRY!" IS...AND IS NOT

Contemptible — Sad — Pitiful — Contrite — Pathetic. These are synonyms for "sorry."[3] Given the connotations of these words, it is no wonder that some healthcare professionals are apprehensive in saying, *"I'm sorry."*

"Sorry" is defined by Merriam-Webster as:

1. "feeling sorrow, regret, or penitence"
2. "mournful, sad"
3. "inspiring sorrow, pity, scorn, or ridicule: pitiful"[4]

As with many words in the English language, the word "sorry" can have several meanings, and that is what can bring confusion to saying, "I'm sorry," in the context of healthcare. If a doctor says, "I'm sorry," and the patient interprets it as meaning, "I was wrong and regret my misdeed," surely it is being misconstrued as an admission of fault, when it is not intended to be so.

In the context of communication with a patient and/or family post-adverse event, "I'm sorry" should not be construed as an admission of fault (except in very limited, specific circumstances). The key is putting "I'm sorry" into *context* post-adverse event. It is what you say after "I'm sorry" that places your statement in context to get to the meaning of sorrow rather than a perception of an admission of fault.

---

3   "Sorry." *Merriam-Webster's Online Thesaurus.* 2006–2007. http://www.m-w. com/cgi-bin/thesaurus?book=Thesaurus&va=sorry (4 Oct. 2007).
4   "Sorry." *Merriam-Webster's Online Dictionary.* 2006–2007. http://www.m-w. com/dictionary/sorry (4 Oct. 2007).

Do not say:

"I'm sorry. It is all my fault."

"I'm sorry...if I just hadn't ...[you fill in the blank!]."

"I'm sorry. This is the first time I've ever done this procedure."

"I'm sorry I made such a mistake."

Do say:

"I'm sorry about this complication. Let's talk about what we think happened..."

"I'm sorry for your loss. I want to review what we know at this point..."

Saying "I'm sorry" should be an expression of empathy, sympathizing with your patient and/or patient's family. It should not typically be an expression of fault. It is important to separate these two concepts. There are times when admitting fault is appropriate and necessary. Fortunately, this is a small subset. Unfortunately, the concept of saying "I'm sorry" has led to confusion between an expression of sympathy and one of responsibility or an admission of fault. Many commentators have been pushing this concept of "I'm sorry" to necessarily require an admission of fault.

Admittedly the terminology can be confusing. Let's set the record straight!

***Always* express empathy post-adverse event.**

"*I'm sorry*" is an expression of empathy.

An "*apology*" is a communication that also expresses responsibility.

Only apologize after due diligence has proven that a medical error occurred.

This is how these terms will be used throughout this book, and it is how the healthcare industry should perceive these terms in efforts to eliminate confusion. We need standardized language so that we can understand each other! Doing so is not new to healthcare. For example, in obstetrics, it was recognized that healthcare professionals, nurses, obstetricians, were attributing different meanings to words used to describe fetal heart tracing, and these differences in meanings could lead to misunderstandings and adverse events. The National Institute of Child Health and Human Development set forth standard terminology and definitions in efforts to have everyone speaking the same language. We need to do the same with "I'm sorry" and apology!

When an admission of fault is expressed, unfortunately, at times it has been expressed in the wrong types of cases. The key is to not always express fault, because that does have serious liability consequences (the ones that healthcare professionals fear), but to express fault in the right circumstances. However, we must always express empathy and communicate early and often post-adverse event.

Let's be clear: Circumstances will exist that will require not only an expression of empathy, but also an admission of fault, an apology. However, this would only be after true due diligence and legal counsel is consulted. In this narrow subset, it is essential to apologize and to accept responsibility in the right way so that you can reach the intended result of open communication, truthfulness, and preservation of the physician-patient relationship. This can lead to closure for the patient and family, as well as the physician. An appropriate example would be wrong site surgery and medication errors, but there are others. Sometimes it is easy to determine whether responsibility should attach; at other times, it is not.

Too often, risks of a procedure or known complications are being perceived or misconstrued as a medical error. It is what makes the patient education and informed consent process so important. The right process will help prevent the jump to the conclusion that a medical error occurred when in fact a known complication, which was discussed pre-surgery with the patient, occurred. A good informed consent process can be a significant aid to disclosure, and this will be reviewed in a future chapter.

> **While "I'm sorry" cannot undo the harm incurred, it can prevent consequences from that harm.**

"I'm sorry" shows respect and is a way of showing empathy. It may diffuse anger and prevent misunderstandings. It can also include acknowledging a complication, an adverse result, or a medical error. While "I'm sorry" cannot undo the harm incurred, it can prevent consequences from that harm. When it comes to healthcare, those consequences may include preventing a strained physician-patient relationship and preventing a claim or lawsuit. This is discussed in more detail in the next chapter. For our purposes here, the key is to understand that you should always express empathy post-adverse event, and whether you also apologize is dependent on the circumstances.

> **For our purposes here, the key is to understand that you should always express empathy post-adverse event, and whether you also apologize is dependent on the circumstances.**

Example of an empathic "I'm Sorry":

"I'm very sorry about your loss. I was saddened to hear of it and offer you my condolences and the condolences of my staff. We all enjoyed your son and caring for him. We will miss him."

When considering whether an apology should be expressed post-adverse event, it is important to understand the differences among adverse events, complications, and medical errors. The lack of uniform definitions for these terms has caused confusion as well, and there are different meanings attributed to those terms by patients and physicians. The Institute of Medicine has defined "medical error" as a "failure of a planned action to be completed as intended or use of the wrong plan to achieve an aim" and defines "adverse event" as "serious injury or death resulting from medical management, not the underlying condition of the patient."[5] JCAHO uses the term "sentinel event," which comes closest to the term "medical error." These definitions just do not work for our purposes.

Understand that the overarching term for any unexpected result, bad outcome, or complication is "adverse event." Think of it is the whole universe of potential negative results from care. A "medical error" and a "complication" are subsets. An adverse event could be the result of a medical error or not. The terms are not synonymous.

Medical errors can have significant liability consequences. An "error," in relevant part, is defined by Merriam-Webster as: "[A]n act or condition of ignorant or imprudent deviation from a code of behavior."[6] When a medical error occurs, it is often negligence (care provided was below the accepted standard of care). However, to be liable for medical malpractice or negligence, not only must an act or omission by a healthcare provider fall below an accepted standard of care but also that deviation must have caused injury or harm.[7] Accordingly, when a medical error occurs, due diligence and consultation with risk management and/or legal counsel will be needed.

When a medical error occurs, you should, as mentioned above, express empathy to patients and/or family. We also know when it comes to medical errors that patients want to hear an apology.[8] A 2003 study showed that when it comes to medical errors, patients want:

---

5   Kohn LT, et al. (eds.). "To Err is Human: Building a Safer Health System." Washington, D.C.: National Academies Press, 1999.
6   "Error". *Merriam-Webster's Online Dictionary.* 2006–2007. http://www.m-w.com/dictionary/error (8 Oct. 2007).
7   It is important to recognize that medical malpractice liability is state-law specific.
8   Gallagher TH, Waterman AD, Ebers AG, Fraser VJ, and Levinson W. **"Patients' and Physicians' Attitudes Regarding the Disclosure of Medical Errors."** *JAMA.* 2003; 289: 1001–1007.

1.   Disclosure of the error
2.   To understand what happened
3.   To understand why the error happened
4.   To know how the consequences of the error will be mitigated
5.   To be assured recurrences will be prevented
6.   Emotional support, including an apology[9]

Remember, an apology is acceptance of responsibility. You should be the one accepting responsibility, but only if it is your responsibility! Oftentimes errors are the result of systems issues,[10] or they may be the result of care provided by another healthcare professional. Proper coordination among healthcare professionals, risk management, and counsel is key. If it is your fault, take responsibility, but consult your legal counsel because of the implications that your statement and/ or wording could have, including insurance coverage issues. Further, risk management and/or counsel can help with language and wording so that the right message is sent to the patient and/or family in the appropriate way.

Example of a fault-based apology:

> *"You received 3 times the dose we anticipated. We do not understand why, but are determined to do so. Your laboratory values are being closely monitored. We do not anticipate any harmful effects. We cannot tell you how sorry we are and how committed we are to understanding how this happened."*

In contrast, you should not accept responsibility for a complication. A complication is a type of adverse event, and one that is a known risk of a surgical procedure or treatment. It is defined by Merriam Webster

---

9   Ibid.
10   Kohn LT, et al. (eds.). "To Err is Human: Building a Safer Health System." Washington, D.C.: National Academies Press, 1999.

as "a secondary disease or condition that develops in the course of a primary disease or condition and arises either as a result of it or from independent causes."[11] This is an important concept since the majority of adverse events are typically known complications of procedures or unfortunate poor outcomes. A known complication or when the intended result is not obtained is not a negligent medical error. Again, empathy or "I'm sorry" is absolutely appropriate and necessary in these circumstances, but an apology (acceptance of responsibility) is not.

It is important to note that other circumstances may arise that fall outside of any of these circles; that is, circumstances arise that are not an adverse event, a medical error, or a complication, but that may require empathy or acceptance of responsibility. Those areas come in the day-to-day activities of customer service, communication, and documentation, which are not associated with an adverse event. For example, it may be a billing issue, an issue with an appointment, or an issue with obtaining results of diagnostic testing. These circumstances require appropriate management as well, which should also include an expression of empathy and may or may not require an apology. It is these types of circumstances that set the stage if an adverse event (medical error or complication) does occur at some later time in the course of true physician-patient relationship. The foundation <u>will</u> have been laid and will help with any subsequent discussion and communications that may need to occur with the patient. If it was not, and you did not apologize for the failure to return a telephone call or for a rude staff person or whatever the service or communication issue was, the patient remembers, and it will often times not be you that the patient turns to when an error or complication occurs, but it will be her attorney! In other words focus on building that loyal relationship that can transcend an adverse event.

---

11   "Complication" *Merriam-Webster's Online Medical Dictionary*. 2006–2007. http://www.m-w.com/medical/complication (8 Oct. 2007).

A strong relationship will continue to hold up during an unfavorable event.

Clarifying what type of circumstance your patient has experienced (a medical error, a complication, or a service issue) will dictate your approach:

- Complication — requires an expression of empathy.
- Medical error — requires an expression of empathy and an apology (when due diligence has established responsibility).
- Service or other risk management issue — requires an expression of empathy and in the right circumstances an apology (in context).

The bottom line here is that "I'm sorry" does not mean "I'm responsible" or "I'm negligent," and apologies accompanied by an acknowledgement of fault are appropriate in certain circumstances. The key is to recognize the difference and prepare an appropriate delivery. Sorry works 100% of the time when done right. Indicating that one is "sorry" in a heartfelt fashion will make every situation better. It may serve to help preserve the relationship so further communication can take place. It may keep the physician on the same side of the table as the patient...a key goal in post-adverse event strategies. It will make both the patient and physician feel better. The particulars on "how" to apologize under these circumstances are explored in more detail in chapter 6.

Review Points

- Say, "I'm sorry," with context for your listener.
- "I'm sorry" is an expression of empathy.
- An apology is empathy plus an acceptance of responsibility or admission of fault.
- An appropriate approach can decrease liability risk, make the patient and physician feel better, and strengthen the physician-patient relationship.
- When a medical error occurs and responsibility has been determined, an apology is needed along with an expression of empathy.
- When a complication occurs, an expression of empathy is needed. No apology should be made.
- Service issues need to also be handled appropriately so you can maintain a trusting physician-patient relationship.

CHAPTER 3
WHY IT WORKS

1. What causes a patient or family to visit a plaintiff's attorney?
2. What impacts whether or not a plaintiff's attorney takes on a case?
3. Why do jurors award large verdicts?
4. Why is a case settled?

Although malpractice cases start with an unfortunate clinical outcome, that may well not be the driver. The short answer to all the questions posed above is an adverse event coupled with an aggravating circumstance. Most often, that aggravating circumstance involves miscommunication or a lack of communication. Hickson reported that poor communication is a primary factor leading patients to sue and has linked both communication lapses and patient complaints to professional liability claims.[12] Levinson has shown that certain physician communication behavior is associated with fewer malpractice claims.[13] Your attorney-authors see this play out in depositions and courtrooms all too often. Further, new research by Stevens & Lee and Press Ganey substantiates that focused risk reduction strategies are successful.[14] Press Ganey evaluated office practice patient satisfaction surveys to identify a relationship between patient satisfaction and malpractice risk. Stevens

---

12   Hickson G, et al. "Patient Complaints and Malpractice Risk." *JAMA*. 2002; 287(22): 2951–2957; Hickson GB, Clayton EC, Githens PB, Sloan FA. "Factors that Prompted Families to File Malpractice Claims Following Perinatal Injury." *JAMA*. 1992; 287:1359–1363.

13   Levinson W, Roter DL, Mullooly JP, Dull VT, Frankel RM. "Physician-patient Communication: The Relationship with Malpractice Claims Among Primary Care Physicians and Surgeons." *JAMA*. 1997; 277: 553–559.

14   Press Ganey Associates, Inc. 2008. Return-on-Investment: Reducing Malpractice Claims by Improving Patient Satisfaction. White Paper: Press Ganey Associates, Inc. Available at: http://pressganey.com/cs/research_and_analysis?white_paper_registration2?id=/galleries/lead-generating-acute/Malpractice_Final_12-14-07pdf&subject=Malpractice_paper.

& Lee evaluated events to analyze the "plus" factors that led to an event. The conclusion reached is that patient satisfaction, or the lack of it, is more of a driver of claims than previously thought. Medical practices can reduce professional liability risk when certain patient satisfaction strategies are genuinely incorporated.

One study has shown that patients simply are more likely to sue when a physician does not disclose an error.[15] Patients and families will reach out to a lawyer in efforts to find out what happened when they do not get answers from their doctor. Chapter 8 of this book is devoted to this very topic — finding ways to encourage patients to seek out their doctor *first* to find out what happened instead of feeling the need to go to a lawyer first. Once the patient and family get to the lawyer, poor communication, service lapses, perceived miscommunication, or worse may become an important factor in whether the plaintiff attorney ultimately decides to take on the case.

One of the country's most prominent medical malpractice plaintiff's attorney, and the past president of the Ill. Trial Lawyers Association, Philip H. Corboy has explained to the authors:

> **When deciding on whether to take on a plaintiff's medical malpractice case, we look for the right theme and a value. The theme is what we will show the jury, and we want to be able to demonstrate for the jury that by making our suggested award, it will be doing the right thing. Issues like failures of a healthcare provider to disclose a medical error, to accept responsibility, to communicate simply and truthfully, and to show empathy are examples of important themes. They are also factors which add value to a claim. Jurors relate with patients and they get angry when doctors fail to admit mistakes.**

---

15   Witman AB, Park DM, Hardin SB. "How Do Patients Want Physicians to Handle Mistakes? A survey of internal medicine patients in an academic setting." *Arch Intern Med.* 1996; 156:2565–2569.

Patients have an inherent right to know about their treatment and when something goes wrong. Keeping information from the patient and his family only makes my case more valuable.[16]

It is not hard to understand that an aggravating circumstance in a case adds value. Value is clearly one factor plaintiff lawyers consider. They can use the lack of information or miscommunication in the courtroom, in front of a jury, who are peers of the patient and not the doctor. Poor communication and poor service can significantly impact a jury's decision on both liability and the size of the award. So-called courtroom drama is used by plaintiff attorneys to make a connection with the patient-jurors so that they relate to what the patient-plaintiff has gone through.[17] At times, jurors perceive a "cover-up" because there has been miscommunication, which could have a major impact on a verdict. Of course, the opposite works as well. If the communication was clear and compassionate it could be very helpful to your defense. The key is to recognize that post-adverse event communication is evidence...it is all evidence! The question will be is it positive or negative, and you, to a great extent, are in control of that.

We know that patients want to hear, "I'm sorry," after an adverse event.[18] It stands to reason that if you give the patients what they want — effective communication including an understanding of what happened and why it happened and show empathy — then you may well prevent your patient from visiting a lawyer in the first place. If for some reason, the patient does visit a lawyer, the aggravating circumstance that may impact the lawyer's evaluation and willingness to accept the case will not be present.

---

16   Interview with Philip H. Corboy, Attorney, Corboy & Demetrio, Oct. 19, 2007.

17   Garrison J. "Lawyers learn to share their pain with jurors: They use a technique called psychodrama to connect better by showing vulnerability." *LA Times,* November 25, 2006.

18   Vincent C, Young M, Phillips A. "Why Do People Sue Doctors? A Study of Patients and Relatives Taking Legal Action." *Lancet.* 1994; 343: 1609–1613.

Studies have supported this concept for over a decade that anger — not greed — is what drives most *customers* to file medical malpractice lawsuits. This is not a new revelation. Dr. Gerald Hickson of Vanderbilt University Medical School, as noted above, and many other researchers have published numerous papers in peer-reviewed medical journals stating this very fact: Anger from poor communication is the key driver of medical malpractice lawsuits. There is the potential to reduce the potential of a claim and value of a claim by embracing this concept.

> **"It has actually been known and understood for over a decade that anger — not greed — is what drives most *customers* to file medical malpractice lawsuits."**

Doctors and insurance companies have fought for appropriate tort reform, which should continue, but that is treating the symptoms of the problem and not the root cause of it: Anger. Disclosure, enhanced communication, and a stronger physician/patient relationship goes to the heart of this issue.

Accordingly, if we reduce patient anger, we can reduce the number of lawsuits filed and achieve other benefits, including decreased litigation costs, reduction in medical errors, better public relations, and physician benefits. While this may not be new information, new *energy* is needed!

Remaining on the same side of the table is optimal for all.

Eliminate anger and many lawsuits will be eliminated, others made less valuable. It can be just that simple. Consider some of the additional benefits:

- **Defense litigation expenses reduced**
  Defense litigation expenses are a major cost factor for medical professional liability insurance carriers and self-insured hospitals and are part of the reason for the spike in medical professional liability insurance premiums over the years. If you review an insurance company's closed claims, you will find that defense litigation expenses often dwarf settlement costs. With empathy, apology, and disclosure, defense litigation expenses could be reduced dramatically. The University of Michigan Health System has reported a dramatic reduction in their defense litigation costs of $2 million annually, or two-thirds, because of their disclosure and transparency program. One of the reasons for the

reduction is that cases are resolved earlier, in a matter of months rather than years through the court system. Further, depositions, discovery, motions, and court appearances are largely eliminated from the expense budget for the claim. Even if a lawsuit is initiated after disclosure and an attempt to compensate, the scope of the litigation can be reduced to focus on damages, which also has a beneficial impact on defense litigation expenses. On the flip side, cases where no error occurred are less likely to see a nonmeritorious lawsuit filed (more directly below).

◆ **Nonmeritorious litigation reduced**
Nonmeritorious medical malpractice lawsuits account for 60 percent to 80 percent of all medical malpractice lawsuits filed in the United States. When healthcare professionals cut off communication after adverse events, patients perceive a lack of caring or even a cover-up — even if no error occurred! Again, this is typically when patients seek out a lawyer. The lawyer hears the patient's side of the story, obtains the medical records, and obtains an expert review to determine whether a case exists. Sometimes, information needed to determine liability cannot be gleaned from the records, and the lawyer will need to name nurses, doctors, and the hospital in a case and take discovery and depositions to determine if there was an error and/or who was at fault. You can prevent this scenario by enhancing communication post-adverse event with empathy, apology, and disclosure. Not only is communication post-adverse event your opportunity to explain what, how, and why something went wrong, but also why everything went right (why no fault exists even if there

was an adverse event or a perceived adverse event) and make things "right".

- **Errors reduced**
  With a disclosure program supported by an event management program, mistakes, near misses, and errors are discussed openly and treated as golden learning opportunities. It is a living, learning laboratory. Use the adverse events as an opportunity to prevent future, similar events from occurring. We know patients want reassurance that the event will not recur. Do a root cause analysis, institute remedial measures, and educate staff and physicians. When errors are reduced, so is future liability exposure.

- **Better public relations**
  Healthcare facilities in the United States spend enormous sums of money promoting their services.
  "We're the heart hospital…a five star place to deliver your baby…a better cure for your cancer…mend your kid's broken leg…."
  You cannot open a newspaper or turn on the television without seeing multiple advertisements from hospitals. It is understandable, because healthcare facilities and professionals are businesses and business people — they need customers.
  However, angry customers not only tell sad tales to their attorneys, but they also vent to family, friends, neighbors, the lady on the bus, the mailman, and other any other sympathetic ear.
  "That hospital is nothing more than a Band-aid station. You won't believe what they did to my husband Frank. I am going to own that damn hospital by the time me and my lawyer are done!'

Word of mouth is one of the strongest advertisements. Over time, word of mouth reflects the culture of an organization.

However, with a disclosure program, you can draw patients and families closer after an adverse event with good customer service techniques. You can also save relationships. The Lexington, VA Hospital reports story after story of patients and families coming back to their facility after an error, even when they had other healthcare choices. Why did this happen? Simple: The facility and professionals had enough character to own up to their mistakes and fix the problems they created. Patients and families respect and admire that kind of character in an institution.

Healthcare professionals invest a lot of money and time building relationships. An adverse event does not mean that investment has to be lost. Rather, it will mean that the relationship can transcend the event.

> **Healthcare professionals invest a lot of money and time building relationships. An adverse event does not mean that investment has to be lost.**

◆ **Better morale for the medical staff**
Medical errors produce three victims: The patient, the family, and the healthcare professionals. The popular media, the trial bar, and politicians focus almost exclusively on the pain and suffering experienced by

patients and families (and their pain is very real), but almost no one discusses the trauma visited upon healthcare professionals after errors. Doctors and nurses literally suffer in silence. A disclosure program can provide emotional support, closure, and healing for healthcare professionals involved in medical errors.

We have worked with physicians throughout the country after an adverse event. Their lament is often heart wrenching: *"I've done 2000 laparoscopic cholecystecomies in my career and I've never cut the common bile duct." "We've done over 5000 procedures here and have never had such a significant event."*

This second victim concept is very real and causes skilled health practitioners to second guess their concerns.

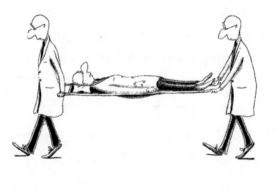

"The way you carry yourself may determine whether you become the second victim."

Conclusion

Recognizing why "sorry works" means that we can now start the process of setting up a communication framework for reducing liability risk associated with poor communication. A proactive and aggressive customer service program that mitigates anger, reduces litigation and associated expenses, provides healing for all sides, and that increases patient safety is the key.

F. Dean Griffen, M.D., Chair of the American College of Surgeons Patient Safety and Professional Liability Committee, has been among the surgeon leaders moving patient safety in surgery to heightened levels. According to him, patient safety can be positively impacted by appropriate pre- and post-adverse event communication, particularly when events are used as part of the education and learning process to prevent future events. A complete program is key. Also, remembering that this post-adverse event activity is evidence upon which the circumstance will be judged is important too. Done well, a claim can be prevented, positive evidence created, and a relationship preserved. Finally, it is simply the right thing to do. [19]

"Preserve your relationship with patients
and the driving force behind them – families."

---

19   Saxton JW, Finkelstein MM, Wojcieszak D. "ESSAY: Ethics Training Needs to Emphasize Disclosure and Apology". HealthCare Ethics Committee Forum; An Interprofessional Journal on Healthcare Institutions' Ethical and Legal Issues, Volume 20, No. 3, September 2008, Springer.

- An adverse event coupled with an aggravating circumstance (poor communication or miscommunication, service lapse) is the driver of frequency and severity.

- Controlling and mitigating anger felt by patients and families after adverse events is the key to reducing lawsuits and settlement costs. Anger — not greed — is the key factor!

- An effective disclosure program can reduce causes of litigation with additional benefits for the patient, physicians, and healthcare organization.

- Attack the medical liability problem with risk management strategies for prevention, rather than just treating the symptoms.

CHAPTER 4

EVENT MANAGEMENT PROCESS: THE PLATFORM FOR A DISCLOSURE PROGRAM

As set forth in the previous chapter, the reasons empathy, apology, and disclosure work are really twofold: (1) Strengthening the physician-patient relationship by providing answers to the patient and/or family and thereby diffusing anger and (2) Creating the appropriate evidence to be used for you instead of against you. While many healthcare professionals and organizations can get on-board with the concept, they always ask, now what? How do we do this? How do we make it practical? How do we make sure apology and disclosure happen? How do we make sure apology and disclosure occur in the right circumstances? How do we make sure apology and disclosure are done the right way?

The answer is to first implement an apology and disclosure infrastructure in your organization that will support this post-adverse event communication. How to implement a disclosure program is discussed in the next chapter, followed by literally how to apologize and disclose. This chapter focuses on "event management," which is the foundation to support your disclosure program.

What is it?

People often ask, *"What do you mean by 'event management'?"* Event management is a process where support can be given after an adverse event occurs in an effort to ensure that good communication and appropriate documentation occur and that patients and families are kept informed. It is about coordination and collaboration between healthcare professionals for the benefit of patients. Event management is what will support your apology and disclosure program. It may mean having a meeting with a patient and/or family to discuss the patient care so that questions can be asked and answered; it may mean coordinating the information coming from different providers so the patient and family receive a clear message; and it may mean following up with them and being a continued resource for tough questions ("*What about the bills? Did someone do something wrong?*"). Every circumstance will be different and may need to be managed differently. In some circumstances, an apology may be needed. On other occasions it can be diffusing the angry patient who has suffered a known complication of a procedure. When any of those circumstances arise, having in place an event management program will help the process move forward in a methodical and organized fashion. Our point is that the time to plan for what you're going to do, what the process will be, is now – not when the adverse event occurs!

What are the benefits?

A true event management program will help in your efforts to reduce liability risk, but it has other benefits as well. While in the first instance, an event management program addresses the immediate event — managing the communication issues — it also provides a means for a living, learning laboratory for continuous quality improvement: Could we have done something differently to have prevented the outcome? Can we incorporate a tool or strategy to reduce future similar events? This quality assurance aspect of event management can lead to reduced medical errors and increased patient satisfaction. Doing so affects the two factors that cause claims: (1) the injury or clinical circumstance and (2) the aggravating circumstance. This is why it is a positive tool for risk reduction.

"We have found a strong association between patient satisfaction and risk management," says Dr. Melvin Hall, President and CEO of Press Ganey Associates, Inc. *"Those providers who excel in providing patient-centered care — from communication to involving patients in treatment decisions to treating patients with dignity — reduce the likelihood of litigation. Bottom line — satisfied patients are less likely to sue."*[20] Press Ganey has found that a one-point decrease in a practice's satisfaction score is associated with a 5% increase in the rate of risk management

20   E-mail communication with Press Ganey (November 1, 2007).

episodes. Press Ganey is the nation's leading provider of health care performance improvement services.

More recently, Stevens & Lee and Press Ganey collaborated in a new analysis of patient satisfaction and its impact on professional liability risk.[21] Press Ganey analyzed patient satisfaction survey data obtained from medical practices between January 1, 2007 and December 31, 2007. This data revealed a link between dissatisfaction in communication with a physician and physician service to negative comments about malpractice. Stevens & Lee analyzed claims and adverse event data collected over a five-year period. This data led to the conclusion that "plus" factors are linked to adverse events and claims. Together the data reveals that communication, service, and patient satisfaction are more of drivers of medical professional liability risk than previously thought.

Further, Press Ganey has shown a direct correlation between employee satisfaction and patient satisfaction. Increasing employee satisfaction bolsters productivity and staff retention. *"There is a strong demonstrated relationship between an organization's patient satisfaction and the satisfaction among the organization's employees,"* says Dr. Hall. *"Health care organizations that focus on the needs of their employees find staff members are able to more fully engage in their roles and better focus on providing high quality care. Improving the quality of care and 'making a difference' is the reason most professionals enter the health care field."*[22]

Benefits of a true event management program include other positives for the physicians, hospital, counsel, and, most importantly, the patient. For the patient, it can lead to improved care, improved safety, and a stronger physician-patient relationship. For physicians and other healthcare providers, the relationship with the patient is maintained and even transcends the adverse event. The risk reduction benefit also comes from the evidence created in the process. This allows defense counsel to defend the case with confidence without the so-called plus

---

21   Saxton JW, Finkelstein MM, Bravin S, Stawiski S. "Reduce Liability Risk by Improving Your Patient Satisfaction." (2008) (accessible at http://www. pressganey.com/galleries/default-file/MD_White_Paper-Malpractice_0808. pdf) (last visited Sept. 11, 2008).
22   Ibid.

factor. That evidence may be a note in a medical chart pertaining to a discussion with a patient and/or family about the complication that occurred, which acknowledges the patient's understanding of the same, for example.

Any event management program should address confidentiality issues. There may be some physician-patient confidentiality issues to work through, but more significantly confidentially of the investigation process and communications between the physicians, hospital, and counsel. Event management is most effective when it can be done in a framework of this type of confidentiality. This helps to allow for a more open communication and analysis to truly to get the root cause. It also provides you with the ability to control the information. Programs exist where this is accomplished through collaboration with legal counsel. Again, just another reason to work and think through the process now and develop a methodical process with counsel's advice.

In summary, benefits of a true event management program include:

- Decreasing professional liability risk
- Decreasing claims and lawsuits
- Creating positive evidence to be used for you – not against you
- Decreasing medical errors — continuous quality improvement
- Increasing patient satisfaction
- Strengthening the physician-patient relationship
- Enhancing your bottom line
- Increasing staff retention
- Becoming the employer of choice
- Becoming the provider of choice
- Creating a peer-review/attorney-client privilege process

How do you accomplish it?

With all of the positive benefits associated with event management, what can you do to ensure an effective event management program exists? First, incorporate an event management policy, then educate your physicians and staff on the policy, and follow it! Policies are important whether you are a hospital or a physician-office practice, because they provide a standardized and consistent process for handling difficult circumstances. They also serve to provide employees and staff with direction and can be the basis for support. Use policies also to orient new employees or physicians. Following a carefully drafted policy is critical to risk reduction.

How do you ensure that your policy is followed? Provide education and training to your physicians and staff. You can hold organization-wide educational programming for staff and a separate program for physicians. Outside speakers could be brought in who can describe event management and show its benefits. To reinforce the policy, provide in-services and annual educational programs.

One of the best methods for bringing physicians and staff on-board is to create a collaborative event management program. By collaborative, we mean that it transcends the hospital and the physician's practice. One area your attorney authors have worked extensively with this concept is in obstetrics. For example, coordinate and collaborate with the obstetricians, pediatricians, neonatologists, labor hall, anesthesia, and nurses. Event management facilitators are provided extra training and provide support as events occur. Such an event management program brings everyone on-board with the concept.

What needs to be done when an event actually occurs?

Perhaps you now have an event management policy, you have had education, but what do you do when an event actually occurs? Again it is very fact sensitive, but consider the following points:

1. Ensure that the patient is safe and ensure that an appropriate treatment plan in response to the event is formulated and in place. This should be the initial primary concern.
2. Follow your event management policy and notify the proper individuals. For example, you may need to notify hospital risk management, and you may need to notify your insurance company

as well. Notice to your insurance carrier could impact coverage for any event or claim. Some innovative insurance companies or captive insurers require notification of events within a certain time period and then will provide event management support.

3. Initially, ensure that the patient and/or family has a response to the pending issue. Often, you will only have initial information, and more investigation will be needed, letting the patient know candidly that this is part of the process. When no contact occurs, remember, they will often seek out their attorney to get answers if too much time passes.

4. Gather information so that you can provide it to your risk management and/or insurance company, who can provide you with support. For example, what happened, what were the discussions pre-event with the patient, what is documented in the medical record? Specifically, as an example, if a known complication occurred, what did you discuss with the patient about the risks of the procedure? Was it you who had the discussion or someone else? Is it documented that the patient understood these risks? What discussions were had with the patient after the complication occurred? What is documented in the medical record about those conversations? As you can see, we are essentially gathering the *evidence* that will support (or not) your care.

5. Review the care. In an objective fashion, review your care. It is important to remember that this should not be done with the retroscope. It is always easier after the fact to say, "*I could have...; I wish I had...; I should have...*" However, you need to review the care as if it were contemporaneous with the facts known at the time treatment and care decisions were made and provided, not in retrospect with new facts and knowing the outcome of the care.

6. Collaboration among providers, risk management, and perhaps legal counsel may be needed in certain cases. This is not the time to place blame. Be respectful of one another. You will also

need to collaborate on who takes the lead in discussions with the patient/family; who will be at the meeting or discussion; who will document the meeting or discussion; who will be the contact after the patient/family meeting or discussion.

7. Collaboration in significant events involving many providers can be difficult. Physicians may have different insurers and counsel. These situations take leadership but it is worthwhile to try to get all interested parties together in a conference room and review the information you have and that you need and begin to set forth a communication plan so the patient and family can appropriately get all the information they need. It is in these types of circumstances that collaboration is essential. You can see how easily misinformation or conflicting information could get to the patient/family if collaboration does not occur.

8. Leave this collaborative endeavor with a plan. Include discussions about what and how information will be relayed to the patient/family. For example, *"Mrs. Smith, I have met with the other healthcare providers that have been involved with your care since your admission here at Sacred Heart Hospital. We reviewed your care, including the medical records. We also had an independent, objective third-party cardiologist review your records. We are very sorry that you incurred one of those risks of the procedure that we discussed before your surgery. We want to answer any questions you may have."* This does not necessarily come easy, especially when you are emotionally involved in a situation.

9. In determining who is best suited to communicate with the patient and/or family, most often it will be the doctor (that's who the patient wants to hear from), but consideration should be made of both the relationship with the patient and the communication skills of the provider. Although rare, sometimes the provider may not be the best-suited individual. Alternatives could include a nurse with a good relationship with the patient, another physician, risk manager, or patient safety advocate.

10. After any meeting or discussion with the patient/family, document it in the medical chart. Include who was present, a summary of the conversation/meeting, the time, the date, the location, the patient/family's understanding of what occurred and the next steps, and what the next steps are. For example, *"On February 22, 2007, at 12:11, in her hospital room, I met with Mrs. Smith to discuss the stroke she incurred following a cardiac catheterization that was performed this morning. We discussed her treatment plan of rehab and admission to a rehab facility, which she was in agreement with. I also discussed with her the fact that the stroke was a potential complication that we had discussed prior to the surgery. She recalled that discussion. She will be discharged to rehab, and I will follow her there."*

11. All conversations with patient and/or family should be documented, *objectively*. Documentation should be limited to the facts and should not include emotions. If your organization requires that an incident report be completed, do so, but again, only provide objective facts.

12. After any meeting, provide the patient and/or family with contact information for a point person should any questions arise after the initial discussion or communication. It can simply be that you provide them with one of your business cards. Include on the back your cell phone number or an alternative method of reaching you if you are not available at the number listed on the business card. You want them to be able to reach you.

13. Follow up with the patient and/or family! So often we see this step falling through the cracks. Physicians and facilities do a great job of initially talking with the patient and even investigating what occurred, but then fail to circle back to the family or provide additional subsequent support. They are then surprised when they receive a records request from an attorney, and now it is just too late. You can schedule a subsequent face-to-face meeting, or if a telephone call is all that is needed you can do that as well; or perhaps it is a letter. Oftentimes, a subsequent face-to-face

meeting would be most beneficial. For example, perhaps you were waiting for the results of an autopsy report to discuss the cause of death with a family. Once the autopsy report results are in, call the family and schedule a meeting. At the meeting, you can show them the autopsy report and, importantly, explain what it means. *"The medical examiner has listed the cause of death as a pulmonary embolism. A pulmonary embolism occurs when clots break loose from the vein surface and block pulmonary blood vessels. Primary symptoms are chest pain and shortness of breath, which your son did not have. Sometimes pulmonary embolisms do not exhibit any symptoms, as occurred here. A pulmonary embolism is a risk of the gastric-bypass procedure performed, and a risk that we discussed with your son prior to his agreeing to move forward with surgery. Unfortunately, he experienced one of those risks, and we are very sorry for your loss. I would be happy to answer any questions you may have about this report or the care of your son. Do you have any questions? Perhaps you will have some after you leave and this new information settles in. Please call me if you have questions after you leave here today and I would be happy to discuss them with you."*

14. While the exact mechanics of "disclosure" are discussed in chapter 6, any time you speak with a family and/or patient after an adverse event, you need to expect that they will be anxious, nervous, and upset. They do not know what happened! You will also be nervous and upset, but you need to be a calming force — they are looking to you!

15. Keep the lines of communication open with the patient/family. Make yourself available and make sure they know how to reach you. You can touch base with them. A balance does exist though. You do not want to harass them.

16. Ensure that systems are in place and followed to prevent reoccurrence. This should be done within your organizational systems. Perhaps there is a patient safety officer in charge of this, or a committee or risk manager. If you are a physician in a physician practice, work with your office manager to implement

new strategies, tools, and/or processes. For example, you may have a patient who incurred a pneumothorax after receiving a trigger point injection. Your office hears from a lawyer who wants the patient to be compensated for a hospitalization, pain and suffering, and time off work. The patient's attorney alleges that a pneumothorax is a known risk of a trigger point injection. Your office agrees to pay to help the patient. Your attorney tells you if the patient had signed an informed consent form that noted that a pneumothorax is a known risk, you probably would not have had to make any payment. The data and literature indicate that it is a known risk. Internally, you can create and implement a procedure-specific informed consent form for trigger point injections, which also sets forth the known risks of the procedure (including a pneumothorax). Next time a pneumothorax does occur as a result of a trigger point injection, and you discussed that risk with the patient, who has signed a procedure-specific form, you will be able to explain to the patient that it is a known risk of the complication, you discussed it previously, and remember the informed consent form that was signed.

How is disclosure a part of it?

As you can see, event management can provide you with appropriate evidence to be used for you through documentation and communication. What you say to the patient, how you say it, and what you document will affect whether all the benefits of event management are attained. Empathy, apology, and disclosure are forms of communication. (In chapter 6, details of the communication aspect of disclosure are addressed.) True event management is the framework that allows for disclosure, or effective communication, to take place. With an event management infrastructure in place, it will be easier to incorporate an apology and disclosure program.

+ A true event management policy and program are needed to support your apology and disclosure program.

+ A true event management program is a process where support can be given after an adverse event occurs in an effort to ensure that good communication and appropriate documentation occur and that patients and families are kept informed.

+ Implement (or update) an event management policy.

+ An appropriate event management policy, if consistently followed, is beneficial in increasing patient satisfaction, increasing patient safety, providing continuous quality improvement, strengthening the provider-patient relationship, decreasing liability risk, and importantly to this book, providing the framework to support an apology and disclosure program, which comes with its added benefits.

CHAPTER 5

How to Implement a Sorry Works! Program in Five Steps

Apology and disclosure are more than a policy — they are a program. Many healthcare institutions across the United States have adopted disclosure policies in the wake of the 2001 JCAHO standard on disclosure,[23] but few organizations have actual disclosure programs in place. Policies are fine, and are needed, but they are only part of the equation. Policies do not make disclosure happen. Programs do, particularly with the combination of a disclosure program and an existing event management program.

For healthcare and/or insurance organizations to experience disclosure success stories similar to the University of Michigan (and elsewhere), a disclosure *program* has to be implemented. Such programs need the buy-in and support from the leadership of the hospital, physicians, and insurer(s) as well as the legal and risk management staff. Everyone has to be on the same page and committed to making the program a success. In fact, in our experience, for the program to work, there needs to be a champion who can start the process of putting a program in place.

There is nothing ad hoc about disclosure. The disclosure program should be consistently and uniformly applied to all adverse events, whether perceived as small or large in value, be they known or unknown to the patient and family. Successful disclosure programs involve consistent and constant high ethical standards. Consistent ethics translate into credible disclosure programs. Patients and families - the *customers* - and their attorneys, when involved, must feel they are receiving the whole truth at all times.

---

23   JCAHO. "Ethics, Rights, and Responsibilities," in *Comprehensive Accreditation Manual for Hospitals: The Official Handbook* (Oakbrook Terrace, Ill.: JCAHO 2003), Patient Rights Standard RI. 2.90, RI-12.

> **There is nothing ad hoc about disclosure. The disclosure program should be consistently and uniformly applied to all adverse events, whether perceived as small or large in value, be they known or unknown to the patient and family.**

The program must also include training and tools as well as support in how to keep the process going so it can take hold. Just going to a seminar is a start, but it does not itself facilitate the change that needs to take place. The program structure must assure that appropriate, effective disclosure takes place consistently.

Consider the following five steps as you implement your disclosure program:

Step 1: Sorry Works! Starts With a Few Committed People — Get the Decision Makers On-Board!

Developing a disclosure program begins with you! Be the champion! Disclosure programs begin with a few "champions" who carry the flag and get the rest of the institution excited. They use the powerful data and combination of easily definable benefits of appropriate disclosure to bring the management on board (see chapter 9 for disclosure success stories). We see it time and time again. Disclosure not only makes economic sense, but it is also in keeping with most healthcare organizations' and physicians' values and culture.

Your job is to be the voice for disclosure, as often it takes someone willing to push for a cause. People like to join in causes where enthusiasm is pervasive. You need to drive the concept and ultimately its success. It may actually be YOU who gets the concept into a program at your institution. YOU may be the one to handle the typical questions and challenges to disclosure (see Questions and Challenges at the end of this book). It may be YOU who pushes the next steps to obtain the organizational commitment. It will also then be YOU who will get the quiet sense of accomplishment when it happens and helps so many patients and medical staff members.

Leadership

Obtaining the commitment and buy-in from the leadership may be the single most important action that can lead to a successful disclosure program. If your leadership is not on-board, your program will never work.

In order to obtain this necessary buy-in, education is key. Educate the key leadership — the hospital or insurance company CEO, board president, risk manager, patient safety officer, and in-house counsel. Educational programs are available. The concept of disclosure and its *benefits* must be conveyed and understood. Further, they must understand that commitment is required, and more — training for the physicians and staff. It is not simply getting behind the concept of disclosure, but actually making it work, and that requires adequate training and education for those on the front lines. To be effective, disclosure must be done in the right way.

You can also incorporate conference calls with key disclosure and patient safety leaders who can answer any questions that the leadership may have. We have seen naysayers become supporters! It is just a matter of education.

You might hear from your leadership... *"Our staff and physicians do not want this."* It may be because doctors do not understand what "it" is. Discuss disclosure with your doctors. Your leadership and you may be surprised to find very receptive ears. The fact is that many healthcare professionals are tired of being told to run away or hide from patients and families after adverse events. Providers are also tired of trying to convince politicians to fix their liability problems. Disclosure offers providers the chance to begin to address their liability problems on their own, which is refreshing and different.

"Eliminate the appearance of avoidance."

Committee

Create a committee to move the concept forward to reality. The committee is often comprised of physicians, nurses, risk managers, attorneys, and administrators who help develop the disclosure program. The committee will develop a policy and procedure, as outlined below, and importantly, ensure not only that the disclosure program occurs, but also that once it does, the program is kept alive! In part, this is done by incorporating a workable policy and program and making sure an education process takes place. Workable, practical and user friendly.

Some members of the steering committee could later form the nucleus of the disclosure team that leads the program, helps assure continued education, and helps determine who is going to be on the disclosure team.

Defense Counsel

Use your committee to obtain the buy-in of defense counsel. Oftentimes, the defense counsel's initial reaction to disclosure may be reluctance. You need to educate your defense counsel that in fact your disclosure program will help them. By disclosing in the right way, you actually can create favorable, appropriate evidence that will help your defense counsel should a case be pursued. Truly, most defense counsel at this point in time know that enhanced communication post-adverse event is the only option. Disclosure programs include enhanced communication and a whole lot more.

Insurer

As with the defense counsel, use your committee to obtain the buy-in of your insurer. In the present day, most hospitals are self-insured, so this happens through your risk manager, but if not, involve your insurer early, including insurer(s) that cover independent contractor physicians. When it comes to disclosure and apology programs, oftentimes insurers believe that the insured (doctors, hospitals) are not in favor of disclosure, and the insureds believe that the insurer will be opposed to disclosure. Sometimes that is the case, but you need to find out!

"As an insurance company, we think disclosure has a lot of promise. It certainly would seem to help our bottom line, but our doctors will never go for it. The 'a word' is not in their vocabulary."

"As a doctor, I think Sorry Works! is good for my patients and me, but the insurance company will say no. There's no way they'll go for this disclosure stuff. Insurance companies always say no to innovative ideas."

Everyone is in their silo, assuming that the other side will automatically say no. Doctors and hospital administrators can get this started. It only takes a phone call or an e-mail to their insurance carrier(s) with a question: *"Would you support implementation of a program that can increase patient safety and satisfaction at the same time reduce professional liability risk?"* They might be surprised to learn that their insurance company is already studying the issue (chiefly because of the potential cost savings), and receiving support from their insureds will help. If the insurance company is not studying Sorry Works! or flat out says "no," then physicians and administrators need to realize that they are the customers and should demand that a disclosure program be considered and that they help. Write letters, send e-mails, make phone calls. It is your practice... your hospital... your patients... your liability problem... take control! Done the right way, and that is our whole point, there is very little downside.

Make no mistake, Sorry Works! is a culture change, and changing culture is never easy. We are asking healthcare and insurance organizations to shift from deny and defend to openness, honesty, and transparency. Some people will not like the change. Some individuals will resist, but the benefits are worth it.

Action Steps:
- Be the champion of disclosure
- Obtain the buy-in of your leadership — provide an educational program
- Obtain commitment from the decision makers (leadership, insurers, and in-house counsel)
- Identify other disclosure champions and form a disclosure committee
- Create your disclosure committee

Step 2: Adopt a Disclosure Policy and Procedure

It is important for the policy and procedure to be in place before you move forward with announcing the commitment to disclosure to the entire organization. You can find disclosure policies adopted by organizations by simply "Googling" the Internet (for example, the Veteran's Administration Directive or the University of Michigan). However, any one policy may not be the best fit for every organization. It is important to tailor a policy to suit your facility's needs and requirements and that it is consistent with your other policies that are in place. You may need to do some hard work when drafting your policy. While disclosure may seem like an easy issue, there are legal and risk implications and language and definition challenges. This is exactly what your committee can work through. The American Society of Healthcare Risk Management (ASHRM) has provided some guidance.[24]

---

24   Perspective on Disclosure of Unanticipated Outcome Information," ASHRM whitepaper/monograph, www.ashrm.org, Nov. 2003.

You need to recognize that any policy that is created may end up being evidence in litigation. Many states throughout the nation recognize a corporate negligence theory of liability against hospitals, and that can be based on whether you have a policy, and if you have one, if it is followed. The policy may be requested in the discovery process of litigation. You therefore need to ensure that your policy does the job it is intended to do — provide guidance for your healthcare providers — but at the same time, it is drafted in a way that is less likely to be used against your healthcare providers and/or the facility. When drafting a policy, consider the following:

1. <u>A statement on the purpose of the policy.</u> What is the purpose of your policy? Is it to increase patient safety, provide open communication with patients and their families, ensure that patients are kept informed of their health status, and/or provide guidelines to support your healthcare providers? Your disclosure policy's purpose could be:

   > It is the goal of [insert name of institution or practice] to involve patients in their care and treatment through effective communication. This policy is intended to provide guidelines for disclosing certain adverse events to patients and/or their families.

2. <u>What "events"' are covered by the policy?</u> It is important to analyze and consider what your disclosure policy will cover. Will it include complications? Will it include near misses? You need to have agreement on this before rolling it out to your staff.

3. <u>Defining terms.</u> Much confusion in this area of disclosure has also presented due to varying nomenclature and the varying definitions that are attributed to those terms. For example, near

miss, anticipated outcome, bad outcome, unanticipated outcome, adverse event, medical error, and so on. It's confusing!

4. <u>A policy statement.</u> You will need a policy statement, which should consider the subject matter of the policy and embrace its goals and the goals of the organization. Your policy statement may be:

> Our [insert facility] is committed to open communication and honesty with our patients. Patients, at all times, have a right to know their medical status. Patients will be provided with timely and accurate information with respect to outcomes of care, including adverse events, whether anticipated or unanticipated, and our healthcare providers will provide information with regard to medical errors with clinical consequences or when a reasonable person would want to know, whether or not there was a negative clinical consequence.

5. <u>How much guidance you want to provide.</u> How much detail are you going to provide? Will you include actual sample language to use in discussions with family, for example, or are you going to provide general guidance and provide other resources?

6. <u>"Who" the policy applies to.</u> Does it apply to all healthcare providers?

7. <u>"What" events must be disclosed.</u> Is it only medical errors? Will you include near misses?

8. <u>If there are some circumstances that are mandatory while others are discretionary.</u> For example, your organization may want all

medical errors to be disclosed, or you may consider disclosure on a case-by-case basis.

9. "How" to disclose. Consider whether you want to provide information to your healthcare providers on "how" to disclose, and if so, how much information you will provide to them regarding the mechanics of disclosure.

10. Addressing "when" to disclose. Consider whether including information on when disclosure needs to take place. Is it as soon as possible after the event?

You may struggle with some of these issues. Reach a consensus with your committee. Next, follow through with your organization's approval and implementation process. When you roll out your disclosure program to your organization, your policy will be in place and you can provide educational programming for your healthcare providers.

Action Steps:
+ Have your disclosure committee develop your disclosure policy.
+ Work through the analysis of what you want your policy to address and how.
+ Adopt the policy and procedure through your organizational structure.
+ Publish it to the organization.

Step 3: Roll Out the Program to the Entire Organization

Now let's obtain the commitment of the entire organization to successfully launch your disclosure program. This means education. Hold organization-wide seminars for your physicians and nurses. This is another good opportunity to get trainers or consultants involved in the process to assist you. **At a minimum**, providers (physicians, nurses, and technicians) should understand the disclosure concept and its benefits, know about the policy, and know who to call for advice and counsel on disclosure after an adverse event.

Critical to the success of this is that everyone understands how disclosure is a positive concept for *them* and patients. Medicine is a stressed profession with a lot of demands. If disclosure appears to be just more mandates — more work — then it will meet with resistance or worse. The reality is that when doctors and nurses understand disclosure, they will be fine with it ... back to education and its importance.

The educational program should stress the importance, the roots, and the value of disclosure. The message of the training for providers should be that disclosure is something you intuitively want to do, will put you in a better liability position, and is great for patients!

Other options exist for rolling out your disclosure program, and what you do is dependent on your organizational structure — number of facilities, providers, and staff. It may be a combination of live educational programming along with video educational programming, train the trainer, webcasts, and/or in-services. You may decide to hold live programs for all physicians and follow that by live educational programming for staff. Train-the-trainer programs can be incorporated and are useful for larger organizations.

Action Step: Provide educational programming to your healthcare team.

Step 4: Train the Disclosure Team

Your disclosure program should include establishing a disclosure team, or a group of individuals who receive additional, intense training on disclosure — how, when, what.

> **Your disclosure program should include establishing a disclosure team, or a group of individuals who receive additional, intense training on disclosure — how, when, what.**

You should carefully select your disclosure team, and they should be individuals committed to disclosure. At a hospital system, the team could include physician leaders, risk managers, a head nurse, a chaplain, and many others. Within an insurer, the team could include leadership from risk, claims, and legal. At a doctor's practice, perhaps it is simply that everyone is a member of the disclosure team! The size of your disclosure team will depend on your program and organizational structure. Consider, for example: Will you have coverage 24-7 by at least one of these individuals? Do you need 24-7 coverage by more than one individual? Do you need a department head and an individual from every department? These are the types of issues that a disclosure consultant can help you to determine.

We often call disclosure team individuals "communication facilitators." Disclosure team members should become experts in disclosure and be ready to help providers deliver bad news to patients and to families. The hope is that individual providers will have to disclose on rare and infrequent occasions, so it should not be a surprise that providers will be "rusty" and forgetful of how to properly disclose to patients and families after adverse events. This is where a trained disclosure team helps. Disclosure team members should have hands-on training. Role playing and discussing scenarios are extremely important. Small group workshops can also be held.

You can even implement a train-the-trainer type program. (this will often depend on the size of your organization and can be somewhat fluid).

We have had disclosure teams be a small core but grow to be small teams within every department with additional backup if and when necessary. Do not get bogged down with size — get started with good communication and those champions mentioned earlier in this chapter.

Action Steps:
+ Identify and select your communication facilitators.
+ Provide hands-on training.

Step 5: Keep the Program Alive!

After all your hard work, you will need to focus on keeping the program alive! If principles are not kept at the forefront, they will be forgotten or become "stale." If disclosure does not occur, everyone will lose faith. It will become another initiative that everyone thought was a good idea and was excited about ... but lost steam. Do not let this happen! Consider the following suggestions:

- Start your disclosure program small and publicize your success stories internally! (Remember to do so in a way that protects the confidentiality of the physicians and providers involved and the patient.) This can be done in educational programming to your physicians and staff.
- Provide support to those involved in a disclosure event. Unexpected or adverse events also take a toll on the providers and those providing the disclosure. A post-event support system can help providers who have disclosed receive the help and healing they need so they can effectively return to serving patients and families. This is actually an underestimated concept. When outcomes are not realized, the doctor feels a rainbow of emotions — none of them good.
- Keep educating. Hold in-services on disclosure and annual educational programs. Gear the programs specifically to nursing staff, to physicians, to new employees, and to the disclosure team. Each will have different educational needs.
- Importantly, learn from the process. Disclosure is really a part of event management. Use the lessons learned to reduce the risk of future similar occurrences. This must be done in a blame-free manner. Review and discuss disclosed cases so that process improvements can take place. Learn from your mistakes and improve your healthcare delivery systems! Risk managers, patient safety officers, and business managers will value this aspect of your disclosure program.

- Educate the local trial bar about your disclosure program. The message is simple: Legitimate cases will be handled fairly and swiftly, but non-meritorious claims will never be settled. Consider the following quote from Richard Boothman of the University of Michigan Health System:

> "I believe the word is out that if they (the trial bar) have a legitimate case, they share all the details with us, including their experts' reports and interviews with the family. I also believe that if they have a marginal or questionable case, they do not bother any more because they know we will fight those aggressively with the best of lawyers and best of experts."[25]

- Finally, please share your story. The more hospitals and insurers that tell Sorry Works! and disclosure success stories, the sooner disclosure and apology will be the norm. Share your story at conferences and with trade and popular media, always carefully protecting confidentiality but letting your peers know ... it works! Share your story with us!

Action Steps:
- Publicize your success stories
- Continue with education
- Provide support

Remember, the end goal is development of a program — not a policy. Policies sit on the shelf and collect dust, whereas programs are

---

25   Boothman, R. "Apologies and a Strong Defense at the University of Michigan Health System." _The Physician Executive._ March/April 2006.

literally living, breathing creatures. You need a plan, and this chapter provides you with the framework to accomplish a successful disclosure program.

Review Points:

- Leadership commitment and buy-in.
- A disclosure policy and procedure.
- Roll out the program to the entire institution.
- Train the disclosure team.
- Keep the program alive!

CHAPTER 6

HOW TO APOLOGIZE TO PATIENTS AND FAMILIES

Remember, "I'm sorry" (or an expression of empathy) is different than an "apology" (or accepting responsibility). What you do depends on context. How you do either takes skill and training. This chapter provides you with the "how to's" of "I'm sorry" and "apology."

While the number of stories about Sorry Works! are promising and extremely compelling, a nagging question still persists for many healthcare professionals. How exactly do I say, "I'm sorry," without the patient getting the idea that I am admitting negligence? How exactly do I apologize to a patient or family? How do I accept responsibility in the right way? These are fair questions: Empathy and apology are not found on the course syllabi at most medical schools – or law schools (although they should be!). Physicians are not alone with this feeling. Although we are a forgiving nation, most Americans have trouble saying, "I'm sorry." All you have to do is pick up a newspaper or magazine to see politicians, athletes, movie stars, and others trying to apologize:

"For me to be at a comedy club and flip out and say this crap, I'm deeply, deeply sorry."[26] Michael Richards (you recognize him as Kramer from the TV show *Seinfeld*) apologized to the nation on the David Letterman show for racially charged language used during a comedy routine. This was part of his statement...and he hired a crisis expert before apologizing!

"It is with a great amount of shame that I stand before you and tell you I have betrayed your trust."[27] Marion Jones, Olympic gold medalist,

---

26   Lucas S. "'Kramer' Apologizes for Racist Comments." (accessible at http://www.associatedcontent.com/article/90041/kramer_apologizes_for_racist_comments.html) (last visited October 10, 2007)

27   "Tearful Marion Jones Apologizes, Announces Retirement." (Associated Press) (accessible at http://www.kvia.com/global/story.asp?s=7176191) (October 5, 2007; last visited October 10, 2007).

apologized to the nation for lying about using steroids. Alex Rodriguez of the New York Yankess apologized as well. *USA Today* did not buy it.[28]

Of course, bedrooms, kitchens, and coffee shops across America are the scenes of poorly delivered apologies day in and day out too:

"Honey, I don't understand why you are getting so emotional about this...I am sorry if I hurt your feelings. But, you know, you have some blame in all of this too! Can't you get over it so we can move on?"

Relationship experts can help couples apologize, but what is important in apologizing to your significant other is not necessarily important when a healthcare provider apologizes to a patient. We are here to help you empathize and apologize to your patients!

How to Say, "I'm sorry" — Expressing Empathy

"I'm sorry" showing empathy is always appropriate. This is true no matter what the circumstances, whether or not a medical error has occurred, and whether or not you are at fault. Your empathy must be heartfelt, and it must be a thread or theme through every discussion with the patient and/or family. This means if an adverse event occurred without error or liability attaching, say, *"I'm sorry."* In other words, it is a powerful tool when a known complication of a procedure occurs. *"I am so sorry. Your Mom suffered a complication known as an anastomatic leak."* However, this also means if an adverse event occurred where responsibility does attach (standard of care was breached and was the cause of injury or harm) then you must also apologize. So, in the second instance, you will need to both show heartfelt empathy and accept responsibility (which is discussed later in this chapter). However, at the outset, how do you say, *"I'm sorry"*?

Immediately after an adverse event occurs, your disclosure team may be alerted and can help with the initial step of empathy. The provider should always express empathy, and remember that context is essential. Perhaps your conversation could go like this:

---

28   Saraceno J. "Jones' Apology Sounds Like Another False Start." (accessible at http://www.usatoday.com/sports/columnist/saraceno/2007-10-07-marionjones-comment_N.htm) (last visited October 10, 2007)

"I am sorry this happened. I want you to know that we are conducting an investigation to learn what happened, and as we learn information you will learn information. OK?

Here is my business card if you have any questions or need assistance. The number on the card rings to a live person 24 hours a day/7 days a week. Also, as relatives come to the hospital please have them call the number on the card if they have any questions or concerns...myself or someone from my staff will be happy to speak with them.

The nurses and physicians attending to the care of your son understand his current condition, and they are committed to working with you and your family.

Is there anything else we can do for you or your family at this point? Do you need food, lodging, transportation, phone calls? We also have counseling services available that may help you, including pastoral services.

Do you have any questions? If not now, but questions later arise after I leave, please call the number on the card, and I would be happy to answer your questions."

Notice that we said, "Sorry," but no blame was accepted or assigned. The first step of the disclosure process is not a true apology...it is simply empathy and compassion. It is also good customer service. In reading the dialogue above you can see that the speaker literally trying to pull the family closer to the institution, just like a good customer service program will literally make the injured/aggrieved customer feel appropriately as if they are on their side (after all they are). Also, you can see that we said only what we know. We do not infer or make guesses... we simply stay in the proper zone of being empathetic and promising an investigation to learn the facts.

> **The first step of the disclosure process is not a true apology... it is simply empathy and compassion.**

This initial disclosure is all about rebuilding trust with customers. Patients and families place an enormous amount of trust in healthcare professionals. Indeed, there is no other service relationship in our society where one party places so much trust (and faith) in another party. When an adverse event occurs (whether there was an error or not), the trust is put to an extreme test. In many cases, trust is broken and has to be earned back. Following an adverse event, a healthcare institution and their insurer should do everything to bring the patient and family closer and embrace them. That is good customer service, and the first 24 hours after an event are the most critical. It is what any good customer-centered company does for their customers after mishaps — think Disney, The Ritz-Carlton, or Southwest Airlines. What do these companies do after something goes wrong? Answer: They make the customer their best friend.

Below are some more examples of expressing empathy:

+ *"I'm very sorry about your loss. I was saddened to hear of it and offer you my condolences and the condolences of my staff. We all enjoyed your son and caring for him. We will miss him."*
+ *"I'm sorry you feel this way. I want to talk about what happened and help you understand it and what we are going to do next so that you can be assured that we are doing everything we can to care for you and support you."*

Some phrases to stay away from:

+ *"These things happen all the time. It just happened to a patient of mine yesterday."*
+ *"You are going to just have to tough it out."*
+ *"You're overreacting."*
+ *"You should have known that the pill was not the right one. You should have told the nurse."*
+ *"If I had seen the lab report results, I would have ordered a CT scan, but I did not. It's all my PA's fault for not letting me know."*
+ *"It's all the radiologist's fault."*
+ *"I wish I hadn't ignored the symptoms of abdominal pain. I just thought they were not significant."*
+ *"It's not my fault. You should have..."*

- *"I'm never going to work with that doctor again. The next time I need a cardiology consult, I will refuse to work with him."*
- *"I should have listened to the rumors. I heard that consultant had three patients die last year."*

Blaming others or jumping to a conclusion is not a positive step. Typically we do not have all the facts. Stick with initial heartfelt empathy and only the facts you know. More can come at a later time. If you do have QA concerns, of course follow up with an appropriate peer review process. However, jumping to the blame game without all the facts does not help the situation.

With empathy and information shared with the patient/family, you are ready to investigate the circumstances and determine whether an apology is warranted. Apologizing may seem like an easy task, but when it is you that is at fault, when it is your reputation on the line, when it is your insurance that is affected, when it is your privileges at risk, it is a very difficult task emotionally.

Please note: An apology, which includes admission of fault, only happens after an investigation reveals that the standard of care has been breached and it is causally related to the injury. Do not make an apology until you are ready! You cannot take it back!

How to Apologize and Accept Fault

Any effective, meaningful apology has four basic elements:[29]

(1) Empathy or "sorry"
(2) Admission of fault (*"I made a mistake — It's my fault"*)
(3) Explanation of what happened and how it will be prevented from happening again
(4) As necessary, an offer of compensation or some sort of fix to the problem that has been created.

---

29   Lazare A. "On Apology." Oxford University Press. 2004.

Effective, meaningful apologies have four basic elements:

1) Empathy or *"sorry"*

2) Admission of fault (*"I made a mistake — It's my fault"*)

3) Explanation of what happened and how it will be prevented from happening again

4) As necessary, an offer of compensation or some sort of fix to the problem that was created

These elements, in the right cases, eliminate anger felt by the aggrieved party. Relationships and trust will be restored. It is important to explain what happened and how it will be prevented from happening again. This should all have been part of your investigation process. True change cannot occur without knowing exactly what happened. Patients want to know what happened. They also want to know how it will be prevented again. If you tell patients how it will be prevented from happening again, you must ensure that those steps are taken. It may be a new process, incorporation of a new tool, a new hire, education, or even firing.

When it comes to compensation or a fix, we are really talking about resolution. How can you bring closure to this situation? Words alone may not be enough. Patients will have real problems as a result of the error that need to be fixed — by you, your organization, and/or your insurer.

"The apology is one thing, but my husband will be laid up for six months because of their error. Who is going to pay the bills and put food on the table? I guess I will have to sue these doctors!"

Sometimes it will simply be monetary compensation, but think outside the box. Listen to their issues and think of creative ways to resolve them:

- Lodging, meals for loved ones
- Continuing medical education for the healthcare provider
- An endowment in a loved one's name
- A scholarship in a loved one's name
- Paying off a house mortgage
- Remodeling a home for wheelchair access
- A structured settlement for children of the patient
- Childcare expenses
- Lost wages for the period of recovery
- Naming a lecture series on errors in honor of their loved one
- Involving the patient/family in quality improvement processes at the hospital

"Take a different perspective by placing yourself in <u>that</u> position."

Recognize that it is not necessary for a "fix" to be discussed at an initial meeting or discussion with the patient and family when you accept responsibility. In fact, it is probably better not to do so.

Also, consider the need for a release that releases you and perhaps others from future liability if you do make a payment. However, this may not be necessary in all circumstances, and must be considered on a case-by-case basis. Therefore, it is essential to consult an attorney in this process. Further, if a release is needed, legal counsel should be involved to ensure that the release is valid and will hold up in court should it be challenged. The release will provide protections from any future claims made by the patient and/or family based on the underlying negligence. It's not a lottery. The patient should not be able to reach an agreement with you and then later decide that he wants more money and sue.

Word of caution: As has been mentioned, an apology involving the four elements should only be delivered to a patient or family after an investigation has *proven* an error or breach of standard of care occurred, as well as a causative connection. It is hard, if not impossible, to "un-ring" the apology bell. Make sure you have all the facts in place before apologizing. Remember, "I'm sorry" just by itself can be and is very meaningful. It makes every situation a little better, assuming it is part of an overall enhanced communication strategy. The four steps of apology are reserved for those cases as explained above where due diligence has been completed.

"OK, great, I understand the four elements of apology and when I should apologize, but how do I actually deliver an apology should an investigation show that an error was committed?"

> **"Make sure you have all the facts in place before apologizing."**

It starts with the right attitude, which includes the understanding that disclosure and apology is not about the doctors, nurses, hospital, or the insurance company — it is about the patients and family: The customer. You must think how your words and nonverbal communication and other actions will be received by your customers.

"Have I taken all the steps of disclosure before ringing the bell of apology?

Your customers are going to be closely scrutinizing you and your colleagues throughout the disclosure and apology process. Their emotions are raw. They are literally mourning the injury or death caused by the medical error. The trust they placed in you, your colleagues, and the institution has been violated. The relationship has been damaged. They desperately want to rebuild their trust in you, but any slip up (even unintended) will send them tumbling back down the hill. Be careful. Think this through.

We have already discussed how to effectively empathize, and you will need to continue to empathize in your apology discussion.

Remember, you have in place an event management infrastructure to support your apology and disclosure. Use it and use the information below as your checklist. First, let's set the stage.

+ **Select a neutral meeting to apologize and to disclose.**

    Schedule a disclosure meeting at a time and place convenient and comfortable for the patient/family. It may well be at the hospital. Remember, disclosure is all about the customer. Make it convenient for them, but also make it private and comfortable.

+ **Clear your calendar — do not put a time limit on the meeting.**

    Set aside enough time. Do not assume the disclosure meeting will last an hour and schedule a patient or another meeting immediately afterwards. You may either rush through the disclosure meeting (which is bad) or you may be forced to cancel on the other patient, which is poor service for that individual. More importantly, you will not feel comfortable in the disclosure meeting and the customers will pick up on your negative verbal and nonverbal cues. You do not want to rush through the disclosure meeting — take all time you need and the family needs. Furthermore, after the meeting, you and your colleagues will want time to decompress and review, including taking time to appropriately document the disclosure meeting. Take all the time necessary!

+ **Provide food, drinks, mints, tissues, and other necessary items.**

- **Provide comfortable chairs, good temperature, and a clean meeting room.**

  This almost seems like common sense, but many a meeting has been destroyed by uncomfortable chairs, a room that was too hot or cold, or a table that was covered by crumbs, half-eaten cookies, and spilled drinks from the previous meeting. Make sure the room is ready for the disclosure meeting.

- **Special needs? Know your customers!**

  Scout out the patient and family ahead of time. Know them. Understand them. How many members of the family plan to attend the meeting? Is the room big enough to accommodate everyone? Are there enough chairs? Is the table big enough? Does anyone have a wheelchair or other special needs? Know your customers!

- **Details, details, details.**

  It sounds morbid, but think like a funeral home director. Walk into a high-quality funeral home and every detail is covered so the family can focus on their one job: Mourning. Dealing with an adverse medical event involves mourning too, especially if there is a death or major injury. So, when planning the meeting make sure every detail is covered so the customers can focus on the apology and disclosure and begin the process of healing and moving on with their lives.

  OK, so the stage is set for a successful

> "Remember, disclosure is all about the customer."

> "...When planning the disclosure meeting, make sure every detail is covered so the customers can focus on the apology and disclosure..."

apology and disclosure meeting. So how exactly do you apologize? Again, below is an important checklist.

+ **Have a plan.**

    Have a plan in place: What will be discussed, who will be present, who will take the lead, what is the desired result, and how are you going to get there? This should be coordinated through your event management program.

+ **Practice.**

    Practice what you are going to say and how you are going to say it before the meeting/discussion. Use a mirror so that you can see how you may be perceived by others. You can even work with legal counsel to practice through videotaping. If you do practice with video, be sure to do so with legal counsel involved so you can protect those practice sessions under attorney-client privilege. You do not want a plaintiff's lawyer using your practice sessions, your goof-ups, in front of a jury!

+ **As you start the meeting, remember to turn off cell phones and pagers.**

    "Mrs. Jones, I want to tell you how sorry we are about the mistake that injured your BEEP! BEEP! BEEP! BEEP! BEEP! Now, where was I? Oh, yes, your husband and how we injured him. We are so... BEEP, BEEP, BEEP, BEEP..."

    Get the idea? Just like the movie theater, put your pagers and cell phones on mute at the start of the meeting. Do *not* set your pager to vibrate, because your customers will hear that too and wonder why you are not answering it. A better idea is to leave your pager and/or cell phone with a responsible person

> **"Just like the movie theater, put your pagers and cell phones on mute at the start of the meeting."**

who can monitor it for you during the meeting, and if there is a real emergency that person can slip you a note or whisper in your ear and you can politely excuse yourself from the meeting.

+ **Sit down with the patient and family. Do not stand or lectur**

Physicians are used to being authority figures. Sit down at the same table with the customers and look them in the eye. Act respectful and courteous. If you feel the urge to lecture or stand up, do not do it. In this meeting, you are *not* the chief of staff or head of anesthesia with an advanced degree. You want to relate: One human being apologizing to other human beings and asking for forgiveness. Be humble, be contrite, and show it. Get on the same side of the table!

> **"Sit down at the same table with the customer and look them in the eye."**

+ **Talk slowly, and do not dominate the conversation. Allow the patient and family to interject and ask questions.**

Healthcare professionals have a tendency to dominate a conversation. Not here, not in this meeting. Talk slowly and deliberately as you work through the apology. Use common language. Do not use too much scientific or medical jargon. Use common language: It was a heart attack that was missed, not a myocardial infarction. Also, allow and even encourage the customers to interrupt with questions and statements. Remember, this meeting is all about the customer, although we often find it helpful and therapeutic to the doctor.

> **"Use common language. Do not use too much scientific or medical jargon."**

- **Silence is OK!**

  Silence and "pregnant pauses" in meetings can feel painful, especially when you are a busy person who is used to being in charge and talking really fast. But silence is OK and even necessary in disclosure meetings. Silence gives your customers time to absorb what you are saying and formulate questions or responses…the questions and responses you will need to hear to ensure you are connecting. Silence is OK…silence is respectful.

  > "Silence is OK and even necessary in disclosure meetings."

- **In effect, ask your customers to repeat back what you said by asking them questions.**

  You want to make sure your patients and families are correctly receiving the information you are trying to convene. Remember, your customers are likely in an emotionally traumatized state, so you need to make an extra effort to make sure you are connecting by occasionally asking them to repeat back what you said or ask them some simple questions. If they are not receiving the information, you will need to review the information, or you may even need to schedule another meeting when they are emotionally ready to listen better. Use your judgment.

  > "Make sure your patients and families are correctly receiving the information you are trying to convene."

- **The "s" word: "Sorry". Say it!**

  Say you are sorry. Do not say you *"regret the mistake," "feel bad,"* or *"wish the episode hadn't happened,"* but say, *"I'm sorry."* Patients and families want to hear you say the "s" word. It is literally the gold standard and has special value to injured patients and families. They want to hear the word from you. Look your customers in the eye and say, *"I'm sorry."* To understand the importance of the "s" word versus words like regret, consider the story from the October 25, 2008 *Dallas Morning News*. A woman sat in an ER for 19 hours for a fractured leg, never saw a physician, and was sent a $162 bill. The hospital later retracted the bill after media publicity about the story, and in the letter to the patient wrote the following: *"We regret any inconvenience this may have caused you."* That does not make you feel so good!

A better apology could have read like this:

> ## "Patients and families want to hear you say the "s" word."

"We are very sorry for our poor service and the frustration and additional pain you suffered during your visit to our emergency room. Furthermore, we are sorry for the additional frustration and anger caused by our errant billing. I can assure you we will learn from the mistakes we made in your situation, improve our services, and hopefully, in the future, you will give us a chance to regain your trust. We have eliminated the bill sent in error to you.

- When appropriate, as discussed earlier, admit fault. Take ownership of the mistake.

> ## "Admission of fault is necessary for patients and families to forgive you."

"I made a mistake"... *"It was my fault"*... *"I accept full responsibility for this unfortunate situation"*... *"We committed an error"*...etc, etc.

"Sorry" is one word, but admission of fault shows people you have real character and are truly owning up to the problem. Admission of fault is necessary for patients and families to forgive you. Sorry without admission of fault will ring hollow and heighten anger and suspicion with your customers in the circumstances where an apology is needed.

+ **Explain — slowly — how the error happened, to the extent you know, and how it will be prevented in the future.**

> "Customers want to know that their suffering was not in vain and medicine will improve."

Tell customers how the error happened and how you, your colleagues, and the institution have learned from the mistake(s) and what you will do to make sure the same mistake(s) are not repeated. Patients and families desperately want to hear this information from healthcare providers. Customers want to know that their suffering was not in vain and medicine will improve. This is a very important to patients and families, especially when they expect and desire to receive treatment in the same hospital again.

+ **Answer all questions truthfully and honestly. It is OK to say you do not know the answer to a question.**

The explanation of events that caused the error(s) will undoubtedly lead to questions from the customers. Take these questions seriously and behave in a correct manner if you do not know the answer to a particular question.

Medical school teaches physicians to always be on their toes and be ready for difficult questions thrown by an instructor or senior physician. The fact is that life is an open-book exam. Nobody knows all the answers to all the questions, and customers understand this truism. It is OK to say I do not know.

"I don't know the answer to your question, Mrs. Jones, but I can assure you we will continue to research this, and I will be back in touch with you in the next day or so. Is this OK?"

Very acceptable. But if you try to fake your way through a question, most customers will detect it and resent you, and once you are caught with inconsistent responses, get ready for a lawsuit.

+ **Allow customers to vent and rant — do not take it personall.**

Patients and families will receive a wealth of emotionally charged information in a disclosure meeting. Their initial response may be anger, shock, and rage, and they may express these feelings with shouting, cursing, crying, and accusations. Do not take any of it personally. Let your customers vent. Do not engage in a shouting match, become defensive, or get sucked into an argument. Simply respond by saying, *"I can only imagine how this feels for you, and being angry at me, my colleagues, and this institution is completely understandable. I am so sorry about all of this. I am truly sorry."*

> "Let your customers vent."

Let them continue to vent and allow the anger to drain out of them. Look for the appropriate opening to continue the discussion. If no opening presents itself, the disclosure process may need to continue with a second meeting on another day. Provide space and time for cooler heads to prevail.

+ **Communicate.**

Communication is not just what you say, but it is also how you say it. Be mindful of your word choice, the tone of your voice, and your demeanor. Patients recognize insincerity. Be sincere. It has been reported that as much as 90% of all communication is non-verbal. Do not look at your watch (it only suggests that you are in a hurry). Even if the discussion is over the phone, patients, while they cannot see you, they can get a sense of the tone of your voice and determine whether you are being sincere. Do not become angry or judgmental.

- **Listen.**

  Truly listen to what the patient/family has to say. This means not only what they say but also how they say it. Patients will know when you are not listening and are not taking them seriously.

- **Express gratitude.**

  Express gratitude for bringing a situation to your attention, if that is the case.

- **Compensation discussions may take several meetings.**

  Compensation may be discussed and negotiated over several meetings. The first meeting may involve simply asking questions and getting a better understanding of the customers' financial situation and needs. Between the first and second meetings, you and your disclosure team may develop a compensation proposal. Be sure to involve people on your team from risk management and legal counsel who understand the value of injuries and wrongful deaths.

  It is a process. You will try to meet their needs by making an offer. Undoubtedly, your customers and their counsel will counteroffer with a number that is on the higher end of the scale. Listen to what your customers and their legal counsel say constitutes fair compensation. Even though their number is higher than your original offer, it does not mean they are necessarily trying to be unfair or fleece you. Ask questions and listen. Because anger has dissipated (or even eliminated), you can have a discussion about what is fair and reasonable compensation. Take advantage of the situation and talk with your customers and their attorney! It is a process. Try to keep the discussion on an objective level. Risk managers are experienced and often very good at this, as are representatives of your insurer.

- **Be fair but firm – you're not an open checkbook!**

  You want to be fair with your customers and their legal counsel, but you must be firm. All unreasonable and outrageous requests will be denied, and if they persist, let them know you are not afraid to have the courts make the ultimate decision. That decision will be basically limited to determining the value of damages.

- **Disclosure may be an extended affair — stay in touch with the patient and their family.**

  Medical errors can be long-term affairs. One or two disclosure meetings *may* not completely resolve the situation. You may need to continually reach out and communicate with patients and their family members for an extended period of time to make sure they understand all the issues and are comfortable with the resolution. Remember, disclosure and apology are ultimately about rebuilding trust and relationships, so be a friend and stay in touch with people! Do not ever let patients and families feel abandoned or they may pay you back with litigation or other acts of retribution. This is often times the biggest complaint of patients – how do I know you will keep up the change one, two, three years from now?

- **Summarize the discussion and next steps.**

  At the end of the disclosure meeting, summarize for the patient/family what was discussed, what their concerns were, how they will be addressed, and what the next steps are.

- **Document.**

  Consistent with the discussion on event management, document the meeting/discussion.

This extensive checklist of items list should not overwhelm you and your colleagues. Yes, disclosure and apology can be a lot to think about, especially if you have not been trained or experienced in these matters. Prior to a disclosure meeting, the participants should engage in role plays to "practice" what they are going to say and how they will react to customer feedback. However, you do not want to develop a script...disclosure and apology must come from the heart. Customers will detect scripted apologies and may feel like they are being snowed over. Practice, yes; but scripting, no.

Examples of effective apologies:

- *"I'm sorry that you are experiencing side effects from the medication dosage. I accidentally wrote 30 milligrams instead of 3.0 milligrams on your prescription. I have taken steps in my practice to ensure that this does not happen again. We have implemented JCAHO recommendations for number nomenclature on prescriptions that should reduce future risk of similar incidents. The important thing for you to know with your care is that the side effects are temporary and they will not be associated with any permanent damage."*

- *"I'm sorry that I misread your x-ray. I have no excuse, and can only hope that you understand that medicine is not a perfect science. I do my best to read every x-ray with the utmost of care and diligence. Sometimes, a miss occurs. We have looked at ways to reduce this potential and what has occurred with you reminds us our work is not done. We have instituted a new policy that ensures quality assurance reviews every morning of the previous day's reads. What I would like to do for you is pay for your surgery that is now needed to repair the fracture and provide you with compensation that will reimburse your medical expenses associated with this fracture and any pain you have been experiencing. I have received an estimate from your surgeon on the costs of your surgery and related medical expenses, as well as an estimate for medications and rehab that will be needed. Given this, I want to provide you with $15,000."* (Note: this type of discussion is one reserved for a second meeting and after all due diligence has been completed).

- *"I'm sorry that I did not see the results of your mammogram. If I had, I would have referred you to an oncologist at that time. We have reviewed the circumstances, and I have discovered that for some unknown reason, your lab report ended up in the medical chart without being initialed by anyone. We have in place a requirement at our practice that all lab reports are initialed when they are reviewed. It appears that did not happen here. In efforts to reduce the risk of this happening again, I have hired a nurse whose sole job is to review all incoming laboratory reports and x-rays. When she sees a report with an abnormal result, she is required to notify the patient's physician so that appropriate next steps can be taken, including notification to the patient. The good news is that we have not lost much time, I have called in a favor and have gotten you an appointment for tomorrow with an oncologist. The oncologist will discuss with you your treatment options. I would like to stay involved with your care, and your oncologist will keep me informed. Please feel free to reach out to me throughout this process if you have any questions. Again, I am truly sorry for what has happened, but I do feel that we have your care on track now, and that you will have a good result."*

Examples of ineffective apologies:

- *"As the doctor here I can tell you this situation is just horrible for me. I feel terrible. I wish this hadn't happened. You know, I shouldn't be telling you this, but Nurse Betty shouldn't have given those drugs to your daughter...that's the reason she's on life support. OK? Oh, there's my beeper, I need to run."*
- *"I was on call when the leak was discovered. Dr. Jones should have paged me, but he did not. I know he told you he did, but he's wrong. It's all his fault."*
- *"I'm sorry you think something went wrong, but a cut of the common bile duct is a known complication of this procedure. I know I did not discuss it with you prior to surgery, but everyone knows it is a risk."*

- "I'm sorry that I performed surgery on your right leg instead of your left, but it is all the nurse's fault. She placed an "x" on the left leg, and I thought it meant not to touch that leg. She should have put a "yes" on your left leg. Everyone knows that, and that is what our hospital policy says to do."

It all boils down to these steps:

(1) Empathy
(2) Investigation
(3) Apology and disclosure
(4) Resolution

What if your investigation reveals that no liability exists, but the adverse event is significant in other ways?

Recognize that there will be some adverse events that are not medical errors, but that are some type of significant complication for one reason or another where an apology, or admission of fault is necessary. The difference is that the admission of fault is not one as to liability but an admission of fault as to, for example, a miscommunication, a service lapse, or other plus factor.

For example, a patient's family was not kept informed of the patient's deteriorating health where the patient was thought by the family to be a healthy 55 year old man. Unbeknownst to the family, the patient's condition began to worsen, but physicians had no discussion with the family about the worsening condition and therefore not setting the needed and relevant expectations of the family – an imminent death. Conversely, the family thought that the patient was going to be discharged the following day and be sent home. They decided to forgo a visit with the patient until then. However, the patient died in the interim and the family was unable to be with their loved one during his last moments. Despite the communication issues, the medical care provided was appropriate – there was no way to prevent the death. However, the family is very upset that they did not have the opportunity to be with their loved-one particularly as he was dying.

In this circumstance, empathy and apology are both necessary. The physician needs to take responsibility for the lack of appropriate communication with the family. Even though there was not breach of a standard of care, the plus factor involved here is certainly one that could lead a family to a lawyer, after all the patient was 55 years old and the death of a 55 year old can be an attractive case to a plaintiff attorney. Proper post-adverse event communication and disclosure can help the family to heal and prevent them from visiting a plaintiff lawyer who may take on a case.

A full investigation and understanding of what occurred and the issues must be done. Preparation for a meeting with the family must be done. Finally, the meeting must actually take place. You can expect that the family will not be happy and will not leave the meeting initially feeling great, nor will you. However, the communication and open discussion can help them lead to closure. They will have an opportunity to vent their concerns and frustrations, and you will have an opportunity to tell them while they cannot bring back their father, brother, dad, etc., or change what happened, you can work to ensure that similar circumstances do not occur with future patients. And you must! You must follow through with your promises, and you must follow up with the family to let them know what you have done – perhaps at 3 months, 6 months, and one year. It will depend on the circumstances.

The key here is understanding that while an apology, admitting *fault* as to liability, is often necessary when a medical error is involved, an apology, admitting *fault* on key non-liability issue may also be necessary.

What if your investigation reveals that no error occurred and the issue is not one that rises to the level of an apology admitting some type of fault?

You provided initial empathy to the patient/family and have told them you would investigate the matter. Above, we explained how to apologize when the investigation reveals that an error occurred, but what if none occurred? You must still contact the patient or family and schedule a meeting with them. In this meeting, continue with your empathy (*"We are sorry this happened"*) and explain the findings of the investigation. You may also want to share the records of the investigation with the patient/family. For example, if the autopsy report determines that the cause of death was natural, show the family the autopsy report and explain it to them. Answer any questions they may have. In this meeting, you need to show what you did with your investigation, why it was appropriate, and the results. However, no settlement is offered.

What if the patient/family still think otherwise? You have some options, and which you choose will be dependent on the circumstances. You can simply wait to see if a lawyer takes on the case. Plaintiff lawyers in advance of filing suit should request the patient's medical records. When this occurs, it should be a telltale sign that a plaintiff's lawyer is investigating the patient's care, and, at this point, you can have your legal counsel reach out to the plaintiff's counsel in an attempt to dissuade him from filing a lawsuit.

Your lawyer may offer to have the plaintiff's lawyer talk with the expert that reviewed your care and determined that your care was appropriate. Your lawyer may offer to meet with the patient and the lawyer, along with you.

Ultimately, if all of your care was appropriate, your case should be defended to the end. It is the only way the right message can be sent to patients and attorneys: We will not settle cases where our treatment met the standard of care.

Conclusion

Finally, this chapter demonstrates why it is important to have a disclosure *program* that is administered by a team of professionals in your organization from administration, risk management, legal, and the medical staff. This team needs to be trained on all the details of disclosure and through the program be prepared to offer support and help to your medical professionals, who will be disclosing and apologizing on rare and infrequent occasions.

Review Points:

- Say you are sorry immediately after an event without admitting fault.
- After an investigation has proven a medical error with causation, use the four steps of apology.
- Include the four steps of apology when you need to apologize when a non-medical error is your fault – empathize and apologize in context.
- If an investigation reveals no causative error, continue to empathize but do not admit fault.
- Practice!

CHAPTER 7

DO YOU NEED A LAW TO APOLOGIZE?

"I would never introduce a doctor's apology in court. It is my job to make a doctor look bad in front of a jury, and telling the jury the doctor apologized and tried to do the right thing kills my case." —
President, South Carolina Trial Lawyers Association, testimony before South Carolina Senate, September 2005

This quote stands in stark contrast to conventional wisdom, but it is right on the money. Unfortunately, healthcare and insurance professionals have been errantly informed for years not to apologize lest it be used against them in court. *"Say you're sorry and you're dead in court,"* is the mantra. Not so, as mentioned previously, as long as apology and disclosure are done right and healthcare professionals understand the vast difference between a sincere showing of empathy and an apology accepting responsibility. Both done in the right way under the right circumstances have powerful positive legal consequences. Again, it is about <u>context</u>.

Further, across the country, state legislatures have enacted laws that provide some form of immunity to physicians and other healthcare providers for apologies if a lawsuit is initiated. The impact of these laws includes providing the environment in which healthcare providers feel comfortable with apologizing to patients and families with less fear of repercussions. However, when done right, defense counsel may actually **NOT** want to refrain from introducing an apology into evidence during a medical malpractice lawsuit. Remember, at the minimum, disclosure is about building great evidence for the defense! These laws may be useful where a healthcare professional did not conduct a post-event communication in the right way (in other words, not in context). In conclusion, apology laws can make healthcare professionals feel more comfortable about disclosing and apology and can save him from a botched or hurried apology; however, the absence of apology laws (or if a law is not deemed "robust") should not prohibit the development of a Sorry Works! program. Indeed, professionals who adopt Sorry Works! learn so-called apology laws actually have very little legal value.

Disclosure: Medical Ethics and the Law

The reasons to disclose for the patient and family have been discussed and have their grounding in law, ethics, and common sense. Patients have a right to know. Ethical standards have been promulgated by the American Medical Association, the Joint Commission on Accreditation of Healthcare Organizations (JCAHO), and the American College of Physicians Ethics Manual.

The American Medial Association *Code of Medical Ethics* provides:

> It is a fundamental ethical requirement that a physician should at all times deal honestly and openly with patients. Patients have a right to know their past and present medical status and to be free of any mistaken beliefs concerning their conditions. Situations occasionally occur in which a patient suffers significant medical complications that may have resulted from the physician's mistake or judgment. In these situations, the physician is ethically required to inform the patient of all the facts necessary to ensure understanding of what has occurred. Only through full disclosure is a patient able to make informed decisions regarding future medical care.
>
> Ethical responsibility includes informing patients of changes in their diagnoses resulting from retrospective review of test results or any other information. This obligation holds even though the patient's medical treatment or therapeutic options may not be altered by the new information.

Concern regarding legal liability which might result following truthful disclosure should not affect the physician's honesty with a patient.[30]

In summary, the Code of Medical Ethics requires disclosure from an ethical viewpoint and further states that concerns over legal liability that may result from that disclosure are no reason to be untruthful. JCAHO's accreditation standards address the ethical considerations, providing: *"Patients and, when appropriate, their families are informed about the outcomes of care, including unanticipated outcomes."*[31] The value of JCAHO's position is that it means that the movement for healthcare provider disclosure extends to the hospitals, and accordingly, the approach with disclosure can be collaborative between the healthcare professional and the hospital.

However, healthcare providers as noted above have traditionally been fearful to apologize to patients and families, believing that the apology will be construed as an admission of fault or guilt. This fear is not without support as plaintiff attorneys have used healthcare provider words against them in the courtroom; however, it is time to change this view and to have disclosure and showing of empathy used *for* healthcare providers instead of against them, and the apology laws help to fuel the environment needed to effectuate change.

In 1986, Massachusetts was the first state to enact a sympathy/apology law, and it provided:

> *"Statements, writings or benevolent gestures expressing sympathy or a general sense of benevolence relating to the pain, suffering or death of a person involved in an accident*

---

30   American Medical Association. Opinion E-8.12 Patient Information. *Code of Medical Ethics.* American Medical Association. 2006. (accessible at http://www.ama-assn.org/ama/pub/category/8497.html) (last visited August 22, 2007).

31   JCAHO. "Ethics, Rights, and Responsibilities," in *Comprehensive Accreditation Manual for Hospitals: The Official Handbook* (Oakbrook Terrace, Ill.: JCAHO 2003), Patient Rights Standard RI. 2.90, RI-12.

and made to such person or to the family of such person
shall be inadmissible as evidence of an admission of liability
in a civil action."[32]

It was not until 1998 that the next sympathy/apology law was enacted. In total, since the Massachusetts law was enacted, 34 more states have enacted some form of a sympathy/apology law, providing immunity protections to healthcare providers (at the time this book was written). (See Appendix A for a complete list of those states and the relevant statutes.) The most laws were enacted in 2005, with 13 states enacting laws with immunity provisions. The components of the sympathy/apology laws vary, and they generally include:

- Protections in certain actions (i.e., civil actions, wrongful death actions only, arbitrations, administrative proceedings);
- What is protected (i.e., written statements, oral statements, and/ or conduct);
- What content is protected (i.e., affirmations, gestures, expressions of apology or sympathy, expressions of fault, "sorry," offers to undertake corrective action);
- Who is protected (healthcare providers and/or employees of the healthcare provider);
- Who is the statement or conduct directed to (patient, relative of the patient, patient's survivors, healthcare decision maker for the patient, friend of the patient or family);
- What does the apology or sympathy relate to (i.e., an accident, an unanticipated outcome, an event, patient injury or pain);
- What protection is afforded (i.e., inadmissible as evidence of admission of liability, inadmissible as admission against interest, protected from examination in a deposition)
- Most states do *not* protect statements or admissions of fault. Among those, the terminology varies:

---

32   MASS. GEN. LAWS ANN. ch. 233, § 23D (West 2000).

- Statement of fault
- Admission of liability or fault
- Fault
- Statement of fault, negligence, or culpable conduct

At the time this book was written, at least two more states had introduced legislation: New Jersey and Pennsylvania. In Pennsylvania, encouraging an open dialogue in these situations benefits everyone. When something bad happens, we all want to understand why and we want to know how we can prevent it in the future. The goals of the health care provider and the patient are really the same. They both want answers. Our litigious climate shouldn't force people into a courtroom to find them. Sometimes the answer may not be readily apparent and sometimes we may not find one but the more conversations we have, the greater our chances of improving and learning.

The end result is essentially the same and attempts to promote an environment where healthcare professionals feel that their discussions of disclosure and empathy with patients and family will not later be used against them.

Colorado, on the other hand, enacted one of the broader state laws, which includes protections for a healthcare provider's actions and conduct and specifically protects words or acts that express fault. The law was intended to be broad in efforts to promote an open relationship between physicians and their patients.[33] Georgia, South Carolina, Connecticut, and Arizona also recently shielded words such as "mistake" and "error."

Some state laws incorporate a timing element. For example, in Vermont, the statement or conduct must be made within 30 days of when the provider knew or should have known of the consequences of the error, in order to be protected. This approach may take away from some of the goals of the sympathy/apology laws.

---

33   Cohen JR. "Toward Candor After Medical Error: The First Apology Law." *Harvard Health Policy Rev.* 2004; 51:21–24.

The authors believe that a combination of various components of these statutes and more makes for the most effective sympathy/apology law. (A draft model law is contained in Appendix B.)

Beyond the sympathy/apology laws, some states have gone a step further and have enacted mandatory disclosure requirements. To date, eight (8) states have enacted such laws: California, Florida, Nevada, New Jersey, Oregon, Pennsylvania, Vermont, and Washington.[34] Pennsylvania was the first state to require a statutory duty to notify patients in writing of a "serious event." It provides:

> A medical facility through an appropriate designee shall provide written notification to a patient affected by a serious event or, with the consent of the patient, to an available family member or designee within seven days of the occurrence or discovery of a serious event. If the patient is unable to give consent, the notification shall be given to an adult member of the immediate family. If an adult member of the immediate family cannot be identified or located, notification shall be given to the closest adult family member. For unemancipated patients who are under 18 years of age, the parent or guardian shall be notified in accordance with this subsection...Notification under this subsection shall not constitute an acknowledgment or admission of liability.[35]

The concept of these mandatory disclosure laws is premised on the ethical foundation, which can benefit patients and healthcare providers, when the law is satisfied in an appropriate fashion. However,

---

34   CAL. HEALTH & SAFETY CODE § 1279.1 (Deering 2007); FLA. STAT. ANN. §
      395.1051 (LexisNexis 2007); NEV. REV. STAT. ANN. sec 439.855 (LexisNexis
      2007); N.J. STAT. AN. sec 26:2H-12.25 (LexisNexis 2007); 2003 OR. LAWS
      ch. 686, sec 4); 40 P.S. sec 1303.308 (2006); VT. STAT. ANN. tit. 18, sec 1915
      (2007); WASH. REV. CODE ANN. sec 70.41.380 (LexisNexis 2007).
35   40 P.S. § 1303.308 (2006).

admittedly and clearly, they are not without drawbacks. Often patients view these letters as an indication that something "wrong" happened. In fact, the letters, unfortunately, are often written that way (perhaps, according to statute, almost necessarily so!). In these states it becomes critical to have a disclosure program in place so that the mandatory letter becomes part of the process and not the process itself. In this respect, the patient will receive their letter *after* communication has occurred and will read the letter in context. They will have already been told about the letter and the purpose of the letter, and the potential of the notice letter being taken out of context is greatly reduced.

The Pennsylvania law, for example, places the onus on the hospital facility to provide written notification to the patient/family within seven (7) days of the occurrence or discovery of a serious event. It is essential that even though it is the hospital's duty to comply with this law, the physicians be involved in the disclosure. In fact, hospitals should coordinate this process with their doctors. Remember, the letter *is* evidence. Healthcare providers and hospitals should use the letter to their advantage instead of disadvantage. There is a tendency to say as little as possible in the letter for fear of the letter being used against the hospital or healthcare provider. However, an alternative approach could be a well-balanced letter that informs the patient at the same time that it documents positive evidence.

At the federal level, Senators Hillary Rodham Clinton (D-NY) and Barack Obama (D-IL) introduced the Medical Error Disclosure and Compensation Act in 2005. It set forth a two-part approach, requiring expression of sympathy to be provided immediately to a patient and permitting other discussion of accountability to be made only after a full investigation was completed. The bill died in committee. The authors suggest that it is time to revisit federal legislation in this arena.

Sympathy/apology laws encourage physicians and healthcare professionals to overcome their cultural inhibitions about apology by providing the immunity protections that have seemingly held healthcare providers back. *"Hey, it's OK to apologize now…we won't get sued!"* However, the truth of the matter is that it has always been OK to say "sorry." In fact, as mentioned earlier, good communication after an adverse event is an important legal strategy to reduce the potential of the so-called "plus" in the courtroom.

After an adverse event, everything that occurs, but particularly what occurs in the first 24 hours, will often help determine whether or not the patient or family go to see a lawyer. It has been well established that two significant reasons they do so are out of anger or to obtain what they perceive as needed information: *"What really happened?"* When patients do not receive prompt information post-adverse event, they are forced to speculate what is almost always on the negative view. They become suspicious. Worse yet, they can hear different explanations that are not well coordinated and make it appear as if different versions are being offered. Perhaps their questions go unanswered, or worse, phone calls or requests for a meeting go unanswered. These actions (or inactions) drive them to a lawyer.

> **After an adverse event, everything that occurs, but particularly what occurs in the first 24 hours, will often help determine whether or not the patient or family go to see a lawyer.**

This is also the type of behavior that plaintiff lawyers find attractive. It is the "plus" — behavior that when showcased in the courtroom in front of patients (jurors) can anger the jury and result in large awards at times more reflective of their reaction to the behavior than the actual damages! Jury consultants have confirmed this reality and we have seen firsthand.[36]

---

36   *See, e.g.,* Saxton JW, Finkelstein MM, Bravin S, Stawiski S. "Reduce Liability Risk by Improving Your Patient Satisfaction." (2008) (accessible at http://www.pressganey.com/galleries/default-file/MD_White_Paper-Malpractice_0808.pdf) (last visited Sept. 11, 2008).

> **We must begin to realize that not only is disclosure and enhanced compassionate communication post-adverse event best for the patient and family, it is your best legal strategy and the reason apology-immunity laws have little legal value.**

We must begin to realize that not only is disclosure and enhanced compassionate communication post-adverse event best for the patient and family, it is your best legal strategy and the reason apology-immunity laws have little legal value. As the quote at the beginning of this chapter says, trial lawyers like to demonize physician and hospital defendants. A claim of "cover-up" or the fact a family has to go to a lawyer to find out what happened certainly paves the way.

"All that my client wanted to know was what happened. Their son was in the ICU instead of home after what was described as a minor procedure. No one was saying anything. When they asked the nurse, she quickly turned away. One nurse actually asked if my client had talked to Dr. Smith. Well, they tried, but he never returned the call. They lost their son and have to sue to find out what really happened! Can you ladies and gentlemen imagine not knowing? Well, we will all find out this week..."

If apology and disclosure are done right, healthcare professionals and their institutions will reduce and importantly keep patients and families on the *same side of the table in the quest to find out what happened and what we need to do about it.* Patients should not feel as if they need help from a lawyer to do so.

There are cases where fault is not at question — but the parties cannot agree on the value of damages. Value is intensely subjective. Damages include both economic and noneconomic damages. The economic damages are often definable, but the noneconomic damages are far harder to value. For example, noneconomic damages include pain and suffering or loss of consortium (essentially loss of companionship).

Sometimes this inability to easily determine the value of noneconomic damages can lead to nonresolution (because it is too hard!) and a lawsuit being filed. Most cases, however, in the hands of experienced lawyers, can be resolved. At times mediation can help or even arbitrating among defendants who cannot agree on apportionment.

However, if the case proceeds to court, the provider and/or hospital will instruct defense counsel to argue the case only on the damages; fault will **not** be contested. Assuming the provider(s) made a reasonable monetary offer during the disclosure process, the plaintiff attorney will have scant evidence with which to inflame the jury. Always remember, it's hard — if not impossible — for a plaintiff's attorney to prosecute an honest, contrite defendant who made a good faith effort to fix a problem.

"But can an apology ever lead to a successful lawsuit?"

If an apology is hurried or botched, a lawsuit may be in the offing. What's a hurried apology? Admitting fault or assigning blame before an investigation is complete. Consider the following quotes that could be dangerous in the immediate aftermath of an adverse event:

"Sorry, we screwed up."

"I'm sorry I did this to you."

"Sorry. If I had read the lab reports differently, this would not have happened."

You must be careful, because you may be forced to eat those words if your investigation shows no error was committed, and then the family and their legal counsel may suspect a cover-up. Remember, it's hard to "un-ring" the apology bell.

"Well, of course they're now saying they didn't make mistake. But as your attorney, I can tell you the most honest moment in this whole chain of events is when that doctor came out of the operating room and spontaneously admitted to you that he made an error that led to your husband's death. There is a cover-up going on here and we will file a lawsuit to unearth the truth."

There are ways to show empathy without making a statement that will be used against you. For instance:

"During your husband's surgery a complication occurred. We are sorry this happened. We are going to do a complete evaluation to find out what exactly happened. We want to share that with you and answer any questions you have then and now. As far as the complication, remember when we discussed surgery in my office. Yes, that's right. I did draw pictures and gave your husband a copy of the form."

Remember, an apology — which includes admission of fault — is only offered after an investigation has proven an error occurred. Yes, always be in a hurry to empathize, but don't always be in a hurry to apologize.

What's a botched apology? An apology that is not heartfelt or sincere. An apology that deflects blame. Consider the following the examples:

> *"You know your husband shouldn't have had a high fat diet for all those years. He was in horrible shape and we did the best we could. Sorry."*

> *"I know you feel bad about the loss of your wife, but I feel absolutely horrible. You have no idea what this is going to do my career!"*

> *"I shouldn't be telling you this, but Nurse Jones has made several errors, and I think she gave your son the wrong drugs."*

> *"Well, medicine is not only a science, but it's an art form too. This was a medical misadventure and these things do happen from time to time. No one is really at fault; it just happened and we regret it."*

All of this was discussed in greater detail in chapter 6. The important point is that if apology and disclosure are done in a well-thought-through process, the result can be beneficial for the healthcare provider and the patient, and even reduce frequency and severity. You need not have a sympathy/apology law in your state to allow you to feel comfortable to do so; however, if your state does have one, it can only help to make you feel more comfortable. It in no way means you should approach the disclosure process any less carefully.

Review Points:

- The disclosure movement has taken hold, with 35 states currently having enacted some form of a sympathy/apology law.
- However, no law is needed for a physician to show empathy or even apologize.
- Cover-ups and service lapses after adverse events spur litigation and severity, while an honest defendant takes the wind out of a case.
- Apology and disclosure must be "done right" under the auspices of a program to avoid hurried or botched apologies, which can be misinterpreted.

CHAPTER 8

THIS IS A JOB FOR PATIENTS TOO!

There can be little doubt that the real winners of the disclosure programs are patients and their families. One can only imagine (Doug's family does not have to) the cascade of emotions when things go wrong. All of us place tremendous faith in our healthcare professionals. For good reason. We are blessed with healthcare professionals with tremendous talent, and for the overwhelming majority, individuals who are compassionate, caring, well educated, experienced, and "driven for the right reasons." When we go to them as patients, our hopes, dreams, and expectations are all sky high.

Psychologists have shared with us that patients and their families, in the present day environment, almost never envision their surgery, their treatment regime, or their test not going right. They have heard of complications, but they do not imagine it could happen to them! Even with effective informed consent, no patient thinks that they will be the statistic that is reviewed with them. An actual error is even more remote in their mind. When either happens, it is a crushing realization. The procedure that they have been waiting months for, having endured a tremendous amount of pain, hoping that conservative therapy would work, taking time off from work for this one procedure to make their pain go away … causes them to be in worse shape than when they started! It happens. And it certainly happens notwithstanding the fact that the health care professionals had provided appropriate and even excellent care. But that does not make the continued pain and the expense that the patient is going to incur any better.

Psychologists tell us this is a double whammy for patients. Not only are they left with an unfortunate medical or physical circumstance, but are also in emotional turmoil. The individual whom they trusted literally with their life let them down. The individual with whom they had a trusting relationship has breached that trust. Can they trust you further? Will you be honest about what happened? Patients and their families sadly become suspicious. During that period of time when they actually need you more than ever, there is a tendency for the patients to pull away. Unfortunately, their family members and well-wishers can inadvertently help in this negative process. In other words, instead of telling the patient to head back first to the doctor, they feed the suspicion and suggest that they visit "their cousin Vinny!"

We know, post-adverse event, that patients need, more than anything else, their doctor. They need additional support, information, someone to answer their questions and concerns, and someone to hear their frustrations. There is no one better to fill this role than their doctor. If patients stay connected with their doctor, he or she can explain to them what occurred. They can review with the patient again why they feel a complication occurred, if they know. Focus on what they are going to do next. Allay their suspicions. If a true mistake has occurred, the patient needs to know why, to the extent that question can be answered. The patient will want to know what is going to be done to reduce the potential of such a mistake happening again, and the patient will want to be treated fairly. Patients should not have to engage a lawyer simply to find out the information that they badly need and deserve. Patients should not have to engage a lawyer to initiate a lawsuit and go through three or four years of litigation if they are entitled to compensation. The lack of a process that we have referred to as "event management" (see chapter 4) is a gaping hole in our efforts to support patients' and doctors' efforts to maintain solid relationships. *Let's be clear … when there is an unfortunate or even tragic outcome … patients need to go back to their doctor, at least first!*

Patients should be encouraged to return to their providers, first.

The litigation process is hard certainly on the doctor, more than we realize and probably more support should be given to our doctors when this occurs. However, in an under realized way, it is extraordinarily hard on the patient and the family. You heard bits of that in chapter 1 from Doug. Can any of us imagine having to be cross-examined about the worst tragedy of your life? Many have said that their deposition in which they were challenged about what occurred (in some cases actually blaming the patient or family members) is even worse than the incident itself. The litigation process is long and difficult for the patient and family. It includes drafting a complaint that, of course, the patient's counsel would do, but must be reviewed in detail by the patient; responding to discovery; giving up a lot of one's right to privacy; participating in often long depositions; having to review information that is provided by the doctor's counsel; and often, if it gets to a trial, taking between a week and two weeks, sometimes more, to have the case heard by a jury. Perhaps most importantly, this is no closure. No healing. For example, in a death case instead of going through the typical grieving process and moving on to the extent possible, one has this emotional wound opened time and time again for the next 3 or 4 years.

Imagine, as a patient, going through that entire process just to have the jury indicate that they do not feel the doctor was responsible. Various statistics show that physicians win approximately 80% of these cases that go to trial. One can only imagine the lasting effects of having a jury of *your* (the patient's) peers disagree with these allegations that you (the patient) have come to sincerely believe and live with over several years. It is going to not only open the wound, but perhaps sadly prevent it from healing — indefinitely.

Now, let's look at what would happen if we acted in accord with the concepts described earlier in this book. The patient and the family would receive immediate support from their healthcare team. They would receive information about what had occurred and assurances of what is being done to prevent it from occurring again. If compensation was due, they would receive it in perhaps months instead of years (if at all). If not, they would understand better what occurred and why. Of course, there will be good faith differences of opinion, but when everyone is talking, it becomes a smaller subset. The key is rather obvious, but understated and under-realized! We have quite a different process when we all work together.

> **Patients must go back to their doctor at least first.**

For this process to work, both sides of the equation need to be present, with an acceptance by healthcare professionals of the theories and the strategies described in this book, which we are happy to say, has begun to occur around the country and will continue. The first edition of this book was requested by tens of thousands of doctors, policy makers, risk managers, insurers, ethics teachers. However, patients must give their doctors a chance. Patients must go back to their doctor at least first. All too often a doctor reaches out only to find that a patient's lawyer has instructed them not to communicate. When this happens, everyone loses.

Perhaps a grassroots campaign is needed. Perhaps medical societies across the country need to reach out to the patient population and let them know that their doctor is there for them, even when these unfortunate, terrible adverse events occur. Maybe this chapter needs to be in every reception area so that patients know that although medical errors and complications are rare, they do happen. When they do, the relationship should not fracture. We need to stay on the same side of the table, the doctor and the patient, even when expectations are not met or a complication occurs. This has been a recurring theme in this book. There is perhaps no more important fundamental concept. Let's get the word out so we can spread this concept. Let's put it on our website; let's be creative on how we get this positive message out. Of course, it is uncomfortable to discuss "what we do when things go wrong," but years ago healthcare professionals were uncomfortable about discussing informed consent. Now it has become a standard part of patient education. Can we fit in a statement about talking to your doctor *if* a complication occurs? Perhaps it is a first step. Many surgeons around the country have incorporated such a statement as:

"In the unlikely event that one or more of the above inherent complications may occur, my physician(s) will take appropriate and reasonable steps to help manage the clinical situation and be available to me and my family to address our concerns and questions."

The point is that the concept of Sorry Works! and disclosure have always been focused on what the doctor should do and what the doctor's responsibilities entail. Those clearly are important, but let's be clear about the patient and family responsibilities too. Patients should resist the temptation that one must retain counsel immediately. In some subset of cases, of course, it may become necessary, but often that is not the case. Even when counsel is involved, it does not have to mean that there are three or four years of contentious and expensive litigation. Your attorney authors have dealt with many very fine plaintiff's lawyers through a disclosure process sometimes resulting in payments and sometimes not. Let's at least start on the same side of the table!

Review Points:

- Patients and their families are the true winners of a disclosure program.
- When an adverse event occurs, patients need to go back to their doctors first!
- A grassroots campaign by providers is needed!

Chapter 9

The Realized Benefits of Disclosure

Success Stories

Lexington, Massachusetts, is the site of the famous "shot heard 'round the world'" that opened the American Revolution against King George. Lexington, *Kentucky,* is the site of the "shot heard 'round the medical malpractice world.'" To be fair, Dr. Steve Kraman and Ginny Hamm, JD, of the Lexington Veterans Affairs Hospital did not set out to be revolutionaries. They just wanted to develop a better way to treat patients and families after adverse medical events. However, their work has left a legacy that has truly sparked a revolution within healthcare, insurance, and legal fields. The Sorry Works! message was initially modeled after their disclosure program, and Dr. Kraman serves on the board of The Sorry Works! Coalition.

The Lexington Veterans Affair lost two major lawsuits in the early 1980's. Significant sums of money were lost (both in the verdicts and litigation expenses), but more importantly, doctors and patients/families turned into bitter enemies during the litigation process. It was not the way they wanted to run a hospital. So, Dr. Kraman and Ms. Hamm developed a system to quickly identify bad outcomes so they would not be blindsided by lawsuits.

One of the first cases they identified involved the death of a woman who entered the Lexington Veterans' Affairs Hospital with several health complications. The woman's daughters did not suspect anything — their mom was in poor health — and they had her body picked up from the hospital and prepared for burial with no questions asked. However, the woman's death was unexpected, and the hospital staff did a thorough investigation. As it turned out, the investigation found that errors hastened the woman's death. This was a telling moment, because here was a case that could have been easily swept under the rug. The daughters thought it was Mom's time and no attorneys would have been banging down the door. But what is the definition of character? Doing the right thing when no one is watching.

The Lexington VA officials called the daughters and informed them that they had some information to share about their mother's death. The daughters were advised to retain legal counsel, and a meeting was scheduled. In that meeting, Dr. Kraman and his colleagues apologized, admitted fault, explained what happened, and discussed compensation. The case was settled in a few weeks.

The skeptic might say, "*Well, that's a great story, but no wonder the federal government is in debt up to its eyeballs...These guys are handing out money like it's water!*"

Not true. The experience from the woman's death led to the creation of a disclosure program at the Lexington VA in 1987. After seven years of a disclosure program, the Lexington VA, when compared to 35 other similarly-situated VA facilities, was in the top quartile for total claims — because they were disclosing so much — but they were in the bottom quartile for total payments. Over a 13-year period, the program handled over 170 claims, and the largest single payment made was $341,000 for a wrongful death case. According to data from the office of the VA general counsel, in the year 2000, the mean national VA malpractice judgment was $413,000, the mean settlement pre-trial was $98,000, and the mean settlement at trial was $248,615. During that same year (2000), Lexington's mean payment was $36,000.[37]

In fall 2005, the U.S. Department of Veterans Affairs mandated that all of their facilities follow Lexington's lead by implementing disclosure programs.[38]

The skeptic might counter, "*Well, these numbers are fine and the VA should be applauded for mandating this approach system-wide, but we have to remember that this involves a government hospital where cases are adjudicated in the federal court system. This program will never work in*

---

37   Kraman, S., MD, and Hamm, G., JD. "Risk Management: Extreme Honesty May Be the Best Policy." *Annals of Internal Medicine* 1999, 131: 963–967.

38   Department of Veterans Affairs, Veterans Health Administration. VHA Directive 2005-049, Disclosure of Adverse Events to Patients, October 27, 2005

our community hospital that has to deal with the daily realities of unpredictable local judges and juries."

Critics who make this argument fail to understand a basic precept of Sorry Works — this program is about patients and families and controlling anger, not about lawyers, judges, or the courts. When *customers* enter a healthcare facility, be it government, private self-insured, or a community hospital, they enter with the same hopes, expectations, and fears. Patients are patients, families are families, *customers* are *customers*, no matter where they get their care. And if *customers* smell a cover-up after an adverse medical event, they will become angry, no matter what type of hospital is shutting them out. Controlling anger is the reason the Lexington VA was in the lowest quartile for total payments despite being in the highest quartile for claims. They removed anger from the process and in so doing removed customers' desire to financially punish the institution. Anger, not greed, is what drives severity. True, it is easier to establish a disclosure program in a government facility, but the perceived barriers of doing so in community hospitals can be overcome.

> **"Controlling anger is the reason the Lexington VA was in the lowest quartile for total payments despite being in the highest quartile for claims. They removed anger from the process and in so doing removed customers' desire to financially punish the institution. Anger, not greed, is what drives severity."**

It took some time, but disclosure programs began to appear at organizations outside the VA system. Early programs continue to exist, and successes have been reported. This chapter will review the many successful disclosure programs that have been implemented across the country.

University of Michigan Health System. Perhaps one of the most well-known disclosure programs is the one adopted by the University of Michigan (UM) Health System in 2001. Its program is similar in scope and intent to the Lexington program — however, UM's program has an interesting twist. When starting the program, UM staff told trial lawyers who typically sued their system about the program.[39] UM leadership pledged to catch medical errors while patients/families were still under their care and deal fairly with patient/families and their legal counsel. However, UM conceded they were not going to catch every error before a patient/family left their facility, and sometimes medical complications surface days, weeks, months, and even years down the road. UM asked the Michigan trial bar, when people showed up in their offices asking to sue UM, that they (the trial bar), contact UM before filing any paperwork with the courts. UM pledged to meet with trial lawyers in such cases, and if legitimate errors were apparent, settle quickly and fairly. If, however, the complaints were without merit, UM would never settle such cases.

UM's results are extremely promising. Claims are down from 262 cases in 2001 to less than 100 cases in 2006 (back to pre-1990 levels). Reserves have been cut from $72 million to less than $20 million, and transaction expenses have been reduced from $48,000 per case to $21,000 per case. Finally, closings for cases have decreased from an average of 20.3 months to 9.5 months.[40]

In addition to good numbers, UM is changing the culture of medicine and law in the Wolverine State. When the disclosure program started in 2001, the majority of the UM medical staff were suspicious and apprehensive. Five years later, 98% of the UM medical staff support the program, and 55% said the program was a "significant factor" to stay at UM.[41] The UM disclosure program has become a retention program too — fascinating!

---

39   Richard C. Boothman. "The University of Michigan Health System's Claims Experience…and the importance of open disclosure." Presentation to the New Jersey Council of Teaching Hospitals, October 4, 2006.

40   Richard C. Boothman, Chief Risk Officer, University of Michigan Health System. Testimony before the U.S. Senate Committee on Health, Education, Labor and Pensions Committee, June 22, 2006.

41   Ibid.

The Michigan trial bar is also responding in a positive fashion. Seventy-one percent said the program is leading them to settle cases for less; 81% said costs are less, and 57% said they are passing on cases they would have tried in the past.[42] Trial lawyers are saying that since the UM system is honest in their dealings, the good feelings are being reciprocated.

> *"The filing of a lawsuit at the University of Michigan is now the last option, whereas with other hospitals it tends to be the first and only option," said Norman D. Tucker, a trial lawyer in Southfield, Mich. "We might give cases a second look before filing because if it's not going to settle quickly, tighten up your cinch. It's probably going to be a long ride."* [43]

News flash for the medical and insurance communities: Trial lawyers are human beings! Their clients are human beings too. If you treat people with respect, the respect will be returned. If you treat people poorly, the disrespect will be returned. UM has accomplished in six years what 40 years of tort reform has failed to do: Change the behavior of the trial bar. Instead of trying to bludgeon the trial bar, perhaps the medical and insurance communities should learn to treat trial lawyers with respect and professional dignity and see what happens. You might be surprised!

Like the VA program, UM's program is based on three simple principles:[44]

1. Apologize and compensate quickly and fairly when medical care causes injury;
2. Defend medically appropriate care vigorously; and

---

42 Ibid.
43 *Doctors Say "'I'm Sorry' Before 'See You in Court'"*, by Kevin Sack of The New York Times, May 18, 2008.
44 Ibid.

3. Learn from mistakes so they are not repeated, further reducing liability exposure.

> "...for disclosure programs to be successfully implemented the medical staff has to know they will backed up when they do their job."

It is hard for anyone to disagree with these principles. Point #2 is extremely important. Sorry Works! is *not* a no-fault compensation scheme. Well-meaning people often believe that disclosure programs are simply saying sorry all the time with an open checkbook. No! Adverse medical events where a thorough investigation shows the standard of care was met will *not* result in compensation to the patient or family. In such cases, the medical providers will empathize with the patient/family and their legal counsel, answer questions, share records, and dispel any notion of a cover-up while proving their innocence, but no settlement will be offered or approved — ever. Furthermore, if a lawsuit is initiated, the case will be aggressively defended to jury verdict. Healthcare professionals are never sold out in a Sorry Works! disclosure program. In fact, for disclosure programs to be successfully implemented, the medical staff has to know they will backed up when they do their job. Many healthcare providers find this approach refreshing. Alternatively, cases of obvious negligence are settled quickly and fairly, saving everyone time, money, and stress while providing the healing all sides need (healthcare professionals included). Indeed, disclosure programs such as Sorry Works! turn the world of medical malpractice litigation on its head! Providers who have done their job are never forced to settle a claim, while patients and families who have legitimate injuries (be they large *or* small) do not have to wait years for justice.

University of Illinois Medical Center. In 2006, the University of Illinois Medical Center in Chicago developed a disclosure program based on the Michigan approach. In developing its disclosure principles, the University of Illinois adopted the three Michigan principles listed above and added a new one:

1) We will provide effective communication to patients and families following adverse patient events.
2) Apologize and compensate quickly and fairly when medical care causes injury.
3) Defend medically appropriate care vigorously.
4) Learn from mistakes so they are not repeated, further reducing liability exposure.

In the program's first year, 40 disclosures were made, but only one claim was filed. **Please note:** The University of Illinois Medical Center operates in Cook County, Illinois, which, according to the American Tort Reform Association, in the 2008/2009 report was the third-worst judicial hellhole in the United States.[45] If a disclosure program can work in this litigation climate, it can work *anywhere*.

There are other unique elements of the University of Illinois Medical Center disclosure program that are worth noting:[46]

> **The University of Illinois Medical Center operates in Cook County, Illinois, which, according to the American Tort Reform Association, in the 2008/2009 report was the third-worst judicial hellhole in the United States. If a disclosure program can work in this litigation climate, it can work *anywhere*.**

- UI tries to conduct all investigations into adverse events within 72 hours or less, and their goal is to disclose, apologize, and settle all matters in 60 days or less. They have a rapid investigation team as well as a

45   American Tort Reform Foundation. "Judicial Hellholes" Report. 2008/2009. (accessible at http://www.atra.org/reports/hellholes/report.pdf) (last visited February 2009).
46   McDonald T. Presentation: "Full Disclosure: One Hospital's Experience." University of Illinois Medical Center. March 9, 2007, at the Chicago Patient Safety Forum's Annual Meeting in Chicago, IL.

disclosure team trained in communicating bad news to patients and families.

- The biggest barrier faced by UI in establishing their program was outside defense counsel. According to Dr. Tim McDonald, leader of the UI disclosure program, when UI was starting their disclosure program the medical center was also interviewing for new outside counsel. During interviews, a question was posed to the prospective attorneys how they would handle a surgery where the wrong leg was removed. Twelve of the 16 firms counseled deny and defend, and one even advocated altering the medical record to imply that the "wrong leg" needed to be removed anyway! Amazing. Dr. McDonald said you have to hire defense counsel who will accept litigating cases before the courts only on damages.

- Dr. McDonald has shared several moving stories about the UI disclosure program, including an event where a patient was given a massive overdose of cancer-fighting drugs. The patient was in excruciating pain and bleeding everywhere. The providers sat on the incident for a few days and felt horrible. Some of the providers involved in the incident became physically ill, while others could not sleep. However, McDonald's team learned about the event, investigated quickly, and organized a disclosure meeting. The patient could not believe the honesty and candor. She was so glad to hear that she would not be sick anymore and that her illness was not the cause of the problem. Furthermore, she was pleased the mistake was identified and corrected so it would not happen to another patient. Finally, her bills were waived, which pleased her too. As for the providers, they got a huge load of their chest and felt so much better afterwards. It's all about healing!

- Billing is part of the UI disclosure program. With one keystroke all billing is stopped to a patient/family after an adverse event. This is an important point, because often an errant bill or collection notice sent to a patient or family can significantly hurt the relationship. Regulatory billing issues must be discussed with counsel.

+ UI also has a patient liaison to continually work with patients/ families and make sure they never feel abandoned after adverse events.

To conclude on the University of Illinois Medical Center success story, consider the following passage from *The New York Times* article cited earlier in this text:

"In 40 years as a highly regarded cancer surgeon, Dr. Tapas K. Das Gupta had never made a mistake like this."

As with any doctor, there had been occasional errors in diagnosis or judgment. But never, he said, had he opened up a patient and removed the wrong sliver of tissue, in this case a segment of the eighth rib instead of the ninth.

Once an X-ray provided proof in black and white, Dr. Das Gupta, the 74-year-old chairman of surgical oncology at the University of Illinois Medical Center at Chicago, did something that normally would make hospital lawyers cringe: he acknowledged his mistake to his patient's face, and told her he was deeply sorry.

"After all these years, I cannot give you any excuse whatsoever," Dr. Das Gupta, now 76, said he told the woman and her husband. "It is just one of those things that occurred. I have to some extent harmed you."

In Dr. Das Gupta's case in 2006, the patient retained a lawyer but decided not to sue, and, after a brief negotiation, accepted $74,000 from the hospital, said her lawyer, David J. Pritchard.

"She told me that the doctor was completely candid, completely honest, and so frank that she and her husband - usually the husband wants to pound the guy - that all the anger was gone," Mr. Pritchard said. "His apology helped get the case settled for a lower amount of money."

Catholic Healthcare West. The July 2007 edition of *Las Vegas Life* reported the following on the Catholic Healthcare West disclosure program:

"....*Catholic Healthcare West, which operates hospitals in Arizona, California, and Nevada (including St. Rose Dominican Hospitals), instituted a full-disclosure program in 2002. Mike Tymczyn, vice president of communications for St. Rose, said the numbers were encouraging. "Although Catholic Healthcare West cannot for certain link the implementation of the full-disclosure program (to a drop in claims), there has been an overall decrease in claims since that time," Tymczyn said. "It's not an exact correlation, because of the way claims are reported, but there has been a decrease."*[47]

COPIC. COPIC Insurance is a doctor-owned insurance company based in Colorado that has operated a disclosure/early offer program since 2000. It has been reported that COPIC's 3Rs program has cut malpractice claims against physicians participating in the program by 50% and reduced settlement costs by 23%[48].

COPIC does have some serious deviations from the Sorry Works! approach, though, that should be noted. The 3Rs program — which stands for "Recognize, Respond, and Resolve" — is a no-fault system. Furthermore, cases involving deaths are not handled by the 3Rs program. Finally, patients and families cannot be represented by legal counsel nor can there by any written demands for compensation.[49] However, patients and families are not required to sign a waiver of further liability if they accept money from COPIC, preserving their right to file a lawsuit if they still wish. COPIC's theory (and hope) is that patients and families will no longer be angry after completing the program and will forego litigation, even though the option is still available to them. They report positive results. The program has made payments to over 900 injured patients since 2000. Cases in the 3Rs program have settled on average

47   Miller K. "A Sorry State." *Las Vegas Life*, July 2007.
48   Kowalczyk L. "Hospitals Study When to Apologize to Patients." *Boston Globe*, July 24, 2005.
49   "COPIC's 3Rs Program, Recognize, Respond to, and Resolve Patient Injuries." Richard Quinn, 3Rs Medical Director, COPIC Insurance Company.

for $5,300 versus non-3Rs closed cases, which settled for $88,056 in 2003, $74,643 in 2004, and $77,936 in 2005.[50]

COPIC's successes have been with smaller cases (usually $30,000 or less in value). It has been reported that they have not been able to get cases larger in value through the program. The failure of the 3Rs program to attract larger cases is easy to understand: Patients and families with life-changing injuries or wrongful deaths want their own legal counsel to ensure they are being treated fairly. 3Rs says attorneys are not welcome, so these patients and families opt for traditional litigation, which costs everyone enormous sums of time and money. Severely injured patients or families dealing with wrongful death cases are simply not going to trust the insurance company to act in their best interest…they are going to want their own attorney to speak for them. Remember, successful disclosure programs focus on what the *customers* want!

Despite these important differences, COPIC's program shares many philosophical beliefs with Sorry Works! chiefly that anger is what drives patients and families to file medical malpractice lawsuits. Like Sorry Works! COPIC believes that improved communication focused on solving problems and maintaining relationships between healthcare providers and patients/families is the key to controlling liability exposure.

The most critical element of the COPIC success story is that it shows that an insurance company can implement a disclosure and early-offer program that reduces lawsuits and costs by mitigating anger felt by patients and families.

Other Programs. There are countless other hospitals, small healthcare institutions (such as Lasik and orthopaedic surgery centers), and insurance groups that are practicing disclosure and early offer programs — albeit quietly; for example, one alternative insurance vehicle in central Pennsylvania, Central Pennsylvania Physicians Risk Retention Group, which insures nearly 1,200 healthcare professionals in a nine-county region in Pennsylvania. Its risk management program

---

50   Ibid

has adopted the concept of apology and disclosure and works with its physicians as adverse events arise to appropriately manage events. Physicians are educated and counseled on the disclosure concept. When appropriate, claims are placed on fast track, providing quick closure to patients, their families, and physicians as well as reducing litigation reserves and expenses. Early results of this young program (five years) are showing successes!

Other publicized programs include:

+ Stanford University Teaching Hospitals has a disclosure and early-offer program.[51]
+ Harvard Teaching Hospitals are developing a program.[52]
+ Twenty-eight different Kaiser hospitals operating an early-offer compensation program similar to Sorry Works! report positive changes in their liability exposure as well.[53]
+ Children's Hospitals and Clinics of Minnesota — operating in a state without tort reform and treating children (i.e., huge liability exposure) — is successfully operating a disclosure program.[54]
+ In 2001, Johns Hopkins Hospital adopted an apology and disclosure program.

The early data is simply too compelling for healthcare and insurance professionals and their companies not to embrace apology and disclosure. We can learn from the early programs and early successes. We know far more now than we did a decade ago. We can bring physicians, risk managers, administrators, staff, and other healthcare providers on-board to the concept, and we can execute a program that works effectively to

51   Driver J. Presentation to the Greater New York Hosp. Ass'n., May 2005.
52   See O'Reilly KB. "Harvard Adopts a Disclosure and Apology Policy." AMNews. June 12, 2006.
53   Wojcieszak D, Banja J, Houk C. "The Sorry Works! Coalition: Making the Case for Full-Disclosure." *The Joint Commission Journal on Quality and Patient Safety.* (June 2006).
54   Eisenberg D. "When Doctors Say, 'We're Sorry.'" *Time Magazine,* August 15, 2005.

strengthen patient relationships and better an organization's bottom line. We can take what has been learned and even develop disclosure programs that climb to the next level, combining expanded informed consent and patient accountability with enhanced post-event communication and alternative dispute resolution.[55] We can really begin to attack this liability equation and do something good for doctors and patients all at the same time!

New Disclosure Success Stories!

Park Nicollet. In March 2008, a patient was admitted to Park Nicollet Hospital in Minnesota to have a cancerous kidney removed. The surgeon removed the wrong kidney. What follows is a memo from Park Nicollet which explains their disclosure process for this event… the memo speaks for itself:

> TO: All Employees
> FROM: David Wessner, President and Chief Executive Officer
> David Abelson, Executive Vice President, Chief Clinical Officer
>
> RE: *Tragic Medical Error at Park Nicollet*
>
> **SUMMARY:** We are saddened to tell you that Park Nicollet has made a tragic medical error for which we accept full responsibility. We have apologized to the family and are doing everything we can to support them. We also are supporting our involved staff. The family has reviewed this communication and asks that no further information be released. We expect significant media coverage.

---

55   It is this type of program that the authors have created for healthcare organizations nationwide.

DETAILS: On Tuesday, March 11th (2008), a patient with presumed cancer of the kidney had their healthy kidney removed, leaving the affected kidney inside their body.

This is a tragic error and Park Nicollet assumes full responsibility. We have apologized to the patient and to the family. We are working closely with them to support them in every way we can during this difficult and challenging time in their lives.

The error occurred in diagnosis before the surgery took place. The surgery staff followed all appropriate safety protocols, including marking the surgical site and pausing before surgery to confirm the final details. Unfortunately, the side of the affected kidney was incorrectly identified in the medical chart several weeks before the surgery took place.

This event will be reported as required under the Adverse Health Event laws.

This is a devastating tragedy for the family. It is also a tragedy for all of us at Park Nicollet. We know we can say that everyone at Park Nicollet feels this error personally and we offer our thoughts, prayers and support to the patient and family.

The surgeon that performed the procedure has voluntarily ceased surgical and clinical care and will not see patients until a complete Root Cause Analysis has been performed and reviewed. During that time, Park Nicollet's other urologists will assume care of this physician's patients. We will use the Root Cause

Analysis to determine how we can prevent this error from ever occurring again, and we will share our findings with other hospitals so they can also learn from this experience.

Those of us privileged to work in health care know that there are many opportunities to do great good for patients. Unfortunately, in the course of providing care, there are also opportunities to make errors. We work continuously to eliminate errors and will not rest until we reduce them to zero. Internally, we encourage you to talk in your teams about our opportunities to do great good and how we can avoid and entirely eliminate medical errors. Every employee at Park Nicollet has a stake in this, and we will only succeed with the support of everyone.

The patient and family have chosen to remain at Methodist Hospital for their recovery. We have discussed this communication with them and they know that we are sharing this information with Park Nicollet employees. They do not want any additional information released and do not want to speak publicly at this time. They also asked us to share this message with you: "Please respect our privacy and confidentiality during this difficult time." We ask you to respect their wishes.

Shands Memorial Hospital, Florida. Shands Memorial Hospital in Florida administered a massive overdose of growth hormone to a three-year old in 2007, severely damaging his brain and leading to his death. The hospital disclosed, apologized, and took ownership of the mistake in a public fashion by holding a press conference. The hospital is now working with the family to develop a children-only hospital in its area of Florida (Pastor, 2008).

Methodist Hospital, Nebraska. Methodist Hospital in Omaha, Nebraska missed an aortic dissection in a 19-year old man over three separate visits to their ER, even though the family had a history of aortic dissection, the young man's father had an operation the year before to correct an aortic dissection, and the young man and the family pled with their ER doctors to check for aortic dissection. The autopsy afterwards confirmed an aortic dissection. The family sued, however, the hospital quickly took ownership of the mistakes, settled, and then worked with the family to produce a video about the situation. On the video, the hospital chief of staff admits mistakes were made but they have learned from this tragedy and have thus saved at least five patients with similar symptoms. The hospital put the video on their website and is working with the family to distribute the video to hospitals and doctors across the country (website for Methodist Hospital, www. bestcare.org, Summer 2007).

The Institute for Healthcare Improvement. Published a paper in early 2008, which highlighted several success stories.[56] A few excerpts from that article are below.

Geisinger Health System, Pennsylvania.

> "Initially, physicians felt they had to do this (disclosure) because it was the law (in Pennsylvania),' McKinley says, 'but over time their thinking has evolved. Physicians and other providers gradually discovered that this policy actually helps them...
>
> Geisinger has had fewer claims filed than the national average. When they observe the trends in their own data, the number of claims has decreased.

---

56   "Disclosing medical errors: Best practices from the "leading edge" written by Eve Shapiro.

McKinley believes a case is less likely to become a lawsuit because they've had early discussions with the patient or family. 'Patients and families get a full explanation, a commitment from us that we're going to correct the problem, and feedback after the root cause analysis to let them know what we've done,' she says."

Brigham & Women's Hospital, Massachusetts.

'Before this policy, we were concerned about telling patients and families too much; now, we tend to be concerned about telling them too little. There's been a huge sea change. There's no such thing as too much information,' she says. Physicians' fear of lawsuits was a formidable barrier to Brigham and Women's ability to openly and transparently communicate adverse outcomes and medical errors, Barnes believes. 'But,' she says, 'the common theme that runs through patient-family depositions has been that patients and families didn't think they were given complete information. Or they had questions that were never answered. Once something bad happened, they never saw the doctor again.' Barnes tries to help physicians understand that if they don't communicate openly about an adverse outcome, they are more likely, not less likely, to be sued.

'We've seen a decline in lawsuits since we implemented this policy, but I'd be the last person to say it's because of this process. Many other factors could influence this reduction. But there definitely hasn't been an increase in the claims as a result. I think we've been able to resolve some cases more quickly because we've taken on the problems at the very beginning,' she says. Brigham and Women's goal in openly communicating with patients and their families 'is not to decrease lawsuits but, rather, to save the relationship' with patients and families. 'We want patients to continue to come to us rather than go elsewhere to seek care,' Barnes says.

Conclusion

What these examples show is that the disclosure movement is continuing, and that because of disclosure success can be achieved for patient, families, healthcare providers, institutions, and lawyers.

Review Points:

+ Disclosure and apology programs in hospitals and insurance companies have shown early successes!
+ Disclosure and apology programs can help organizations financially at the same time that they strengthen the physician-patient relationship.

Questions & Challenges
in Context

The most common questions and challenges to "I'm sorry," apology, and disclosure are addressed below. Of course, every question is fact-specific, so in this context, we have simply tried to cover general concepts. However, these general concepts will certainly give you a start and be especially helpful in handling doubters and naysayers. Furthermore, the authors are happy to respond to additional questions or challenges. We do it all the time!

QUESTION: *"What do you put in the chart after disclosure?"*

ANSWER: A summary of the meeting: who was present, date, and time of the meeting. The medical chart is for documenting medical treatment and advice, but some documentation should be in the records (plaintiff's attorney and their experts review the record when they decide whether to sue you or liability exists, respectively). If more significant documentation is warranted, consult risk management or counsel. Sometimes, in efforts to protect the information, they will have you write a detailed letter to your attorney.

QUESTION: *OK, we agree with disclosure, including the part about compensating patients and families injured by our errors. But how do you determine what is fair compensation?*

ANSWER: You are describing an event that, after due diligence, you have determined was a breach of the standard of care and causally related; a medication error, for example, where harm is causally connected and substantiated. Your team should reach out early and involve your insurer, if commercially insured, or if self-insured, the risk manager who may be the individual who handles your claims. The risk manager may be on the disclosure team. Valuing the damages is always difficult. The key is to early on diffuse the anger. In this regard you will then be compensating the damages not the anger. Then a couple of suggestions follow. Look to meet needs: i.e. missed work, transportation expenses, waiver of bills under certain circumstances, and/or payment of subsequent expenses. Think about noneconomic activities that often are meaningful, such as a lecture series on safety or a certain aspect of training to show the patient/family you are improving your processes so the mistake does not happen again (a very important point for many patients and families who have suffered medical errors). As to the exact offer, rely on your claims personnel who has experience in these matters, but do not resort to the *"Let's low ball and see if they take it."* Obviously, the amount is going to be less if counsel is not involved, but it must be in the fair range to be credible (and to ensure the long-term credibility of your program). You will present an offer, and then typically the patient/family and their attorney — if they are represented — will counteroffer. It is a process. The key, however, is that it is not done with anger and spite...which often are the key drivers of escalating damages.

QUESTION: *As a hospital, we support Sorry Works! and we are self-insured so we can do this, but the majority of our physicians are independent contractors with their own insurance and we have no control over them. What if we get involved in a case where fault lies with us and the physician – or entirely with the physician – but the physician and his/her insurance company don't want to participate? Or, worse, what if the physician just* *blames everything on the hospital? How do we make this work?*

ANSWER: Education and being pro-active with your physicians and insurers are the keys. Understand that many doctors will want to participate in Sorry Works!, and many insurance companies are very interested in the dramatic reductions in frequency and severity offered by disclosure programs. Reach out to them and sorry can work in the majority of cases. However, there will be times in which the physician and/or their insurer don't want to participate or, worse, blame everything on the hospital. You are no worse off by empathizing, communicating, and working hard to stay connected with your patients and families. You can still meet with the patient or family even without the doctor and explain your role, and refer them to their doctor – who is not present at the meeting – for additional questions. No, you can't point the finger at the doctor for a variety of reasons – including destroying relations with your medical staff. However, the potential good will created with the patient/family very likely will get the hospital out of the case or get the hospital out of the case sooner at a lower price. The important thing to remember is many physicians will want to participate, so don't be held back or deterred by the outliers. Finally, as a hospital, you may consider establishing a captive insurer for your physicians, thereby placing everyone's liability under one carrier and making the disclosure process more seamless.

QUESTION: *As a surgical group, although our quality is quite high, clearly complications occur and, at times, unfortunately, even mistakes. Many of us have always wanted to reach out quickly to patients, but our insurer has discouraged* *the same. How does this work? Do we establish our own fund for these early payments? Where does the money come from?*

ANSWER: The compensation paid should normally come from your insurance carrier, and this is why we recommend you collaborate with your insurance carrier early on. Many enlightened carriers are willing to make a small payment pre-suit, and they will even entertain paying a large claim if warranted and if due diligence has been accomplished. Of course, for most claims insurers will want a general release executed. The topic of a general release can be worked into your discussions with patients and their families. However, if your particular insurer is not interested in an early intervention where appropriate, you ought to tell them about concepts such as disclosure and what is being discussed by Sorry Works! because if they are not interested in a collaborative disclosure program, they may not be doing all they can for you as an insured. Further, in fact many physicians are starting their own self-funded plans or captive insurance programs. Some of the most successful insurance vehicles are what is commonly referred to as risk retention groups. You may be interested to know that the so-called alternative risk financing market (insurance vehicles other than the traditional commercial carriers) now provide insurance for more than half of the healthcare market. Perhaps they are no longer the alternative? However, the dollars often will come from your self-funded program (captive) or from your insurance carrier. The key is early collaboration. Finally, there are decisions to be made about whether or not an individual physician wants their insurance carrier to pay, because it raises

National Practitioner Databank questions. This is something legal counsel meeting with the doctor will review as there are certain legal requirements that will need to be considered. In the end, if your insurance company is not on-board with the Sorry Works! concept, perhaps it is time to shop for insurance – or teach them!

QUESTION: *I thought we did everything right...we disclosed, we apologized, and the patient and family seemed happy. We never heard from them again, so we assumed everything was Ok. And then exactly one day before the statute of limitations was to run, we were served with a lawsuit. How could this happen?*

ANSWER: Disclosure is not a one-time deal! Healthcare and insurance professionals need to keep reaching out to the patient or family in the months (and sometimes years) ahead. Never assume everything is ok, and do not expect patients/families to contact you if they are not ok. Be pro-active! The one thing you can assume is that family, friends, and other people (attorneys?) are speaking to your patient and their family and providing all sorts of "advice"... So, **you** have to remain engaged with your patients, although there is a balance. The key is that the physician-patient relationship transcends the event. Also realize this is not going to work 100% of the time and last, not all is lost because you received suit papers. At least you have prevented the so called "plus". The plaintiff's attorney will not be able to say that you ignored the patient and family.

CHALLENGE: *Doctors will become sitting ducks with Sorry Works!. They will get their pants sued off.*

RESPONSE: After having read the nine chapters in this book, you know this statement is simply not so. Severity is often the product of adverse evidence created either from a service lapse, a lack of communication, or poor communication post-adverse event — not by physicians being honest and open. *Sorry Works!* works 100% of the time. It makes a bad situation a little better. If one does not completely understand the difference between showing empathy and enhanced communication and an actual apology accepting responsibility, you could then inadvertently miscommunicate (see chapter 2). However, this is why we emphasize having a disclosure educational program, a disclosure policy, and a disclosure program so that the entire team understands how to appropriately integrate this powerful concept.

CHALLENGE: *What if "I'm sorry" doesn't work? Hasn't a doctor just admitted guilt? Isn't this going to be problematic in court?*

RESPONSE: Again, one must understand the difference between saying, "I'm sorry," and accepting responsibility. Remember, "I'm sorry" is an expression of empathy. An apology includes acceptance of responsibility. The key is placing "I'm sorry" in context. Certainly, saying, "I'm sorry," for a complication or an unfortunate outcome is not going to put you in harm's way in the court, particularly if you learn simple steps and concepts concerning the same. Even an apology that includes acceptance of responsibility, assuming it is done *after* appropriate due diligence, is also not going to hurt you in the courtroom either. You have already determined that this is a case in which responsibility lies at your feet. These are cases in all likelihood that should be fast-tracked in claims, and all effort should be made to reach a fair resolution prior to a lawsuit being initiated. However, resolution is not always possible because the parties can honestly disagree on the value of a claim. Under such circumstances, the claim has to move forward, but often for simply an evaluation of the damages. There are cases that are argued quite successfully in court on just damages with plaintiffs receiving far less than what is offered to them in the first place. When we say far less we mean literally less, which means that the plaintiff attorney and unfortunately his or her client have truly gone in reverse. To pursue a claim on damages plaintiffs may have to invest $40,000 to $50,000 or more in expenses and years of their own time and effort, all to sometimes receive a judgment less than they could have obtained very early on. Accepting responsibility for something you are responsible for, in collaboration with your insurer, should help you in the courtroom, not hinder you.

QUESTION: *Who makes disclosure or apology in most disclosure programs? Is it the doctor, nurse, or hospital administrator? What if the doctor is not a good communicator?*

ANSWER: Determining the right communicator is part of implementing a disclosure program. It almost always involves the provider with some coaching and help from the disclosure team. However, if the provider is a poor communicator and/or the relationship with the patient/family is severely strained, then it may be appropriate to have another provider with a stronger relationship talk with the patient, or it may be that a patient safety officer or risk manager is the most sensible substitute for the provider. Disclosure literally needs to be evaluated on a case-by-case basis.

QUESTION: *What circumstances require disclosure? Is there any standard? What about situations where there has been*

ANSWER:

an error but no apparent injury, such as a medication error? Perhaps this is better off left unsaid?

The answers to these questions are somewhat dependent on state law. However, the general rule is that if an error reaches a patient, disclosure is appropriate, **whether or not there is an injury.** You have to think of this from the family/patient's perspective and whether or not they would want to receive the information. In almost all circumstances they will. There have been circumstances where doctors have placed their judgment in place of the patient, convincing themselves that no damage occurred and disclosing the medical error would simply alarm the family. However, the family often will find out about the medical error from a third party. Now we have the anger and distrust that we have worked hard to prevent; that same anger that leads patients and/or families to attorneys.

QUESTION:

Is it okay to attend a patient's funeral? Will people get the wrong impression and assume I, the doctor, did something wrong in the medical care I provided?

ANSWER:

Yes, it is absolutely ok to attend a patient's funeral. Such an act shows you are a caring, empathetic person and the family will remember, especially if you have a long-standing relationship with them. Attendance at a funeral or memorial service does not imply guilt or any wrong-doing. Remember, it is all about context! You are simply being empathetic and acknowledging the emotions of the family in a positive, constructive fashion.

QUESTION:

Our hospital has a disclosure policy in place, but how do we get a disclosure program started?

ANSWER:

As mentioned in chapter 5, having a disclosure policy is important, and many hospitals, pursuant to JCAHO

Standards,[57] have adopted disclosure policies in the last several years. However, the true home run is making sure you have a disclosure *program*. This means buy-in to the concept at the most senior level and then literally making sure it takes place on the front line when an adverse event occurs. Following the steps set forth in chapter 5 will help. Starting with education is always critical. This is really an issue of culture. Showing empathy, enhanced communication, and five-star service are issues that sound good but are difficult to consistently apply in the demanding pace our healthcare professionals find themselves. Therefore, if you have a policy, that is a great place to start. Now see if you can transcend that policy to a true program.

QUESTION: *If, pursuant to our disclosure policy and program, we go through each step and offer, for example, $300,000, but the patient and her lawyer counteroffer with $1 million, what do we do then?*

ANSWER: As mentioned in previous chapters, there are cases in which there will be true disagreement on the question of value. However, if you have done what you can to diffuse the anger and the emotional components of the claim and put yourself in the best light possible, these cases are ripe for what is commonly referred to as a mediation. This means getting a neutral third party to hear both sides of the story and determine what the value of the potential claim may be. Often it was thought that only lawsuits are mediated. Clearly, even in the pre-suit stages, mediation can get you to a number both sides can agree on. Often, it is a

---

57   JCAHO. "Ethics, Rights, and Responsibilities," in *Comprehensive Accreditation Manual for Hospitals: The Official Handbook* (Oakbrook Terrace, Ill.: JCAHO 2003), Patient Rights Standard RI. 2.90, RI-12.

number that both sides are not completely happy with ... but happier than moving forward!

CHALLENGE: *Lawyers simply file too many lawsuits in my hometown for disclosure to be successful here.*

RESPONSE: If a region or county is considered to be friendly to plaintiffs' attorneys, it is an area ripe for a disclosure program. Doctors, hospital administrators, and insurers should do everything possible to make sure that patients and families do not leave their offices angry in litigious regions and prevent them from getting to the plaintiff attorney's office in the first place. A disclosure program provides the protocol and methods to alleviate anger and significantly diminish the chances of lawsuits being filed, especially in the most litigious areas. An overly aggressive trial attorney is powerless without an angry, yet sympathetic plaintiff.

CHALLENGE: *But not all bad medical outcomes are the result of errors. Sometimes people just die or are injured despite the best efforts of a medical staff. We can't be handing out checks every time someone dies or doesn't heal completely.*

RESPONSE: You are absolutely correct. Many times the standard of care is met, but people still die or do not completely heal. Doctors and hospitals certainly should not be expected to "hand out checks" under such circumstances, nor should they be expected to deliver an apology that includes an admission of fault or wrongdoing. However, providers still need to communicate with patients and families in an empathetic fashion (*"We are sorry this happened."*). Lack of communication and empathy as well as a perception of a cover-up produces lawsuits even when the standard of care was met. Again, it is understanding the difference between saying, "I'm sorry," and accepting responsibility.

Disclosure programs like Sorry Works! stress communication with patients and families, including in circumstances when an error did NOT occur. They are perhaps most important under these circumstances. Medical staff and administrators should make themselves available to answer questions, provide insight, and empathize with the patient and family — do everything you can to appear honest and transparent ... and be so! But a settlement is not required when no error occurred. If the patient or family attempts to file a lawsuit, the hospital must be clear that it will defend itself vigorously and not settle. This is where your disclosure program pays dividends. Hospitals that practice the Sorry Works! concept develop a reputation for honesty with local plaintiffs' attorneys. If the hospital plans to contest a case (no settlement), local attorneys learn that such cases are probably without merit and not worth pursuing. We call this effect "The Honesty Dividend."

CHALLENGE: *What about "bad-baby cases?" Surely disclosure cannot work for OB/GYNs.*

RESPONSE: Sure it can. There is no question that the so-called tragic "bad-baby" cases are emotional and financially significant and actually speak to larger societal issues (and problems), but Sorry Works! is an excellent way to begin addressing this situation. Every birth with unexpected outcomes or adverse events should be met head-on with excellent customer service and outstanding communication. Such cases will literally test the communication and customer service principles of your disclosure program.

There is no question that bad-baby cases where no error occurred still often result in litigation because the parents have no other financial options to pay for the care of a neurologically impaired child. Some parents are faced with financial ruin, so they try to file a lawsuit. These cases must be tried on the medicine and science. However, evidence of good communication post-adverse event will also be essential to your defense. Remember, you are being opposed by extremely sympathetic plaintiffs. You can have science on your side, but if communication was not appropriate the "plus" will be created. If so, insurer/doctor/hospital will feel forced to settle.

CHALLENGE: *I'm OK disclosing to a patient or their family and even discussing compensation if we caused injury or death, but if they bring legal counsel then the meeting is canceled. All bets will be off.*

RESPONSE: You should not stop the process, but you do need to involve your legal counsel at this point, if you have not already. In this regard, make sure you have counsel who understands what is going to be accomplished, including the potential of arguing the case only on the damages in court should a resolution be unattainable. The disclosure process should not turn into *counsel* taking the lead; it is still between you and the patient. Think of this as the opportunity not only to make things right with the patient, but also to convince plaintiff counsel that either your offer is fair and reasonable or no case exists. If you do not meet, a lawsuit will often result.

QUESTION: *What if my insurance company says "no" to implementing a Sorry Works! program? What should I do then?*

ANSWER: Change their mind or fire them! Doctors and hospitals are customers of insurance companies, and as customers you need to tell your insurer that disclosure programs are in keeping with your culture and you see the value. Make phone calls, send e-mails, write letters, and get other colleagues involved. It's your hospital ... your practice ... your patients and families...your liability problem. Take control by demanding Sorry Works! If the insurer digs their heels in, it is probably a lack of knowledge or a culture that is not a good fit with yours.

QUESTION: *What exactly does Sorry Works! advocate in terms of the timing of disclosure? The investigation may take weeks to months, and on the basis of that analysis one decides whether the standard of care was met and then discloses accordingly. It strikes me that there are situations where even from the get-go you know the adverse event was due to error, for example, wrong site surgery. At this point in time, that would consistently fall below the standard of care. Can you advise as to timing of disclosure? It seems unreasonable to wait a few weeks for the details when the error is so blatant and obvious. What about this situation?*

ANSWER: You are correct. Cases where gross/obvious errors happened need to move a little more quickly; however, not too quickly. After an obvious error (say a wrong-site surgery, as you reference), the patient/family needs to know that an error happened, that you are sorry, and that you/your staff are going to evaluate and determine what happened and will share this information with them. But do not assign blame to individuals or systems — yet. Instead, focus on attending to the immediate needs of the patient/family (food, assistance with phone calls, bills, lodging), give them your contact information, and answer any calls or inquiries for information quickly and friendly. Do not ever give a patient or family any reason to suspect a cover-up. Stay on the same side of the table.

You need to do a complete evaluation and learn exactly what happened, who was involved, how the mistake occurred, and how the problem(s) will be fixed so that the potential for a similar error is reduced. You should, however, keep the family/patient informed as the investigation continues. You do not want them to think that you are doing nothing or are just putting them off. After you have gathered this information, recontact the patient/family and tell them you want to schedule a meeting. In the second meeting, you will explain everything that happened, apologize, and accept responsibility and continue discussions about their needs. This will lead to a discussion about settlement and a number. Expect, as mentioned before, for there to be some back and forth.

QUESTION: *At what point do you initiate conversations regarding compensation? Do you come prepared to offer compensation at the time of full disclosure? If so, how do you evaluate for damages if you don't have information regarding wages, children, etc.?*

ANSWER: Do not make it all about compensation. First, talk with the family or patient, and empathize ("We are sorry this happened .... we feel very badly for you and your family"). Attend to their immediate needs, let them know you will do a quick and thorough investigation, and promise to get back to them at a certain date. Provide contact information for them (do not ever let them feel abandoned ... they must feel connected to the facility and staff at all times).

If the investigation shows there was an error, then you need to consider compensation.

Compensation may require investment of time to complete, but you should involve your insurance carrier, legal counsel, and/or risk manager. The circumstances will need to be evaluated for actual damages.

Some medical providers are understandably slow in discussing compensation — some because they think it "cheapens" or degrades the disclosure event and others because they are still uncomfortable having to pay for errors. However, families and patients want to hear their economic problems are going to be addressed. If all patients and families hear at the beginning is, *"We're sorry and we'll do better next time,"* they might start to think that they are being snowed over with a phony, meaningless apology. Think about this issue from the customer perspective: *"Hey this apology is nice, but my husband can't work for six to twelve months — who is going to pay the bills and put food on the table? I guess I am going to have to sue these doctors!"*

However, you do not want to look like you are buying people off — that is completely understandable. Please understand though, when you apologize, admit fault, and explain what occurred then you look very sincere and credible when you say, *"And we also intend to offer fair compensation for your injuries, and we will be discussing the amount of this compensation with you."*

QUESTION: *If we disclose, apologize, and compensate a patient/family for an error, do we have the patient/family sign a general release? Would making a patient/family sign*

	such a waiver anger them and reverse all the progress that has been made?
ANSWER:	Again, you have to judge each situation separately and know the players involved. Also, as part of your disclosure program, you should have discussions about such circumstances ahead of time with your insurers, attorneys, and administrators. If you are contemplating a settlement, you will often need the patient/family to sign a release. You can approach the patient/family in a way that does not anger them. It may simply be: *"Please understand. Any time one of its doctors provides compensation, my insurance company requires a release. You can have an attorney review the release before you sign it."*
QUESTION:	*What role can/should nurses play in disclosure and apology?*
ANSWER:	The medical malpractice crisis is to a great extent a customer service crisis — not just a legal problem. If you subscribe to this philosophy, then you should believe that nurses play a big role in disclosure and apology and an even larger role in providing excellent customer service to patients and families throughout their stay at the hospital. After all, nurses are usually the front-line employees who have the most frequent contact with the customers.
	Nurses need to be educated to be on the lookout for small problems and address them quickly with good customer service. TV will not work in the patient's room? No problem — we will get a technician up to fix it right away. Food is slow coming to the patient's room? We will get the food there right away and provide a free plate with dessert for the patient's spouse. These events may sound trivial, but small problems can lead to a major blow up if an adverse

event occurs. An already strained relationship may break and a lawsuit will be in the offing:

"Oh, that nurse has been so cold and uncaring. It seemed like she never answered the call button, and when she did she acted like she was doing us a favor. Now this! Something has gone wrong. I just know she and that Doctor Smith screwed up! Where's Vinny?"

Good customer service is so important and will lay the ground for successful disclosure and apology, when needed and appropriate. And nurses can lead the way!

CHALLENGE: *Sorry, but Sorry Works! is just too much of a leap of faith for the medical community.*

RESPONSE: Disclosure programs like Sorry Works! are based on data and research. It really is not hard for any of us to understand and believe. Being open and honest carefully will drive a better result and is clearly the right approach to take at this point. There are just too many success stories to doubt the economic promise of this concept. Clearly it is best for both doctors and patients.

The litigation crisis, in part, is a customer service crisis, which can be helped by doctors, hospitals, and insurers any time — not necessarily a political problem to be solved by politicians. When doctors, hospitals, and insurance companies focus on their patients and families with excellent customer service, it can bring an end to the medical malpractice crisis. Sorry Works! provides the framework to deliver excellent customer service in the minutes, hours, days, weeks, and months after an adverse medical event. **Good customer service is your new focus!**

"Never forget, patients never forget!"

Sorry Works! represents culture change. It won't happen overnight, and it won't happen without good people willing to fight the good fight. The good news is that Sorry Works! works both ethically *and* economically. The arguments waged against Sorry Works! are often emotional, knee-jerk reactions that do not hold water when examined and challenged. The key is to keep spreading and sharing information. Share this book, share the website (www.sorryworks.net), contact Stevens & Lee (jws@stevenslee.com), and share other resources about disclosure and apology. Bring speakers and trainers into your institution or organization. Take time to answer questions of well-meaning people and assuage their fears and concerns. Over time your colleagues and associates will come around and learn how sorry truly does work. **Persistent educational efforts are the key!**

In pushing for inclusion of Sorry Works! into a hospital or insurance company, settle for nothing less than a program. Obstructionists will try to appease reformers by offering policies or arguing that physicians and nurses can "do disclosure on their own." Could you imagine Disney or Southwest Airlines telling their associates to do customer service ad hoc? They wouldn't be Disney or Southwest Airlines. **Accept nothing less than a program!**

As you implement Sorry Works! and begin to experience successes, please share your success stories. The more facilities and organization that adopt disclosure and apology, the sooner reluctant institutions and individuals will begin to feel left behind. We need more people to share their success stories with trade and popular media and through personal communications with colleagues and friends. **Share your disclosure success stories!**

Thank you for reading this book, and good luck in making disclosure and apology part of the culture of your institution. The Sorry Works! Coalition and Stevens & Lee stand ready to help you with any questions or problems you may have. Call or e-mail us anytime. **You can do this, and we are here to help!**

Cheers,

Doug Wojcieszak
Founder/Spokesperson
The Sorry Works! Coalition
www.sorryworks.net
618-559-8168

James W. Saxton, Esq.
Chair Healthcare Litigation
Co-Chair Health Law
Stevens & Lee
www.stevenslee.com
jws@stevenslee.com
717-399-6639

Maggie M. Finkelstein, Esq.
Stevens & Lee
mmf@stevenslee.com
717-399-6636

CME POST-READING QUIZ

SORRY WORKS! DISCLOSURE, APOLOGY, AND RELATIONSHIPS
PREVENT <u>MEDICAL MALPRACTICE CLAIMS</u>

Instructions

The post-reading quiz must be completed individually after having read *Sorry Works! Disclosure, Apology, and Relationships Prevent Medical Malpractice Claims*. The answers provided should be based on personal knowledge gained from reading the book. The quiz contains both true/false and multiple-choice questions, and you should circle your answer directly on the quiz. There is only one correct answer. An answer key to the quiz is provided with explanations for the answers so that you can score your own quiz.

---

1. True or False: When you say, "I'm sorry," you are really saying, "It's my fault."

2. An overarching term for any unexpected result, bad outcome, or complication is:

   a. Complication
   b. Medical error
   c. Adverse event
   d. None of the above

3. When it comes to medical errors, patients want:

   a. To understand what happened
   b. An apology
   c. To know how similar situations will be prevented in the future
   d. All of the above

4. What drives patients to attorneys and attorneys to take on medical malpractice cases?

    a.   An adverse event coupled with an aggravating circumstance
    b.   A desire to get even
    c.   Greed
    d.   They have nothing better to do

5. By eliminating the aggravating circumstance, benefits include all of the following except:

    a.   Defense litigation expenses are reduced
    b.   Frivolous lawsuits continue
    c.   Medical errors are reduced
    d.   Better public relations

6. Event management is:

    a.   Throwing a great party
    b.   Trying to avoid a lawsuit at all costs
    c.   Your platform for a disclosure program
    d.   Not always the best method for managing adverse events

7. When an event does occur, what should you do?

    a.   Avoid the patient; no news is good news
    b.   Immediately apologize for a medical error
    c.   Let the patient know it was not your fault, but that Dr. Smith is the one to blame
    d.   Ensure the patient is safe and follow your organization's event management policy

8. Your five-step process for implementing a disclosure and apology program is:

   a. Roll out the program to the entire organization, adopt a disclosure policy and procedure, get the decision makers on-board, train the disclosure team, and keep the program alive

   b. Adopt a disclosure policy and procedure, get the decision makers on-board, roll out the program to the entire organization, train the disclosure team, and keep the program alive

   c. Get the decision makers on-board, adopt a disclosure policy and procedure, roll out the program to the entire organization, train the disclosure team, and keep the program alive

   d. Roll out the program to the entire organization, get the decision makers on-board, train the disclosure team, roll out the program to the entire organization, and keep the program alive

9. When expressing empathy, which one does not belong:

   a. *"I'm very sorry about your loss. Please accept our condolences."*

   b. *"I'm sorry you are feeling this way. Let me explain what happened and what we are doing to keep your care on track."*

   c. *"These things happen all the time. In fact, it just happened to one of my other patients last week."*

   d. *"We are sorry. We took great care to ensure your son's comfort. Let's go through his care."*

10. The three steps of disclosing a medical error include:

   a. Empathy

   b. Investigation

   c. Apology and resolution

   d. All of the above

11. True or False. Physicians need a law to apologize.

12. Which of the following is false?

    a.   Patients and families are the true winners of a disclosure program.

    b.   When an adverse event occurs, patients need to go back to their doctors first!

    c.   A grassroots campaign by patients is needed!

    d.   Physicians lose when it comes to disclosure.

13. Which of the following are true?

    a.   Early disclosure programs have not seen significant successes.

    b.   Disclosure programs can bring a financial benefit to organizations.

    c.   We can improve on the early success of disclosure programs.

    d.   Both (b) and (c).

14. Identify the correct answer to the following question: *"What if 'I'm sorry' doesn't work? Haven't I just admitted guilt? Isn't this going to be problematic in court?"*

    a.   You are right! Never say, *"I'm sorry."*

    b.   You have admitted guilt, but with the right attorney defending you, it will not be a problem in court.

    c.   Only say, *"I'm sorry,"* if you have committed a medical error; otherwise, it is not necessary.

    d.   Expressing, *"I'm sorry,"* in context will make it most effective in expressing empathy and not expressing guilt. Empathy and responsibility are different. Empathy can help you and help you in court. Not saying, *"I'm sorry,"* when it is expected can hurt you in the courtroom, in front of jurors.

15. After meeting with a patient or family after an adverse event,

    a.   Do not document the meeting. It can only be used against you later.

    b.   Do nothing more. This brings an end to this matter.

    c.   Do document the meeting and discussion in the medical record.

    d.   If you document the meeting, make sure that you put a note in about that angry brother.

CME POST-READING QUIZ
ANSWER KEY

1. False. If given context, when you say "I'm sorry," you are expressing empathy. Do not use this phrase to express fault. Reserve acceptance of responsibility for a true apology, after appropriate due diligence finding liability.

2. (c.). An overarching term for any unexpected result, bad outcome, or complication is an "adverse event." It is important to understand that an adverse event includes all medical errors and complications, but it is only when you have a medical error with liability attaching that an apology is needed. Always express empathy whether it is a complication or a medical error that has occurred.

3. (d.). According to a 2003 study in the *Journal of the American Medical Association*, patients want all of these and more, including to understand why the error occurred, how the consequences of the error will be mitigated, and disclosure of the error. (See Gallagher TH, Waterman AD, Ebers AG, Fraser VJ, and Levinson W. "Patients' and Physicians' Attitudes Regarding the Disclosure of Medical Errors." *JAMA*. 2003; 289: 1001–1007.)

4. (a.). An adverse event coupled with an aggravating circumstance. In the first instance, there must be an injury, and it is the aggravating circumstance that sends the patients running to a lawyer. It may be miscommunication by the provider to the patient, or even a complete failure to communicate with the patient, or a bad physician-patient relationship. For whatever the reason, the patient does not get the empathy and answers needed from their doctor and looks for this from an attorney. As mentioned in the book, perhaps a grassroots effort is needed to get patients to return to their doctor for answers rather than a lawyer.

5. (b.). Frivolous lawsuits can be reduced by eliminating the aggravating circumstances that lead to lawsuits in the first instance. Other benefits do include a reduction in litigation expenses, better public relations, and a reduction in medical errors.

6. (c.). Event management is your platform for a disclosure program. It is the infrastructure to support post-adverse event communication. Event management is about coordination and collaboration among healthcare professionals for the benefit of patients and healthcare providers. You should have in place an event management platform before embarking on a disclosure program.

7. (d.). Ensure the patient is safe and follow your organization's event management policy. Patient safety should always be the first priority. Implement a care plan for next steps and be sure that the patient understands the same. Your steps should also always be consistent with your organization's event management policy. Perhaps you need to notify a risk manager or your insurance company? This would be noted in your event management policy. Do not avoid the patient. It is avoidance that causes patients to fill in the gaps in the story of the care, and often, not the right information. Never place blame on another provider, particularly before any investigation and true due diligence has been completed. Likewise, you should apologize only after due diligence has determined that responsibility and liability has attached.

8. (c.). Get the decision makers on-board, adopt a disclosure policy and procedure, roll out the program to the entire organization, train the disclosure team, and keep the program alive. Following and executing these five essential steps can bring success to a disclosure program. It is essential to initially have champions who get the decision makers onboard! Before rolling out a program, work through the creation of a disclosure policy and procedure, tackle the tough questions early, and find consensus. Then move forward with rolling out the program, bringing the entire organization on-board. Identify your disclosure team and provide them with education and training. Finally, publish your successes!

9. (c.). *"These things happen all the time. In fact, it just happened to one of my other patients last week."* This phrase does not belong! All the other phrases are expressing appropriate empathy. The phrase in (c) is not empathic and makes it seem as though because what occurred now has also occurred in the past is OK. Always empathize with patients.

10. (d.). All of the above. You should always empathize with the patient/family no matter what the reason for the adverse event. It is the initial step, saying, *"I'm sorry."* Next, investigate as appropriate, following your organizational processes, to determine what happened. If an investigation reveals responsibility and fault, apologize to the patient/family and include what occurred, why it occurred, and how similar circumstances will be prevented in the future, along with resolution.

11. False. Physicians do not *need* a law to apologize. Sympathy/apology laws can be helpful, but they are not necessary. Enhanced communication post-adverse event is best for the patient/family, the healthcare provider, and the defense attorney. Apology and disclosure can help to keep the patient/family on the same side of the table and literally prevent a patient from visiting a plaintiff lawyer.

12. (d.). Physicians are not the losers in disclosure. Physicians receive the benefit of maintaining a strong physician-patient relationship, decreased professional liability exposure, fast-tracking claims resolution, and an added emotional benefit as well.

13. (d.). Both (b) and (c). Disclosure programs can help organizations financially, reducing loss expenses and indemnity when effective; and early programs have shown success. We can improve upon these successes in the ways outlined in the book.

14. (d.). Expressing, *"I'm sorry,"* in context will make it most effective in expressing empathy and not expressing guilt. Empathy and responsibility are different. Empathy can help you and help you in court. Not saying, *"I'm sorry,"* when it is expected can hurt you in the courtroom, in front of jurors.

15. (c.). Do document the meeting and discussion in the medical record. Have this *evidence* used for you, instead of against you. Document who attended, a summary of what was discussed, next steps, who was present, the time — date — and location, and the patient understanding of what occurred and next steps.

STATE APOLOGY — IMMUNITY LAWS

State & Year	Citation
AZ (2005)	ARIZ. REV. STAT. ANN. §12-2605 (2005)
CA (2000)	CAL. EVID. CODE § 1160 (West 2001)
CO (2003)	COLO. REV. STAT. ANN. § 13-25-135 (West 2003)
CT (2005, as amended 2006)	CONN. GEN. STAT. ANN. §52-184d (West 2005)
DE (2006)	DEL. CODE ANN. tit. 10, §4318 (West 2006)
FL (2001)	FLA. STAT. ANN. §90.4026 (West 2001)
GA (2005, technical correction made 2006)	GA. CODE. ANN. §24-3-37.1 (West 2005)
HI (2007)	2007 HAW. SESS. LAWS. Act 88 (H.B. 1253) (not yet codified)
ID (2006)	IDAHO CODE ANN. §9-207 (West 2006)
IL (2005)	735 ILL. COMP. STAT. 5/8-1901 (West 2005)
IA (2006)	IOWA HF 2716 (2006)
IN (2006)	IND. CODE ANN. §§ 34-43.5-1-1 to 34-43.5-1-5 (West 2006)
LA (2005)	LA. REV. STAT. ANN. §13:3715.5 (2006)
ME (2005)	ME. REV. STAT. ANN. tit. 24, §2907 (2005)
MD (2005)	MD. CODE. ANN., CTS. & JUD. PROC. §10-920 (West 2004)

MA	(1986)	Mass. Gen. Laws. Ann. ch. 233, §23D (West 2000)
MO	(2005)	Mo. Ann. Stat. §538.229 (West 2007)
MT	(2005)	Mont. Code. Ann. §26-1-814 (West 2005)
NE	(2007)	2007 Neb. Laws L.B. 373 (not yet codified)
NH	(2006)	N.H. Rev. Stat. Ann. §507-E:4 (2006)
NC	(2004)	N.C. Gen. Stat. §8C-1, Rule 413 (West 2004)
ND	(2007)	2007 N.D. H.B. 1333
OH	(2004)	Ohio Rev. Code Ann. §2317.43 (LexisNexis 2007)
OK	(2004)	Okla. Stat. tit. 63, §1-1708.1H (LexisNexis 2007)
OR	(2003)	Or. Rev. Stat. §677.082 (2005)
SC	(2006)	S.C. Code Ann. §19-1-190 (2006)
SD	(2005)	S.D. Codified Laws §19-12-14 (2007)
TN	(2003)	Tenn. R. Evid. Rule §409.1 (2006)
TX	(1999)	Tex. Civ. Prac. & Rem. Code Ann. §18.061 (LexisNexis 2007)
UT	(2006)	Utah Code Ann. §78-14-18 (2007)
VT	(2005)	Vt. Stat. Ann. tit. 12, §1912 (2007)
VA	(2005)	Va. Code Ann. §8.01-52.1 (2007)
WA	(2002)	Wash. Rev. Code. §5.66.010 (2007)
WV	(2005)	W. Va. Code §55-7-11a (2007)
WY	(2004)	Wyo. Stat. Ann. §1-1-130 (2007)

States Not Enacted (15 states)

AL
AK
AR
KS
KY
MI
MN
MS
NV
NJ
NM
NY
PA
RI
WI

Appendix B —

Model State Law — Draft

[1] In any claim or civil action for professional negligence that is brought against a health care provider or health care facility, or in any arbitration proceeding or other method of alternative dispute resolution that relates to the claim or civil action, and in any civil or administrative proceeding against a healthcare provider or health care facility,

[2] Any written or oral statement, writing, affirmation, gesture, activity, action, or conduct, or portion thereof [could label this as any "communication" and then define "communication accordingly]

[3] [A] Expressing or conveying apology, responsibility, liability, fault, sympathy, commiseration, condolence, compassion, regret, grief, mistake, error, or a general sense of benevolence (including "sorry"), *including any accompanying explanation* ; [or include other than an expression or admission of liability or fault]

[3][B] And any offers to undertake corrective actions and gratuitous acts to assist the affected persons

[4] Made by a health care provider or employee of the health care provider [define "health care provider"]

[5] To the patient, relative of the patient, survivors of the patient, health care decision-maker for the patient, or other representative of the patient

[6] And that relates to physical loss, discomfort, pain, suffering, injury or death of the patient as the result of the unanticipated outcome of medical care [we would need to define "unanticipated outcome"]

[7] Shall be inadmissible as evidence of an admission of liability or as evidence of an admission against interest, or in any way to prove negligence or culpable conduct, and the declarant may not be examined by deposition or otherwise in proceedings about the expression or conveyance.

ENDNOTES

1   Kraman, S., MD, and Hamm, G., JD. "Risk Management: Extreme Honesty May Be the Best Policy." *Annals of Internal Medicine*. 1999:131(12); 963-967.

2   Boothman, R. Presentation to the New Jersey Council of Teaching Hospitals, October 2006.

3   "Sorry." *Merriam-Webster's Online Th esaurus*. 2006–2007. http:// www.m-w.com/cgi-bin/thesaurus?book=Thesaurus&va=sorry (4Oct. 2007).

4   "Sorry." *Merriam-Webster's Online Dictionary*. 2006–2007. http:// www.m-w.com/dictionary/sorry (4 Oct. 2007).

5   Kohn LT, et al. (eds.). "To Err is Human: Building a Safer Health System." Washington, D.C.: National Academies Press, 1999.

6   "Error". *Merriam-Webster's Online Dictionary*. 2006–2007. http:// www.m-w.com/dictionary/error (8 Oct. 2007).

7   It is important to recognize that medical malpractice liability is state-law specific.

8   Gallagher TH, Waterman AD, Ebers AG, Fraser VJ, and Levinson W. "Patients' and Physicians' Attitudes Regarding the Disclosure of Medical Errors." *JAMA*. 2003; 289: 1001–1007.

9   Ibid.

10 Kohn LT, et al. (eds.). "To Err is Human: Building a Safer Health System." Washington, D.C.: National Academies Press, 1999.

11 "Complication" *Merriam-Webster's Online Medical Dictionary*. 2006–2007. http://www.m-w.com/medical/complication (8 Oct. 2007).

12 Hickson G, et al. "Patient Complaints and Malpractice Risk." *JAMA*. 2002; 287(22): 2951–2957; Hickson GB, Clayton EC, Githens PB, Sloan FA. "Factors that Prompted Families to File Malpractice Claims Following Perinatal Injury." *JAMA*. 1992;

287:1359–1363.

13 Levinson W, Roter DL, Mullooly JP, Dull VT, Frankel RM. "Physician-patient Communication: The Relationship with Malpractice Claims Among Primary Care Physicians and Surgeons." *JAMA*. 1997; 277: 553–559.

14 Press Ganey Associates, Inc. 2008. Return-on-Investment: Reducing Malpractice Claims by Improving Patient Satisfaction. White Paper: Press Ganey Associates, Inc. Available at: http://pressganey. com/cs/research_and_analysis?white_paper_registration2?id=/ galleries/lead-generating-acute/Malpractice_Final_12-14-07pdf&subject=Malpractice_paper.

15 Witman AB, Park DM, Hardin SB. "How Do Patients Want Physicians to Handle Mistakes? A survey of internal medicine patients in an academic setting." *Arch Intern Med*. 1996; 156:2565–2569.

16 Interview with Philip H. Corboy, Attorney, Corboy & Demetrio, Oct. 19, 2007.

17 Garrison J. "Lawyers learn to share their pain with jurors: They use a technique called psychodrama to connect better by showing vulnerability." *LA Times*, November 25, 2006.

18 Vincent C, Young M, Phillips A. "Why Do People Sue Doctors? A Study of Patients and Relatives Taking Legal Action." *Lancet*. 1994; 343: 1609–1613.

19 Saxton JW, Finkelstein MM, Wojcieszak D. "ESSAY: Ethics Training Needs to Emphasize Disclosure and Apology". HealthCare Ethics Committee Forum; An Interprofessional Journal on Healthcare Institutions' Ethical and Legal Issues, Volume 20, No. 3, September 2008, Springer.

20 E-mail communication with Press Ganey (November 1, 2007).

21 Saxton JW, Finkelstein MM, Bravin S, Stawiski S. "Reduce Liability Risk by Improving Your Patient Satisfaction." (2008) (accessible at http://www.pressganey.com/galleries/default-fi le/MD_White_Paper-Malpractice_0808.pdf) (last visited Sept. 11, 2008).

22 Ibid.

23 JCAHO. "Ethics, Rights, and Responsibilities," in *Comprehensive Ac-*

creditation Manual for Hospitals: The Official Handbook (Oakbrook Terrace, Ill.: JCAHO 2003), Patient Rights Standard RI. 2.90, RI-12.

24   Perspective on Disclosure of Unanticipated Outcome Information," ASHRM whitepaper/monograph, www.ashrm.org, Nov. 2003.

25   Boothman, R. "Apologies and a Strong Defense at the University of Michigan Health System." *The Physician Executive.* March/April 2006.

26   Lucas S. "'Kramer' Apologizes for Racist Comments." (accessible at http://www.associatedcontent.com/article/90041/kramer_apologizes_for_racist_comments.html) (last visited October 10, 2007).

27   "Tearful Marion Jones Apologizes, Announces Retirement." (Associated Press) (accessible at http://www.kvia.com/global/story. asp?s=7176191) (October 5, 2007; last visited October 10, 2007).

28   Saraceno J. "Jones' Apology Sounds Like Another False Start." (accessible at http://www.usatoday.com/sports/columnist/ saraceno/2007-10-07-marionjones-comment_N.htm) (last visited October 10, 2007).

29   Lazare A. "On Apology." Oxford University Press. 2004.

30   American Medical Association. Opinion E-8.12 Patient Information. *Code of Medical Ethics.* American Medical Association. 2006. (accessible at http://www.ama-assn.org/ama/pub/category/8497. html) (last visited August 22, 2007).

31   JCAHO. "Ethics, Rights, and Responsibilities," in *Comprehensive Accreditation Manual for Hospitals: The Official Handbook* (Oakbrook Terrace, Ill.: JCAHO 2003), Patient Rights Standard RI. 2.90, RI-12.

32   MASS. GEN. LAWS ANN. ch. 233, § 23D (West 2000).

33   Cohen JR. "Toward Candor After Medical Error: The First Apology Law." Harvard Health Policy Rev. 2004; 51:21–24.

34   Cal. Health & Safety Code § 1279.1 (Deering 2007); Fla. Stat. Ann. § 195.1051 (LexisNexis 2007); Nev. Rev. Stat. Ann. sec 439.855 (LexisNexis 2007); N.J. Stat. An. sec 26:2H-12.25 (LexisNexis 2007); 2003 Or. Laws ch. 686, sec 4); 40 P.S. sec 1303.308 (2006);

Vt. Stat. Ann. tit. 18, sec 1915 (2007); Wash. Rev. Code Ann. sec 70.41.380 (LexisNexis 2007).

[35] 40 P.S. § 1303.308 (2006).

[36] *See, e.g.,* Saxton JW, Finkelstein MM, Bravin S, Stawiski S. "Reduce Liability Risk by Improving Your Patient Satisfaction." (2008) (accessible at http://www.pressganey.com/galleries/default-fi le/ MD_White_Paper-Malpractice_0808.pdf) (last visited Sept. 11, 2008).

[37] Kraman, S., MD, and Hamm, G., JD. "Risk Management: Extreme Honesty May Be the Best Policy." *Annals of Internal Medicine* 1999, 131: 963–967.

[38] Department of Veterans Affairs, Veterans Health Administration. VHA Directive 2005-049, Disclosure of Adverse Events to Patients, October 27, 2005.

[39] Richard C. Boothman. "The University of Michigan Health System's Claims Experience…and the importance of open disclosure." Presentation to the New Jersey Council of Teaching Hospitals, October 4, 2006.

[40] Richard C. Boothman, Chief Risk Officer, University of Michigan Health System. Testimony before the U.S. Senate Committee on Health, Education, Labor and Pensions Committee, June 22, 2006.

[41] Ibid.

[42] Ibid.

[43] *Doctors Say "'I'm Sorry' Before 'See You in Court'",* by Kevin Sack of The New York Times, May 18, 2008.

[44] Ibid.

[45] American Tort Reform Foundation. "Judicial Hellholes" Report. 2006. (accessible at http://www.atra.org/reports/hellholes/report. pdf) (last visited February 2009).

[46] McDonald T. Presentation: "Full Disclosure: One Hospital's Experience." University of Illinois Medical Center. March 9, 2007, at the Chicago Patient Safety Forum's Annual Meeting in Chicago, IL.

[47] Miller K. "A Sorry State." *Las Vegas Life,* July 2007.

[48] Kowalczyk L. "Hospitals Study When to Apologize to Patients." *Boston Globe*, July 24, 2005.

[49] "COPIC's 3Rs Program, Recognize, Respond to, and Resolve Patient Injuries." Richard Quinn, 3Rs Medical Director, COPIC Insurance Company.

[50] Ibid.

[51] Driver J. Presentation to the Greater New York Hosp. Ass'n., May 2005.

[52] See O'Reilly KB. "Harvard Adopts a Disclosure and Apology Policy." AMNews. June 12, 2006.

[53] Wojcieszak D, Banja J, Houk C. "The Sorry Works! Coalition: Making the Case for Full-Disclosure." *The Joint Commission Journal on Quality and Patient Safety*. (June 2006).

[54] Eisenberg D. "When Doctors Say, 'We're Sorry.'" *Time Magazine*, August 15, 2005.

[55] It is this type of program that the authors have created for healthcare organizations nationwide.

[56] "Disclosing medical errors: Best practices from the "leading edge" written by Eve Shapiro.

SOUTH AFRICA
Twelve Perspectives
on the Transition

THE WASHINGTON PAPERS

... intended to meet the need for an authoritative, yet prompt, public appraisal of the major developments in world affairs.

President, CSIS: David M. Abshire

Series Editor: Walter Laqueur

Director of Studies: Erik R. Peterson

Director of Publications: Nancy B. Eddy

Managing Editor: Donna R. Spitler

MANUSCRIPT SUBMISSION

The Washington Papers and Praeger Publishers welcome inquiries concerning manuscript submissions. Please include with your inquiry a curriculum vitae, synopsis, table of contents, and estimated manuscript length. Manuscript length must fall between 120 and 200 double-spaced typed pages. All submissions will be peer reviewed. Submissions to *The Washington Papers* should be sent to *The Washington Papers*; The Center for Strategic and International Studies; 1800 K Street NW; Suite 400; Washington, DC 20006. Book proposals should be sent to Praeger Publishers; 90 Post Road West; P.O. Box 5007; Westport, CT 06881-5007.

The Washington Papers/165

SOUTH AFRICA
Twelve Perspectives on the Transition

Edited by

Helen Kitchen
and J. Coleman Kitchen

**PUBLISHED WITH
THE CENTER FOR STRATEGIC
AND INTERNATIONAL STUDIES
WASHINGTON, D.C.**

 PRAEGER

**Westport, Connecticut
London**

Library of Congress Cataloging-in-Publication Data

South Africa : twelve perspectives on the transition / Helen Kitchen
and J. Coleman Kitchen, editors.
    p. cm.—(Washington papers ; 165.)
  "Published with the Center for Strategic and International Studies
(Washington, D.C.)."
  Includes bibliographical references and index.
  ISBN 0–275–95086–7 (alk. paper). —ISBN 0–275–95087–5 (pbk. :
alk. paper)
    1. South Africa—Politics and government—1989– . 2. South Africa—
Forecasting. 3. South Africa—Race relations. I. Kitchen, Helen A.
II. Kitchen, J. Coleman. III. Center for Strategic &
International Studies (Washington, D.C.). IV. Series.
DT1970.S685 1994
968.06'4—dc20   94–35607

British Library Cataloguing in Publication data is available.

Library of Congress Catalog Card Number: 94–35607
ISBN: 0-275-95086-7 (cloth)
     0-275-95087-5 (paper)

First published in 1994

Praeger Publishers, 88 Post Road West, Westport, CT 06881
An imprint of Greenwood Publishing Group, Inc.

Printed in the United States of America

∞™

The paper used in this book complies with the Permanent
Paper Standard issued by the National Information Standards
Organization (Z39.48-1984).

10 9 8 7 6 5 4 3 2 1

Contents

Foreword

In mid-1982, shortly after I succeeded Chester Crocker as director of the African Studies Program at the Center for Strategic and International Studies (CSIS), we published the first of a series of monthly briefing papers modestly entitled *CSIS Africa Notes*. The title of this first issue—"To Demystify and Unsimplify"—remains the guiding principle of the publication (and the CSIS African Studies Program) in 1994. As stated in the masthead of each of the 164 issues published over the ensuing 12 years, *CSIS Africa Notes* is "a briefing paper series designed to serve the special needs of decision makers and analysts with Africa-related responsibilities in governments, corporations, the media, research institutions, universities, and other arenas." It has, over time, established a wide readership in all of these categories within the United States and in some 30 other countries.

The lasting relevance of the content of the briefing papers is demonstrated by the fact that two collections of issues published by Praeger in the 1980s—*Angola, Mozambique, and the West* (1987) and *South Africa: In Transition to What?* (1988)—have not outlived their pertinence to the still-unfolding story of southern Africa's political evolution.

Following the format of our previous volume on South Africa, each of the chapters in *South Africa: Twelve Perspectives on the Transition* was previously published as an issue of *CSIS Africa Notes*, focuses on a specific segment or segments of the jigsaw puzzle from which South Africa's future will be assembled, and is datelined (to emphasize that this is how the situation, event, or issue being addressed appeared through a particular set of lenses at a particular time). The authors come from a range of geographical and professional bases but meet one important qualification: residence or repeated physical presence in South Africa. We are looking here through prisms focused on the whys and wherefores of South Africa as seen from within.

Although none of the chapters address directly the issue of U.S. policy, one of the objectives of publishing this collection has been to impress upon readers (especially Americans) that the postapartheid South Africa now in the process of emerging will be primarily determined by internal factors. Evidence has accumulated over the years that "Eminent Persons interlocutors," "constructive engagement," distinguished advisory committees, made-in-Washington "comprehensive" antiapartheid legislation, disinvestment, selective economic and diplomatic sanctions by European trading partners, Sullivan principles, expanding support of black education programs, and other externally devised initiatives affected but could not mandate how or whether South Africa's long-fractured society would be able to find a way to avoid a lemmings scenario.

The U.S. inclination to address South Africa (among other issues) as "a problem to be solved" has run the risk of oversimplifying both dynamics and personalities. South Africa is more than a morality play. It is one of the world's most complex societies – and becoming more so every day.

Helen Kitchen
Director of African Studies
and Editor of *CSIS Africa Notes*
Center for Strategic and International Studies

July 1994

Contributors to This Volume

Millard W. Arnold was appointed in April 1994 to a newly created U.S. Department of Commerce position as minister counsellor to the southern Africa region. Based in Johannesburg, he is responsible for developing and managing U.S. commercial activities in the area's 10 countries. A lawyer by profession, he has served in a range of Africa-related positions over the past 19 years, including deputy assistant secretary of state for human rights and humanitarian affairs in the Carter administration, senior associate at the Carnegie Endowment for International Peace, and director of the Southern Africa Project for the Lawyers' Committee for Civil Rights Under Law.

Herbert M. Howe is director of African studies at Georgetown University's School of Foreign Service, Washington, D.C. His extensive on-the-ground experience in Africa began with a Peace Corps assignment in Nigeria in 1966–1967 and has included (since the early 1990s) periodic research in South Africa on connections between developments in the security area and political reform.

Robert S. Jaster's two chapters in this volume, "Pretoria's Nuclear Diplomacy" and "The South African Military Reassesses Its Priorities," were based on extensive research conducted in South Africa and Namibia on behalf of the London-based International Institute for Strategic Studies (IISS). His publications include *South Africa in*

Namibia: The Botha Strategy (Harvard Center for International Affairs, 1985) and two IISS Adelphi Papers, *South Africa and Its Neighbors: The Dynamics of Regional Conflict* (1986) and *A Regional Security Role for Africa's Front-Line States: Experience and Prospects* (1983). Mr. Jaster was a 1984–1985 fellow at the Smithsonian Institute's Wilson Center in Washington, D.C., and a visiting fellow at the IISS in 1985–1986. He has taught at the U.S. Naval Postgraduate School and the University of Cape Town and served in the late 1980s as a consultant to the Ford Foundation's Developing Country Programs.

Steven McDonald has been executive vice president of the African-American Institute (New York) since 1992. He previously served (1988–1992) as associate director of the Aspen Institute's Southern Africa Policy Forum; as executive director of the United States-South Africa Leader Exchange Program (USSALEP) from 1982 to 1986; on the staff of the late Senator Stuart Symington before and after three years in the U.S. Army that included combat service in Vietnam; and as a U.S. foreign service officer (1970–1979), serving in American embassies in South Africa and Uganda and as the State Department's desk officer in Washington for the then-Portuguese territories of Angola, Mozambique, and Guinea-Bissau.

J. Coleman Kitchen is research coordinator and senior text editor for the books and other publications of the CSIS African Studies Program and deputy editor of *CSIS Africa Notes* – the monthly periodical in which the chapters of this book were originally published. A graduate of St. John's College, Annapolis, Maryland, he received his Ph.D. in mathematical sciences from The Johns Hopkins University. His many contributions to *CSIS Africa Notes* have included "Some Key Dates in Liberia's Political History," "Where Does the OAU Go From Here?" "OAU Assembly XXII," "OAU Assembly XXV," "The Enduring French Connection," "France and Africa in the 1990s," "Zaire and Israel," "Chad's Political History in Brief," "Sudan's Political History in Brief," and "Iran and Africa."

Bruce McKenney received his B.A. from Brown University in 1990 and subsequently served as an intern in the African Studies Program at CSIS and as a research assistant for the Center's Science and Technology Program. He has traveled extensively in southern Africa and did a year of graduate work (in African Studies) at the University of Cape Town. He is now continuing his graduate studies at Harvard University's John F. Kennedy School of Government.

Marina Ottaway is a visiting professor at Georgetown University in Washington, D.C. From 1990 until 1992, she lectured at several universities and carried out research in South Africa (where her husband, David Ottaway, was the *Washington Post*'s correspondent). She was a member of the African-American Institute team that monitored mid-1992 district and regional assembly elections in Ethiopia. Dr. Ottaway's published works on Africa include *South Africa: The Struggle for a New Order* (The Brookings Institution, May 1993), *Soviet and American Influence in the Horn of Africa* (Praeger, 1981), *Ethiopia: Empire in Revolution*, coauthored with David Ottaway (Africana: 1978), and *Afrocommunism*, coauthored with David Ottaway (Africana: 1981 and 1986).

Brian Pottinger, formerly parliamentary correspondent and now deputy editor of the *Sunday Times* (Johannesburg), spent the 1989–1990 academic year in the United States as the twenty-ninth South African Nieman Fellow in Journalism at Harvard University since 1961. His contribution to this volume is based in part on his book, *The Imperial Presidency: P.W. Botha, the first 10 years*, published by Southern Book Publishers (Johannesburg) in 1988.

Witney W. Schneidman, senior coordinator of the CSIS Working Group on South Africa since 1991, joined Samuels International Associates, Inc., as senior vice president in 1992. He is an adviser to the Standard Bank of South Africa and has served as a consultant to the World Bank in the office of the vice president for the Africa region as well as the Southern Africa department. From 1987 to 1990 he was a South Africa analyst in the Department of State's Bureau of Intelligence and Research. He received his Ph.D. from the University of Southern California's School of International Relations, where he wrote his dissertation on U.S. policy toward Portugal, Angola, and Mozambique. His master's degree in political science is from the University of Dar es Salaam.

Frederik van Zyl Slabbert was leader of the parliamentary opposition (then called the Progressive Federal Party) until he resigned as an MP in 1986 to found the Institute for a Democratic Alternative for South Africa (IDASA) and focus on narrowing the gap between the extraparliamentary opposition movements and the government. An early IDASA initiative was a Slabbert-led visit by a delegation of 50 prominent Afrikaners to Dakar, Senegal in June 1987 to meet then-exiled senior officials of the African National Congress – the first-ever such meeting and, in retrospect, a turning point in South Africa's recent history. Dr. Slabbert's chapter in this volume is derived from his presentation at the January 1992 inaugural session of the CSIS African Studies Program's Working Group on South Africa.

Patti Waldmeir has been South Africa correspondent of the *Financial Times* (London) since 1989. She previously served as a Reuters correspondent in West Africa from 1980 to 1982 and from 1984 to 1986 as a *Financial Times* correspondent for all of the sub-Saharan region. Her chapter in this volume was written while she was on sabbatical as a visiting fellow with the CSIS Russian and Eurasian Studies Program in 1992.

SOUTH AFRICA
Twelve Perspectives
on the Transition

1

Why Racial Reconciliation Is Possible in South Africa

Steven McDonald

March 1990

It was 1976, a year that appears on every chronology of South African milestones. A 14-year-old, bespectacled and intense, undertook to convey the feelings of the township students with whom I was discussing the significance of the Soweto and post-Soweto riots of that troubled year. Reaching for words that would leave a lasting impact, the youngster stood up, paused for effect, and then said: "The tree of liberty shall be watered by the blood of black South Africans." What the young black revolutionary did not realize was that he was echoing, almost word for word, the declaration attributed to Afrikaner nationalist hero "Jopie" Fourie just before his death by firing squad in 1914.

Fourie had been part of a short-lived revolt by Afrikaners bitter about the Boer War and opposed to any form of cooperation with the British. The revolt was sparked by the commitment of South African troops to the World War I campaign in the neighboring German colony then known as South West Africa (now Namibia). Several of Prime Minister Louis Botha's fellow generals from the Boer War had balked when the invasion was ordered at British request. They fomented a rebellion of some 12,000 Boer War veterans that ended in hundreds of deaths and detentions. Most of the survivors joined the newly formed National Party, and the incident stands in Afrikaner mythology as one of the great moments of nationalist fervor.

The lesson to be learned from this vignette is not in the prediction of bloody resistance in both cases, but in what these strikingly similar statements of 1914 and 1976 say about their propounders, so far removed from each other both in time and, seemingly, ideology and aspiration. Or are they? Those of us with the patience and inclination continue to find a surprising coincidence of historical, societal, and cultural experiences and current value systems in South African society, black and white, that could augur well for the ability of that country eventually to heal itself.

I lived in South Africa for several years in the 1970s and have continued to make frequent visits through the 1980s. In my quest for a genuine understanding of the South African kaleidoscope, I have sought out and established friendships across the racial, political, and cultural spectrum and have enjoyed extended home hospitality among all racial groups and economic strata. It was in the homes of these diverse South African friends that I began to realize how intertwined are the histories and cultures of black and white in South Africa. It was when the guard was down and the talk informal, turning from politics to the quotidian, that I became conscious of the striking similarities across ethnic and class lines in taste, style, mannerisms, and aspirations. Although my findings are totally unscientific, they have been repeated too often to be ignored.

The Braaivleis

When invited to the home of a South African—whether in the white Johannesburg suburb of Sandton, the black township of Mdantsane in the Eastern Cape, or the "Coloured" township of Belleville in Cape Town—I am invariably hosted to a *braaivleis*. This is the South African variation of our barbecue, and the emphasis is on the *vleis* (meat).

All South Africans love their meat and serve plenty of it, well done. *Boerewors* (sausages), chops of lamb or pork, steaks an inch thick, *sosaties* (spicy meat on skewers) — these foods are prepared over hot, often roaring, fires of wood coals (not charcoal) and served with mealie pap (a white corn flour, eaten grits-style, with a stiff mashed potato consistency) and salads. The variations are only in quantity and quality. Even in the poorest black home, some meat, often of undetermined cut and origin, is always found to *braai* on an open fire.

After the food, there is the drink. Whether black or white, South Africans drink alcohol socially and with a connoisseur's relish. The norm is cold beer for the men and white wine for the women. According to the host's financial ability, glasses never go empty.

Social patterns are also strikingly similar. Whether gathered around a landscaped swimming pool deck in a white suburb or a dusty, grassless, postage-stamp-sized yard in a township, the men always cluster near the fire. The host cooks with a steady stream of good-natured ribbing, advice, and criticism from the other men. The women invariably gather to the side or even in the house and talk to each other about domestic or family concerns. Even in professional circles, where the conversations might be more work-related, the same patterns of gender grouping are found.

Leaving aside any value judgments on diets of inordinate amounts of red meat, drinking (and South Africans are all too often heavy drinkers), or gender-based social segregation, I have long since concluded that these are a part of South Africa, black or white.

Sports

Aside from politics, what subjects are of shared concern to South Africans? The answer to this question also cuts across ethnic boundaries. Sports are a mania throughout the land. Blacks might like soccer more than rugby and whites vice versa, but every sport is followed and understood. Even supposedly elitist games such as cricket or lawn bowls are followed and played by blacks. One of my most striking memories is that of rounding a corner on a dusty street in Soweto to see before me a well-manicured green lawn with older men and women, all of them black, dressed in white skirts or slacks, cardigans, and wide-brimmed hats, chasing bowling balls up and down the pitch. Whether it is a little black boy kicking around a deflated soccer ball on a hard dirt field in the rural Orange Free State or an immaculately dressed white boy overhanding a cricket ball toward a wicket on a green field in Durban, South Africans are sports addicts and continue to talk sports as they grow older and less active.

Love of the Outdoors

Black or white, South Africans consider themselves rugged, close-to-nature types. How this is manifested depends on various factors, including financial means.

Land has almost a mythical quality for South Africans. Urban whites, where possible, have farm properties, seaside villas, or even private game farms and spend as much time there as possible. Blacks, largely restricted from such ownership, still visit the shore or commercial game reserves when possible and treasure their family connections to those still on the land. Life-styles revolve around outdoor imagery, land ownership is a driving goal, and conservation is taken seriously. A culture and history founded in rural traditions, common to blacks and whites, continues to mold attitudes and aspirations, even as more and more South Africans are permanently urbanized.

Religion

Also common to most South Africans is a belief in a God. According to the official 1980 census, the latest available, slightly over 78 percent of all South Africans (white, African, Coloured, Indian) are Christian, 1.4 percent Muslim, 2.1 percent Hindu, and 0.5 percent Jewish. Of the Africans, 76 percent are Christian and the remainder predominantly of "indigenous" religions. (The African figures exclude the residents of the four "independent" homelands, which are left out of the official South African census.)

To use an Americanism, South Africans are real "church-goers." Most Afrikaners (as well as more than a million blacks and over 500,000 Coloureds) belong to the NGK—the Nederduitse Gereformeerde Kerk (Dutch Reformed Church). The Roman Catholic Church numbers well over 2 million members, and the Anglican total is around 2 million.

Among Africans, Christian churches have long played an influential role. Early missions, many of them American in origin, were the first to bring Western education to blacks and remained the bulwark of African education until the 1950s. The early leaders of nationalist and liberation movements were church educated and often church leaders. Much of Afrikaner and African political leadership as we move into the 1990s is church trained or inspired. The role of the church extends to the grass roots, where secular events such as funerals or political meetings customarily include a significant component of religious symbolism.

Today, as in the past, and particularly in rural areas, much of white social life revolves around Sunday worship and after-church gatherings. In black townships, the churches are jammed on Sundays. Among both whites and blacks, the church is the venue for elaborate ladies' hats, spit-shined shoes, and the best clothes one can afford. Even in the white suburbs where black domestic workers are far from their congregations, one sees them, decked out in bright, clean uniforms, holding Sunday services in small groups in an open field.

Although the history of the NGK and other churches has been (and in the case of the NGK still is) marked by the existence of separate branches for Africans, Coloureds, and whites, their members have long shared common cores of beliefs and customs. It is not surprising that the churches have surged into the forefront in leading change in South Africa. From the act of desegregating church schools in defiance of law to the opening of an increasing number of congregations to all races to the challenging of the theological underpinnings of apartheid to the leading of direct protests against the system, the churches have had an important role. They have provided a language, a set of values, and a historical focal point around which South Africans can communicate.

These factors are reflected in the moral values that predominate in both white and black society. Traditional African and Afrikaner family and social units not only have a strong religious focus but are morally conservative. The central, patriarchal family is the norm. Men rule and elders are sacrosanct. Promiscuity is not acceptable (although definitions of promiscuity may differ). Extended families are the rule and are accepted as responsibilities and opportunities. The young and the old are cared for. Hospitality is a social obligation and no one is turned away or goes unfed. One does all one can to help a family member or a neighbor.

The Historical Backdrop

The shared tastes, values, and customs of white and black South Africans derive from a unique historical backdrop. The two key modern-day protagonists, the Afrikaner and the African, have come through the last four tragic, exciting, and awesome centuries in a sweeping current of interaction.

When the whites who would become Afrikaners first arrived in Cape Town in 1652 under the auspices of the Dutch East India Company, they set forth in a land already peopled with strong, proud, independent Africans. The early history was one of co-option and conflict in relation to the Khoi-Khoi and the San, who populated the Cape area. The Afrikaners were a rural people, however, and over time moved inland—partly to escape political control by the European colonial powers and partly to seek land and opportunity.

In the hinterlands they encountered the great African kingdoms of the Xhosa, Zulu, Tswana, and Sotho. Although the history of the establishment of the Afrikaner republics is one of conflict, the conflict was seldom racial per se. Both the Afrikaners and the Africans of this area were herder, gatherer peoples who interacted economically, socially, and sexually. They stole each other's women and cattle. They formed alliances and they betrayed each other. The Xhosa were conquered by Englishmen, Afrikaner "Voortrekkers," Mfengu (refugees from Zulu empire building), and Khoi-Khoi remnants. The Swazis fought the Pedi and the Venda alongside whites. Indeed, every major campaign was fought by entangled alliances on both sides, with Zulu helping to defeat Zulu in the famous war of 1878–1879.

The importance of this history as we view prospects for a postapartheid South Africa is in the interaction and understanding it generated between Africans and Afrikaners – often bitter enemies, but not unknown quantities to each other. Whites grew up speaking African languages and blacks learned Afrikaans. Their vocabularies took on each other's words and phrases. There was some intermarriage. Yet the African never lost his identity. Zulu stayed Zulu and Xhosa stayed Xhosa, living in proud and independent interaction with the Afrikaner. Until the onset of modern apartheid, ascribed to Afrikaners but rooted in British colonial policy, the African was not threatened with extinction, either physically or culturally, by whites. African "defeats" during the numerous wars that took place between the 1770s and 1908 were, as often as not, no more than a decision to stop fighting because food supplies were being interdicted or there was an obligation to return home for planting or other social needs.

In this attempt to "unsimplify" black-white relations in South African history, I do not mean to suggest that the roots of apartheid were not evolving. Early on, the British colonizers in Natal were setting the stage for segregation with the creation of the African reserve system. With the discovery of diamonds and gold in the Transvaal, a migrant labor structure as well as residential, workplace, and economic discrimination began to emerge. The treatment of African workers (by both Afrikaners and the English) was patronizing and sometimes cruel. Although some early diamond mine owners, as well as suppliers of produce and livestock to the mines, were black, these tentative steps toward racial justice were nipped in the bud. The forces of urbanization, industrialization, and nationalism were artificially channeled along racial lines.

It is noteworthy, however, that the Afrikaner was also left out of the early modernization of South Africa, which was largely in the hands of the British. In fact, blacks were more involved in the emerging modern economy of South Africa, albeit initially as laborers only, than were Afrikaners, most of whom stayed on the land as subsistence farmers and hunters. Until after the ascension to power of the National Party in 1948, the Afrikaners remained (as did most of the African population) rural and largely poor.

Other Afrikaner-African Parallels

The African and the Afrikaner paralleled each other developmentally in some other often overlooked ways. Although African languages were centuries older than Afrikaans (a mixture of early Dutch, Huguenot, Malay, English, German, and various African influences that did not gel into a widely accepted language until the late nineteenth century and an official language until 1925), the written and grammatical structuring of these two language groups took place in roughly the same period. Missionaries were beginning to record the Nguni language groups in the first half of the nineteenth century, about the same time that Afrikaans was evolving from a patois to a widely spoken and written language.

Another point of similarity between the Africans and Afrikaners has been nationalism—a prime moving force for both groups through much of the second half of the nineteenth century. As the twentieth century began, both gave their nationalism organizational structures.

Although Africans had formed earlier organizations with nationalist overtones, the movement that remains the embodiment of African nationalist aspirations nearly 80 years later is the South African Native National Congress, formed in 1912 and renamed the African National Congress in 1923. Afrikaners waged a war against the British at the turn of the century, but remained a divided people until the National Party, formed in 1914, finally evolved into the vehicle that brought them to power in 1948. Their long struggle against the British and subsequently English-speaking South Africans for political recognition and power has many parallels with African nationalism's history. In the critical economic sphere, blacks are only now beginning to draw on the Afrikaner experience of establishing financial institutions and other businesses within and for the community.

I was stunned during the 1970s by the number of young black radicals who cited the Afrikaner nationalistic struggle as a strategic model and by the admiration and understanding they accorded the struggle of the "Boers" for identity. Also unexpected was the opprobrium they heaped on English-speaking white liberals whose objectives, to this outsider, seemed most in tune with black aspirations. These "liberals," they said, took advantage of and profited from a system that served them, spoke in high moral rhetoric against the system, but would depart South Africa with their profits if the political stress became too uncomfortable. The fact that the English-speaking white community is also the most wealthy in South Africa only reinforced their point. When I sought to defend specific liberals whom I knew to be dedicated and willing to sacrifice, a sloganeering student retorted, "When I'm arrested for a pass violation, they don't ask if I'm liberal or conservative. When the revolution comes, we won't care who is *verligte* or *verkrampte*."

Trust over Race

It has been my experience over time that trust is a critical
ingredient in relations within South Africa—more important, I would venture, than race. There are dozens of anec-
dotal examples I could cite to illustrate this point, but one
that stands out most vividly in my memory occurred a
dozen years ago.

In 1978, I learned that a person I wanted to see was
going to be at a house party in Orlando, Soweto, on a particular evening. She was an important political leader, currently banned, and her appearance at the party would be in
violation of her banning order. Given these circumstances,
I did not call around in advance to tell anyone of my coming for fear that the security police might be alerted and
become suspicious. I decided just to show up at the party.
I knew the address but did not know the owner of the
house.

As I approached, I could hear rhythmic music and the
babble of conversation. I knocked on the door. When it
opened, the house went deadly silent. The needle was lifted
from the revolving record. A hundred black people focused
their eyes on me and did not move or speak. Here I stood
in the doorway, a burly, bearded white man who probably
matched each one of their stereotypes of the typical security policeman.

Suddenly my friend, the guest of honor, jumped from
her seat and ran up to greet me warmly. Without hesita-
tion, the music began again and people turned to their
drinks and conversation as if nothing had happened. In the
course of a very pleasant evening, I was not confronted or
questioned once but made to feel right at home. Had I been
black—and unknown to them—I believe the initial reaction
would have been the same.

Over the years and after hundreds of observations
such as those I have recounted above, it became apparent
to me that there was a true bridge, a camaraderie born of
shared histories and struggles, between black and white

(especially the Afrikaner). This has never been so clear to me as since I returned to live in the United States, where I associate with a broad circle of South African friends, both black and white. Leaving aside public meetings with a specifically political purpose or venue involving adherence to a certain view, political divisions and ethnic considerations do not stop South Africans from getting together and enjoying themselves. This is especially true for the members of the exiled community, who are always hungry for "a touch from home," as they say.

South Africans will cook for any reason and, if the ingredients are available, dishes from home will be the fare. Black or white, they relish stories or news of an event or an individual. They worry about drought in the Karoo or laugh over snowfall in Johannesburg. The price of real estate or the value of the rand will bother them equally. They will share, wistfully, stories of the South Africa they left behind and its people. And, whether black or white, the language used will, as often as not, be Afrikaans, despite the fact that a decade ago black children died in the streets of townships to protest the use of Afrikaans as a medium of instruction. They will tease each other mercilessly and mix uninhibitedly, in a way that black and white Americans have seldom learned to do. Unselfconscious and open, black South Africans are sure of their identity and their waiting inheritance. They are proud of their past and feel no threat from a white in any personal way. Whites, perhaps sensing this lack of tension, interact without any signs of apprehension.

What Does All This Mean?

One thing these observations are not intended to imply is that everything is going to proceed smoothly to the almost proverbial nonracial democratic South Africa. Entrenched power interests and segments of the population, both black and white, who do not (or inadequately) share the outlook

I have been describing here may well make trouble. The modalities of transition and the final structuring of post-apartheid South Africa will require intense negotiations to accommodate varied interests. Years will probably elapse before this society can come to grips with its fears and stereotypes and can break down its "Berlin Wall."

What these musings do mean is that, once those barriers have been hurdled, there is real hope for South Africa. The common wisdom is too often that the interests of black and white cannot coincide and that conflict is inherent in the absence of domination. Whites have dominated in the past, and in the future it will be blacks.

My experience counters this view. Blacks hate the "system" but not whites. Whites are accepted as "Africans" and assumed to have a role and a right in South Africa. Whites fear a loss of power but mostly for reasons unconnected to race per se, although racism and racial patterns have given birth to these fears. The society, they know, must undergo vast changes and this probably applies no matter who is in political power. This inevitability has to do with changing demographics and an inequitable distribution of land, wealth, and opportunity; whites know this will mean a readjustment of their life-styles.

The unknown that awaits South Africa inspires legitimate fears, but neither blacks nor whites fear each other in a personal way. Certainly there is patronization in the general attitude of whites and stridency in that of blacks, but their claims to understand each other are not farfetched. Above all, they know how to survive. When surviving meant fighting each other, they did it. A day has now dawned when survival means interdependence. It is my view that the majority of black and white South Africans realize this and that the historical, social, cultural, and personal interactions that have formed their respective values and aspirations will, in the end, allow them to come together in peace.

2

The Botha Era:
An End or a Beginning?

Brian Pottinger

October 1989

The years from 1978 until 1989 saw profound changes in South Africa that, cumulatively, might prove as important to the region as the events currently sweeping Eastern Europe and China.

For the white ruling elite, it was an era that witnessed the death of an ideology. The cold and cerebral idealism of Dr. Hendrik Verwoerd, modern apartheid's chief architect, had by 1978 given way to a growing acceptance that apartheid was impractical and costly. Increasingly, whites were launched into a quest for a future in which power was shared but not surrendered, privilege dispersed but never lost. This government retreat from the old orthodoxies took place hesitantly by way of a program of reform and repression. It was an ambiguous mix demanding a high degree of management skills – a skill, events were to prove, that was sorely lacking.

There were also significant shifts among black South Africans – shifts away from rhetoric and spontaneous protest toward a more considered exploration of available levers of power. An educated and assertive black political elite emerged in the trade union movements and local-level bodies to challenge the state directly through a variety of methods and forums. Between 1984 and 1986, South Africa experienced its longest, bloodiest, and most sustained wave of antigovernment resistance in its history. The government's comprehensive, vigorous, and often ruthless response succeeded in the short term in smothering the revolt.

All of these changes were framed by two other important factors: (1) a declining domestic economy that severely circumscribed the government's maneuverability while inflaming political passions in both the black resistance and the white right wing and (2) a changing global picture that placed South Africa in increasing isolation.

Presiding over the country during these crucial years was President P.W. Botha. It is the nature of his stewardship and its legacy that this chapter addresses.

The Man

Pieter Willem Botha was 62 years old when he became prime minister of South Africa on September 28, 1978. He brought to the office a dominant conviction, a style, and a modus operandi.

The conviction was that whites (Afrikaners in particular) had an ordained role to lead the people of South Africa, and indeed the southern region of the continent, to a new and prosperous future. Yet his inclinations were xenophobic. He grew up in a staunchly anti-imperialist family where both parents had suffered in the Anglo-Boer war of 1899 to 1902, and he showed little indication during his tenure of liking, or even understanding, black Africans. His universe, in short, was gravely limited.

His style was a peculiar mixture of bombast and flexibility. It was bombast that dominated in both the early and the latter part of his tenure — initially to harry a reluctant bureaucracy and party into accepting adaptive reform and then, by an ironic inversion, to alienate and eventually isolate him from a party caucus that had overtaken him in reformist mood by the end of the 1980s.

The modus operandi was drawn heavily from Botha's experience as minister of defense from 1966 until 1980. It implied a reliance on technocratic approaches to the country's looming social, economic, and political crises. It was the military as well that informed his counterrevolutionary "total strategy" – an orchestration of military, political, social, economic, psychological, and cultural forces in opposition to what was seen as a pervasive and imminent threat from "world communism."

In essence, Botha was neither a convinced reformist nor a visionary. Although he accepted the need for adaptation, he never seriously countenanced any significant loss of power. His strength lay, rather, in the capacity to identify crises and his willingness to address them. Time would prove that, although he had both tactical sense and moments of rare genius, he was blessed with neither the conviction nor the ability to comprehend the sweeping changes that were demanded in South Africa – and of him personally.

The Plan

By 1978 the legacy of 30 years of National Party rule was becoming abundantly obvious in a range of crises. These included a growing skills shortage as a result of a hugely defective black educational system; a daunting housing shortage created by state policies limiting black residency in "white" urban areas; a continuing impoverishment of the semi-independent homelands as a result of the "dumping" of black people from common South Africa and archaic tenure systems; the patent failure of government attempts to stem the tide of black peasantry flowing to the urban areas; the growing power of an emerging black industrial class; and, again, the bubbling resistance of political elites within the disenfranchised black, mixed-race Coloured, and Indian-descended population.

Reduced to its crux, the Botha doctrine proposed the co-option of leadership elites in the disenfranchised communities as allies of white power and the sweetening of the broader population by a program of socioeconomic uplift — the resources for this program to come, meanwhile, largely from the private sector. It was a fairly sophisticated strategy of co-optive domination in which the Botha administration sought to reach out across racial lines and rally allies in defense of a set of basic values. Although these values were most frequently described by Botha in terms of Christian ethics or "civilized" norms, they largely boiled down to a defense of the capitalist system, an acceptance of the principle of gradualism in political change, and the premise that individuals were best served by their "own" racially segregated residential areas, schools, and local-level political institutions.

The Institutional Actors

As self-serving as many of the adaptive changes were, they nevertheless constituted to a significant body of white South Africans an ominous departure from the hallowed orthodoxies of rigid apartheid.

In the first seven years of his administration, Botha was to recognize the black trade union movement, scrap the pass laws (thus allowing freedom of movement for black South Africans), drop prohibitions on mixed marriages and sex across the color line, end job reservation, propose legalized mixed residential areas, proceed significantly in ending segregation in social amenities, and encourage the growth of an urban black informal economic sector.

In 1985, he was to pass an important political milestone when he committed his government to the principle of one citizenship, one constitution, and one country for all South Africans (irrespective of race) while at the same time offering the renationalization of black South Africans who had been arbitrarily designated citizens of the nominally independent "national states" (homelands). Despite many anomalies, the shifts in government thinking clearly heralded a move from orthodox apartheid with its exclude, divide, and rule policy to a more subtle program of co-optive domination.

To carry out these reforms in the social, economic, and subsequently constitutional spheres, Botha was obliged from the early days of his administration to stamp his authority on an inert bureaucracy and an intuitively conservative party.

The former he achieved by creating a category of elite and highly paid departmental "super secretaries" (directors general) on contracts and by phasing out hotbeds of reactionaryism in various layers of the bureaucracy (particularly those relating to black administration) by simply devolving their functions to other departments. But central to his approach was the concept of adding an overlay of security-dominated structures to short-circuit problem identification and solving in the civil service.

This system, proposed as far back as 1975, consisted of a National Security Management System reporting directly to the State Security Council (a powerful sort of minicabinet comprising security ministers and others) and operating through a descending hierarchy of "management centers" charged with the responsibility of identifying security-related problems in the country and initiating steps to solve them jointly with other civil departments. This structure was to prove of crucial importance during the 1984–1986 uprisings.

In regard to the National Party, Botha adopted a variety of tactics aimed at marginalizing its impact on policy-making. These steps involved initiating a distinction between "policy" and "principle" (the former to be decided by Botha and the latter by the party congresses, although in fact most major reform steps were decided by Botha unilaterally); stage-managing party congresses; introducing the idea of white national referendums on important constitutional issues so as to overshadow party decisions; and promoting younger, more loyal, members of the party over the heads of older stalwarts.

By 1981, the groundwork for the rearrangement of the bureaucracy had been completed and in February 1982 the last remaining conservative dissidents in the National Party were driven out. These recidivist émigrés would form the new Conservative Party that emerged in 1982. The party they left behind, meanwhile, would for the next seven years be largely sidelined by an increasingly imperious Botha.

Consolidation of Power

Having once secured his dominance in the two primary support sectors (the bureaucracy and the party), Botha moved on to attract other constituencies. These included, for a short while, the South African private sector, which was initially entranced by Botha's enthusiastic but often uncomprehending embrace of free enterprise. He also won the support of many English-speaking South Africans and the Afrikaner intelligentsia, who appreciated his attempts to urge whites into accepting the principle, if not always the reality, of reform. A third constituency came from elements of the Coloured and Indian communities—a small group of politicians who, whether out of principle or in hope of patronage, agreed to serve in a racially divided tricameral parliament in which limited power was shared with Coloureds and Indians.

But none of this support could have a focus unless consolidated in structural terms. Thus Botha turned his attention to reordering the constitutional system. In a November 1983 whites-only referendum, two-thirds of the votes endorsed a new constitution that provided for a legislature made up of white, Coloured, and Indian houses, with the dominant power held by the white chamber.

The new constitution, which went into effect in September 1984, also created the position of an executive state president with extensive powers. The original architects of the system proposed that the state president not be associated with any party and that his cabinet not serve in the

legislature, a concept based on the hope of creating a supra-
political presidency capable of winning support across race
and sectarian divides. This was rejected by Botha, who
stayed on as both party boss and executive president—a
welding of considerable powers within one person.

Foreign Relations

Compared to the relatively flexible approach adopted in the
early Botha years regarding domestic reform, the regional
policy during the period from 1978 to 1987 remained firmly
hawkish, emphasizing defense in depth (based on the premise that the best way to control a border is to be on both
sides of it) and reflecting a liturgical suspicion of foreign
interlocution. South African foreign policy throughout this
period was predicated upon one central concern—domestic
and regional security. It was this concern that dictated
nearly all Botha's actions. Only on a very few issues was
he prepared to bow to Western suasion or, in latter years,
direct pressure.

The United Nations Security Council adopted Resolution 435, establishing the terms for Namibia's independence, on September 29, 1978, the day after Botha took
office. The administration of Prime Minister B.J. Vorster
had agreed to the terms of the settlement proposals, but
this was vehemently opposed by Botha, then defense minister, who saw UN-supervised elections as the inevitable
prelude to a victory by the South West Africa People's
Organization (SWAPO). Such a victory, coming so soon
after the collapse of Portuguese sovereignty in Africa and
South Africa's inconclusive intervention in Angola in 1975–
1976, would, Botha and his generals argued, suggest weakness on Pretoria's part, and such a perception would have
incalculable consequences regionally and domestically.

For most of Botha's early tenure, then, attention in the
area of foreign relations was focused on delaying implementation of Resolution 435, weakening neighboring states
through military action by proxies so as to force them to

deny sanctuary to resistance groups such as SWAPO or the African National Congress (ANC), and seeking maximum Western endorsement for the tentative reform steps being undertaken at home.

By 1984, three years of military engagement in neighboring countries, either directly in cross-border raids or by proxy forces, had succeeded in devastating several already weakened regional economies. In 1984, by entering respectively into the Nkomati Accord and the Lusaka Agreement, Mozambique and Angola tentatively signaled their willingness to become more accommodating toward Pretoria's security concerns—the first steps toward tying the countries of the region into a security commonwealth.

Turning Point

The period from mid-1984 until the end of 1985 could well be considered the apogee of the Botha administration. Domestically, he had succeeded in stamping his authority on the party and bureaucracy. He had nudged the country into a process of hesitant, adaptive change that had seen the extension of an industrial and partial social citizenship to blacks and the first breaches in the apartheid dike in regard to the dilution of white political power. In foreign relations, he was able in mid-1984 to visit eight European nations—a reward for his domestic initiatives and the normalizing of regional relations through the Nkomati Accord and the Lusaka Agreement.

Although the change from Pretoria's Prague Spring to the most comprehensive phase of repression in the country's history cannot be pegged to a specific date, milestone events would have to include the detention of United Democratic Front leaders in August 1984, the surge of violent resistance beginning in September 1984, the July 1985 refusal of the Chase Manhattan Bank to roll over loans, the South African Defense Force raids against ANC targets in neighboring countries in May 1986 (which aborted the

Commonwealth's Eminent Persons Group peace initiative), and the start in 1986 of a series of ANC-linked bombings of "soft" targets.

Although substantial reforms continued even during the period of intense repression and reaction from 1984 until 1986, the time from early 1985 until Botha's resignation in 1989 *did* contrast measurably with his earlier years in power. The eruption of large-scale protest actions from September 1984 onward, actions that often spilled over into insurrectionary violence against state institutions and members of the security forces, appalled and angered him. He turned instinctively to military rather than political methods in response.

The counterinsurgency strategy invoked in 1985 amounted to importation to South Africa of the techniques that had been evolved, tested, and refined by the security services in Namibia. Its central pillars were (1) a program of socioeconomic uplift of the most insurrectionary areas, (2) attempts to establish and support "moderate" community leaders, (3) a campaign of disinformation directed against activists, (4) the "decentralization" of repression by invoking the use of proxies against activists, and (5) a massive and systematic action aimed at neutralizing resistance leaders and preventing their mobilizing support. Although the fifth aspect of policing—the detentions, alleged torture, police shootings, and beatings—drew most international attention and condemnation, it was only one component of a much broader counterrevolutionary action.

This counterrevolutionary strategy, however successful in cooling the situation in the short term, was quite unable to deal with the far more intractable problems posed by a highly politicized mass-based resistance. It was Botha's inability to come to terms with the political components of reform (or even repression) that led to a growing disillusionment among his rank-and-file supporters in the government.

The disenchantment with the content of Botha's pro-

gram coincided with increasing resentment of his style —
imperious, abrasive, and often perceived by members of
the caucus of the ruling party as contemptuous of their
views. This personal style also affected Botha's responses
to foreign interlocution. Even governments and individuals sympathetic to the problems of reforming an intensely divided country were given short shrift by Botha, who
became a convinced xenophobe as international pressure
mounted. The patent inability of the administration to
respond creatively to the challenges raised by the resistance groups also lost Botha previous allies — the private
sector, the Afrikaner intelligentsia, reformist elements
within the bureaucracy, and even those members of the
Coloured and Indian communities participating in the tricameral system.

By 1988 there were already maneuverings within the
senior ranks of the National Party to block Botha from
standing again for president when his term expired in
March 1990. His actual exit, however, was precipitated by
an intervention of another order — the stroke he suffered on
January 18, 1989. Although he wanted to retain power, his
indisposition and precipitate resignation as leader of the
ruling party (he had still hoped, implausible as it sounds,
to remain as president) only further excited opposition. The
party rallied behind its newly elected leader, F. W. de
Klerk, and after seven months of uneasy coexistence Botha
was compelled to resign. Botha's own cabinet had swung
unanimously against him. Apparently unaware until the
last moment of the degree of antagonism he had built up
during his imperial presidency, Botha retreated to a glow-
ering, bitter retirement.

The Botha Legacy

The 11-year tenure of P.W. Botha has left his country a
mixed legacy. At one level he has succeeded in making
respectable among most whites the notion of change, re-

form, and (to use the ruling party's favorite word) "renewal." Above all, he has injected into the national debate the concept of power sharing with other races – however imperfectly conceived or implemented.

The challenging of apartheid orthodoxy is no longer regarded as heresy in the ruling elite. It is welcomed as necessary and in some cases obligatory. Even the naming of a square in Pretoria after Dr. Verwoerd now provokes furious debate in the capital city. Under Botha's tutelage, the focus shifted from the peripherals (i.e., maintaining grotesque forms of social and economic discrimination against blacks) to more fundamental concerns – the retention of power and, parallel to that, evolution of strategies that can meet South Africa's development needs and recast a fundamentally inequitable economic order.

In pursuit of these ends, old shibboleths have been cast aside, new allies sought across historic divisions, and new class interests imposed on old ethnic and racial divides. Botha presided over a partial unchaining of the individual to pursue his own economic and social interests. In this lies possibly his greatest contribution. There is no indication that Botha fully understood the nature of the convergent forces he confronted or the consequences of many of the tactical actions he took to defuse their impact. Yet, in the final analysis, his furtherance of the demise of classical apartheid as a compelling ideology and his inability to provide a coherent substitute has forced whites, willingly or not, to embark on a voyage to a new and inevitably much different future. The debate is now only about sequences, time-spans, and methods.

The Challenges

The most urgent challenge that Botha leaves for de Klerk to address is the economy. Structural and historic dysfunctions in the economy would almost inevitably have meant significant stresses, no matter who led the country. Yet

Botha's lack of understanding of economic matters hastened the already organic economic disinvestment taking
place. He failed to understand the connection between political action and economic reaction, was unable to infuse
foreign investors with confidence, and lost the nerve to
reduce a vote-rich but ever-growing bureaucracy.

His centralization of power through the executive presidency has now become a problem in itself. Depoliticizing
the presidency in an attempt to create a nonpartisan and
symbolic figure, including a constitutional change reestablishing the executive primacy of party political leadership,
appears to be on the new government's agenda.

A third disservice of the Botha years lies in the inordinate authority and influence given to the security services—both in routine policing and in participation in policy-making on civil issues through the National Security
Management System. The emergency laws have given considerable latitude to the police—a latitude often used with
so little discernment that attempts by effective black domestic leadership (whether revolutionary, radical, or mere-
ly dissident) to initiate genuine dialogue in the black communities have been severely prejudiced.

The reestablishment of complete political control over
and accountability of the security services will be one of
the first tasks of the de Klerk administration. Steps already taken in that direction include government tolerance
of a number of peaceful public protests in September 1989
and prosecution of errant members of the riot police.

A fourth major unaddressed issue during the Botha
tenure was, quite simply, the failure to engage either the
imagination or support of the majority of black South Africans in the process of constitutional change. Government-
created structures remained weakened by lack of public
support and the questionable motives of many of the participants. This refusal to accept that credible institutions
can only be the consequence of credible negotiating processes explains the collapse, one after the other, of govern-

ment-created forums. Each failure, meanwhile, has served only as a further encouragement to the use of the boycott tactic by the black community and cynicism about white intentions.

Positive Signals

Despite this menu of unmet demands, the Botha era ends with the following tentative, yet important, areas of change emerging in South Africa:

1. The whole question of the role of subnationalism or ethnicity is under review in both the government and in the ranks of the African National Congress. In earlier times, the National Party sought to project tribal or ethnic association as the defining feature for participation in the political system, while the ANC denied any salience at all to tribal or ethnic association. Now the National Party proposes the right of free association (albeit still very circumscribed) while the ANC concedes the relevance of cultural and language interests.

2. A recent seminal report by a working group of the South African Law Commission has come out in favor of a bill of rights, equality of franchise, and freedom of association. Although the government, following a long tradition of opportunism, has selectively adopted elements of the report to legitimize its own amended policies, the report has sparked constructive debate among both whites and blacks about the role of individual and group rights in a postapartheid society.

3. A move toward a more consensual approach to the character of the economic order in a postapartheid South Africa is also evident. The ANC has slid away from the idea of major and dramatic interventionist tactics, while the government and important sections of the private sector are exploring methods of ensuring a more equitable distribution of the national wealth.

4. There is an almost palpable sense among most of the players of what could be termed the limits of traditional power. On the part of the National Party administration, it is the painful realization that force alone cannot solve political problems and that no country, particularly South Africa, is an island. Hence the attempt by de Klerk to "normalize" the domestic political situation by releasing political prisoners and introducing a marginally more benign security regime. Economic constraints force a greater realism about the ability to project military power indefinitely.

The ANC's acceptance of the limits of power is of the same order but from a different direction. The massive state response to the insurrection of the mid-1980s has convinced the more thoughtful ANC leaders, not to mention sympathetic allies in the Kremlin, that a political solution could be more suitable than a military one. This view is reinforced by the fact that the ANC's military wing, Umkhonto we Sizwe, has been forced to relocate its main bases from Angola to distant Tanzania and Uganda as part of the Namibian peace settlement.

The very success of the ANC dictates its own constraints. As its entrée to Western chancelleries improves in inverse ratio to Pretoria's isolation, the ANC leadership is now called upon to present its policies not in terms of what it is against but what it is for. Thus, in recent months, the ANC has turned its attention to drafting constitutional guidelines and debating strategies of opposition. In this debate not even the once-hallowed principle of boycotting government political initiatives is inviolable.

These new limitations on traditional white and black power seem destined to impel both sides toward some form of tentative negotiations. Although the antagonists may be deeply suspicious and hostile, the reality is that their agendas of change are inextricably bound and concession or compromise on the one side inevitably demands response from the other – however grudging. It is in this dynamic that South Africa's greatest hope lies.

In Sum

It would be naive to suggest that the tentative flexibility described in this report or the changes of leadership (either in the National Party or those imminent in the ANC), generational as they may be, will dramatically change the situation overnight. There are too many vested interests and too many ideological barriers to cross—not least F.W. de Klerk's continuing adherence to the principle of group association by race—for there to be any suggestion of Damascene conversions on the part of any of the players.

Neither can one deny the determination of the new administration to use force if it believes its power immediately threatened or ignore the very real concerns that the seriously weakened South African economy may be unable to carry the costs of a major transition—whether initiated by the current regime or a succeeding nonracial one.

There are, moreover, powerful forces that could seriously erode détente doves. On the one hand stands an increasingly outraged white ultra-right wing with the capacity and proven willingness to use terrorism to oppose what it sees as a betrayal of white interests. On the other hand, there remain deeply ideological and traumatized young black urban cadres who may, in some instances, be beyond the control or even counsel of the exiled ANC leadership.

But it would be equally wrong to accept the prescription of those who have made an industry out of proclaiming that nothing has changed in South Africa. The continuing unwillingness of some elements opposed to apartheid to identify and appreciate shifts in government policy has undercut their ability to exploit opportunities to challenge the system further.

Only if South Africa's leaders—black and white—soon muster sufficient vision, compassion, and patience to bridge the remaining divides can the country hope to pull itself free from the prospect of enduring conflict and impoverishment in the region.

3

The ANC: From Symbol to Political Party

Marina Ottaway

June 1990

The unbanning of the African National Congress (ANC) and other South African political organizations on February 2, 1990 opened a complex political process within the antiapartheid movement. Organizations that developed over the last 30 years in exile or clandestinity were faced with the need to reform so as to become legal participants in an aboveboard political game. The difficulties of such a transformation are great, and nowhere as evident as in the case of the ANC. The oldest and most important of the country's political organizations, the ANC is now engaged in the daunting task of consolidating into a single structure the broad but chaotic network of groups that has carried on the antiapartheid struggle within South Africa since the Congress was outlawed in 1960. The task is made more pressing by the imminence of political negotiations with the government headed by President F.W. de Klerk. The hand of the ANC will be strengthened in the negotiating process if it can present itself as a united, well-organized entity.

The reality of the ANC as of mid-1990 falls short of the "united, well-organized entity" prescription. The organization has three distinct faces: (1) It comes to the table as a strong symbol of opposition to the apartheid system. (2) Its exile heritage is reflected in a bureaucratic apparatus, a hierarchical concept of organization, and an aging leadership. (3) It is also connected to a broad, effervescent, effective internal mass movement that is loosely structured.

Many liberation movements in Africa faced similar problems of reconciling the various identities acquired over the years of resistance. Their experience, particularly in the cases of Angola and Mozambique, shows the difficulty of the task and suggests the problems that confront the ANC in the wake of its unbanning.

In brief, the major problems faced by the ANC are how to retain the wide appeal it has long enjoyed as symbol of the antiapartheid struggle while engaged in competition with other now-legal political parties and organizations for members and supporters; how to solve the conflicts that have existed in the external organization while reestablishing a structure inside the country; and how to establish a coherent, disciplined internal party without clashing with, or destroying, the chaotic but strong mass movements that grew up during the years of the ANC's banning. Reconciling the three aspects—establishing better control without losing support and becoming a political party competing with other political organizations without losing its appeal as a symbol of the struggle against apartheid—is the difficult task ahead. Meeting these requirements, particularly under the time pressure created by the negotiations now getting under way, will put the ANC's leadership to a severe test.

The ANC as a Symbol

As symbol of the antiapartheid struggle in South Africa, the ANC has no rivals. This symbolism has given the Congress great strength over the years, but also has negative aspects. It has been easy for politicians, police spokespersons, and the press to blame the ANC for acts committed by any black political organization, or, on the other hand, to see any weakness in the ANC as a weakness of the movement as a whole. To white conservatives, any stone-throwing incident in a township, for example, is now seen as a manifestation of the ANC's decision to continue the armed struggle until specified conditions are met. Continued violence in Natal after Mandela's call to the youth to "throw their pangas into the sea" was seized on as a sign that the ANC could not control its own people. In a perverse logic, even the realization that "the ANC name is a kind of magic" but that other organizations compete for the allegiance of black South Africans is now viewed by some as a sign that the movement is somewhat of a fraud. (See Ken Owen's column, "As the Myths Fall, the ANC Is Cut Down To Size," in *Business Day*, March 19, 1990.) Being a symbol has its dangers as well as rewards.

The position of the ANC as symbol of the liberation struggle stems in part from its longevity. Founded in 1912, the Congress is a familiar organization at home and abroad, and it enjoys the prestige coming from tradition. More recently established organizations have found it impossible to compete with the ANC at the symbolic level. The Pan-Africanist Congress (PAC), which broke off from the ANC in April 1959 and operated legally for barely a year before it was banned, had considerable attraction for the more politicized and radical element of the population with its philosophy of African nationalism, but was not as well known as the ANC to the masses. The Black Consciousness movement, launched by Steve Biko in the late 1960s, made a strong impression on South African youth and was ultimately responsible for the revival of political activity in the 1970s, ending the hiatus caused by the banning of the earlier organizations. But Black Consciousness did not give rise to a strong, well-established, and well-known political party capable of replacing the ANC as a symbol of resistance to apartheid. Its strength was among the youth, and the movements it spawned were initially student organizations, therefore appealing to a specific segment of the population. Moreover, quick government repression of a succession of political organizations, beginning with Biko's South African Students' Organization (SASO), made it difficult for any group to become the household name the ANC was.

Writing in the late 1970s, Gail Gerhart, a respected student of the evolution of black power in South Africa, saw the spread of Black Consciousness as the beginning of apartheid's undoing:

> Today . . . it appears from the widespread outbreaks of urban violence and the ever escalating level of coercion required by the regime, that the South African order is becoming increasingly unstable—and that one of the prime causes of this instability is the ideological reorientation taking place among the younger generation of urban blacks. . . .

The South African order did become increasingly unstable. The organization that succeeded in marshaling the new wave of political agitation after 1983 was not Black Consciousness, however, but the United Democratic Front (UDF), the new internal wing of the banned ANC. The Congress emphatically rejected Black Consciousness and black power, supporting instead the concept of a nonracial democracy embodied in the ANC's 1955 Freedom Charter. Paradoxically, the political revival spurred by Biko's Black Consciousness movement eventually relaunched an ANC languishing in exile.

A discussion of how this happened goes beyond the scope of this assessment, which focuses not on how the ANC acquired its three faces but on the consequences of this triple identity. What is relevant in this context is that, because of the importance of Black Consciousness in the revival of political activity in the 1970s, the position of the ANC as symbol of the liberation struggle rested on somewhat tenuous ideological bases.

There was no reason to believe that all members of the United Democratic Front's many affiliates really understood clearly the difference between the position of the ANC and that of the PAC or the Azanian People's Organization (AZAPO), the party that inherited the mantle of Black Consciousness in the 1980s. It is doubtful that the ANC's concept of a nonracial democracy had greater appeal with the youth—who now constituted the mass of the politically mobilized population—than the "Africanist" position of the PAC and AZAPO. There was substantial evidence in early 1990 that the idea of continuing the armed struggle, the position taken by the PAC and AZAPO, was more attractive to many youths than the concept of negotiations. And it was also evident that very few of the new generation of activists understood the difference between the PAC and AZAPO—a difference the leaders themselves have difficulty defining.

At the symbolic level, the ANC's greatest success in the 1980s was to make Nelson Mandela the personification of the struggle. In a country where political mobilization is far ahead of both formal political organization and political education, the value of a name everybody knows cannot be overestimated. Mandela's name was known to and revered by the mass of the population. Whether or not the majority knew exactly who Mandela was, what he had done before being imprisoned, what specific ideological position he represented—other than opposition to the apartheid system—is a moot point. Symbols do not need detailed analysis.

The release of Mandela confirmed the value to the ANC of such a symbol, providing the occasion for massive, visible demonstrations of support throughout the country. In the first three months after his release, Mandela probably addressed a million people in rallies big and small throughout the country and abroad. It is doubtful that such numbers would have flocked to rallies organized by the newly unbanned ANC without the presence of Mandela. As a young woman struggling to maintain her footing in the crush of the crowd surging toward Mandela at a rally in Port Elizabeth gasped to a friend: "Everybody has to see this man, everybody."

The strength derived from having become the symbol of the antiapartheid movement has provided the ANC with a following to which it does not have to define precisely its political stand, at least initially. Any political settlement without the participation of Mandela and other Congress leaders is unthinkable. Like many African liberation movements at the time of independence in the 1960s and 1970s, the ANC enjoys in 1990 a very high level of enthusiastic support. But like the liberation movements elsewhere on the continent, it risks discovering that support and enthusiasm do not last if organization is lacking.

The ANC as an Organization

It has been typical of many liberation movements in Africa that their success as symbol of the liberation struggle greatly surpassed their effectiveness as political or military organizations. The ANC is no exception. At the time of its unbanning, the organization was much weaker than the symbol.

There were very good reasons for this weakness. The Congress, like all of the antiapartheid movements, has always had many more supporters than card-carrying members, a fact not unconnected to the risks inherent in formal affiliation with a political organization in a police state. And aside from the limitations implicit in a 30-year period of being banned and exiled, the ANC's internal underground structures experienced a great deal of difficulty surviving the confrontation with the well-organized South African security apparatus. Cohort after cohort of leaders was imprisoned for varying lengths of time. These historical facts explain and justify the weaknesses, but there can be no doubt that the consequences of these weaknesses are potentially serious.

The Apparatus

As a formal organization, the ANC in early 1990 existed mainly outside South Africa. In fact, it was a matter of some contention whether an internal, clandestine ANC existed at all. Chris Hani, the chief of staff of the organization's military arm, Umkhonto we Sizwe, admitted the failure to build such an underground in an interview with *New Nation* in February 1990: "Our people inside the country, in fighting . . . to mobilize thousands into active struggle, neglected a basic area of struggle under conditions of fascist or police state: the need to have underground structures which are unknown to the enemy." On the other hand, leaders of the South African Youth Congress (SAYCO) claimed at the opening of their congress in April 1990 that they had received a message of support from the "ANC underground," a message that was dutifully read out to the enthusiastically cheering audience.

This is not to say that the ANC had no presence inside South Africa during the years it was banned. On the contrary, such presence was very considerable. It was not direct, through the ANC's own structures, however, but indirect—residing in a network of literally hundreds of organizations, broadly affiliated with the ANC and supportive of its goals, but organizationally distinct. (See "The ANC as a Mass Movement" on page 41.)

The problems of the ANC as an organization are numerous and multifaceted. Among the most important yet to be resolved are the difficulties of coordinating an organization still spread around a number of countries, the uncertainties involved in an inevitable leadership transition from the aging Mandela generation to the next, and the challenge of reconciling the political and the military wings.

From the time of its banning in 1960, the ANC was forced to operate under conditions unique in the history of African liberation movements: at no time did it have either internal or external safe bases from which it could organize and/or launch military actions. With 87 percent of the land by law in white hands, a well-developed infrastructure, and black "homelands" mostly composed of small entities surrounded by white-controlled territory, South Africa presented major physical barriers to movements seeking to operate relatively undisturbed within the country. There were no liberated zones in South Africa. Even in countries bordering on South Africa, the ANC never really found a safe haven, initially because the host states were still in transition to independence and later because South African destabilization maneuvers forced governments to curb drastically the activity of the ANC, above all of Umkhonto we Sizwe.

As a result, the ANC was forced to operate far from South African territory. All liberation movements have experienced, with different degrees of intensity, conflict between internal and external organization. For the ANC, the organizational problem was further complicated because of the need to spread its operations over several countries. By the late 1980s, the political leadership was divided between Lusaka (Zambia) and London, and Umkhonto we Sizwe between Tanzania and Angola. Camps in Tanzania provided shelter and education for thousands of young students who fled South Africa to join the ANC.

Aside from slow communications, there was the risk of competing centers of power in various countries and also the possibility that branches would become entangled in the politics of the host country. Examples of such entanglement occurred in Zambia in the late 1970s and in Angola in the 1980s. The ANC leadership based in Zambia decided that Umkhonto we Sizwe guerrillas should fight alongside the Zimbabwe African People's Union (ZAPU) of Joshua Nkomo in Rhodesia—not against the regime of Ian Smith, but against ZAPU's rival, Robert Mugabe's Zimbabwe African National Union. In Angola, Umkhonto personnel participated on occasion in operations against UNITA.

In both cases (according to statements made to the press by ANC dissenters on their return to South Africa in May 1990), some of those involved objected to being sidetracked from the purpose of liberating South Africa from apartheid. In Angola in 1984, this resentment led to a mutiny, which met with brutal repression that included torture of some detained mutineers. Although the Angolan episode is an extreme example, each country that harbored a section of the exiled ANC inevitably presented complications affecting the ability of the organization to remain cohesive.

The broad geographical spread of the ANC within South Africa and elsewhere has long posed problems of administration and discipline that extend beyond the military wing. An organization with such geographic dispersion can choose between administrative decentralization (with the possibility of loss of cohesion) or a centralized control that can become a cumbersome, heavily bureaucratic, slow-moving apparatus. The unbanned ANC of 1990 appears to have opted for the latter. Recent ANC documents and statements reveal a concept of organization best described as "democratic centralism."

A revised "ANC constitutional framework for the period of reestablishment leading up to the holding of a national conference," adopted by the National Executive Committee (NEC) in March 1990, called upon the NEC to draw up lists of existing members and to appoint "persons in all regions of South Africa to receive applications for membership." This top-down approach, further confirmed in early April by the NEC's appointment of organizing committees for each region of South Africa, was particularly striking in view of the wealth of grass-roots organizations affiliated with the ANC that already existed.

The cumbersome, top-down approach is also reflected in the slow progress that is being made toward building an internal organization. In May 1990, three months after the ban was lifted, the ANC was only beginning to open regional offices. The PAC and AZAPO appear to be moving faster, in part because they are not burdened by a complicated external apparatus and by the ANC's large family of affiliated organizations throughout South Africa. While the ANC has been holding mass rallies, the other two groups are holding organizational meetings and signing up members. Speaking at the University of Stellenbosch on May 5, Thabo Mbeki, the ANC's director for international relations, expressed concern about this lag: "The ANC has been very slow to organize themselves since they got unbanned. That is correct. We coming from Lusaka have been shouting to our comrades in Johannesburg to say 'why are you moving so slowly?'"

The blame does not lie entirely with ANC officials inside the country, however. The external ANC has moved equally slowly on the return of the exiles, whose presence could provide impetus to development of the internal organization. The delay is not exclusively of the ANC's own making, because in many cases the issue of the legal status of the exiles had to be clarified first, and the government did not introduce legislation on this matter until the end of April. But ANC bureaucratic procedures (which involve a complete census and the centralization of arrangements within South Africa for all returning exiles) have added to the problem. ANC members are being discouraged from returning on their own.

In sum, the circumstances of an antiapartheid struggle that rendered the ANC an organization with segments in different countries, combined with the leadership's concept of a future organization along "democratic centralist" lines, have combined to make the ANC as of mid-1990 a cumbersome apparatus that is having difficulty responding promptly to the challenge of reorganization presented by its unbanning.

The Leadership

In addition to the challenge of organization, the ANC also faces a challenge of leadership. Mandela is a symbolic figure larger than the organization. His influence, and especially the relation he has developed with President F.W. de

Klerk, is a major asset for the ANC, but it could also be a threat if Mandela decided to act on his own initiative, rather than in accordance with the directives of the National Executive Committee. Mandela is acutely aware of the risks inherent in the situation and is walking a narrow line. He is nudging the organization toward negotiations and flexibility, a position not originally supported by all NEC members. At the same time, almost all his speeches contain pledges of loyalty to the organization and exhortations to all ANC members to follow party discipline.

A second consideration is the age of the top leaders. In 1990 the highest posts are predominantly in the hands of those who controlled the movement before 1960. The rallies held by Mandela since his release provide a graphic reminder of the problem. On the dais, the central figures are Mandela and a group of elderly and dignified men in impeccable suits, some of them needing help up the steps. The audiences are largely a mass of chanting and dancing people in ANC T-shirts and khaki uniforms, with young people in their teens and twenties always appearing to constitute the overwhelming majority.

The inevitable generational transition is complicated by the fact that the younger members of the outside organization are little known within South Africa. This could change fairly quickly, particularly for those, like Thabo Mbeki, who are involved in the negotiating process and thus receiving a high level of exposure. But for the time being the names of the younger external leaders are not household words, except perhaps for Chris Hani, Umkhonto we Sizwe's chief of staff. Ironically, the leaders to whom the young comrades at the rallies wish long life are all septuagenarians.

The leadership of the ANC is somewhat out of touch with its internal following not only because of age, but also because of major changes in the body politic during the long years of imprisonment and exile. Beginning in the 1970s, a generation of young militants emerged whose life experience and attitudes were quite different from those of the older leadership. They grew up under different conditions and engaged in a different political battle.

The ANC of the 1950s challenged the authorities in defiance campaigns directed against the pass laws and other policies of the central government. The struggle of the "young lions" of the 1970s and 1980s was much more local but also much more pervasive. It was directed against town councillors and black policemen, school principals and shopkeepers. They organized rent strikes and marches, fire-bombed houses of black policemen and councillors (who were seen as stooges of the apartheid regime), paraded around with toy AK-47s.

Although the returning leaders of the formal ANC and the followers inside the country share the same goal of eliminating the apartheid system, they belong to different worlds. Mandela watches his young followers singing and toyi-toying (dancing) with the benign and bemused smile of an indulgent grandfather. But he is stern and authoritarian when he addresses them, preaching discipline and obedience to the NEC and exhorting them to return to school.

Civilian-Military Relations

Another urgent challenge facing the ANC is to reconcile the interests of its political and military wings while making the shift from struggle to diplomacy. Theoretically, there is no conflict between the two wings. Umkhonto we Sizwe is not a separate organization with different goals. It was organized in 1961–1962 as a clandestine military organization, after the banning precluded the continuation of overt ANC political activity. Nelson Mandela and Walter Sisulu were among its organizers.

In 1990, the ANC leadership still sees the armed and the political struggle as closely connected. Although Mandela emerged from prison as the champion of a negotiated solution, he also called for the continuation of the armed struggle and has not publicly modified his position to date despite considerable pressure from the South African government and also from some high-profile supporters both within South Africa and in the Front-Line states. These have included Archbishop Desmond Tutu, Zambia's President Kaunda, and Alan Boesak. The commander in chief of Umkhonto we Sizwe, Joe Modise, was a member of the 11-member ANC delegation that participated in the preliminary talks with government leaders in Cape Town on May 2–4.

The task of reconciliation is complicated by the fact that the interests of the military and the political wing of the ANC are not identical. Negotiations increase the weight of the political leadership, warfare that of the military leadership. Moreover, the two elements have different organizational needs: Umkhonto as a military organization is bound to maintain a hierarchical structure and strong discipline, but these two features would detract from ANC overall management's attempts to project an image as a democratic political movement. The previously cited revelations concerning the suppression of dissent within Umkhonto in Angola undoubtedly hurt the ANC politically.

Although the official position is that the issue of the continuation of the armed struggle caused no stresses within the ANC in the lead-up to the Cape Town meeting, closer reading of the statements emanating from various leaders suggests a more complex situation. In January 1990, for example, ANC Secretary General Alfred Nzo was quoted in the *Star* (Johannesburg) as having stated that "[the] military wing does not have the capacity within South Africa to intensify the armed struggle in any meaningful way at a time when it sees a tactical need to do so." Meanwhile, Umkhonto Chief of Staff Chris Hani, who in January was calling with great vehemence for the intensification of the armed struggle, moderated his rhetoric a few weeks later, as the entire South African press was quick to notice. Joe Modise announced on the eve of the preliminary talks in May that Umkhonto was still recruiting inside South Africa.

The real issue seems to be that the ANC cannot just

follow a policy of mothballing Umkhonto, but has to find a new role for it. Hints that a solution might be to integrate Umkhonto cadres into the South African Defense Force have been rejected with outrage by the South African security establishment, but not by Umkhonto leaders such as Hani.

The ANC as a Mass Movement

The mass movement that has unofficially represented the ANC inside South Africa is very different from the external organization. Politically and emotionally affiliated with the ANC, the mass movement has a diversity of organizational structures, with characteristics quite distinct from those of the external ANC.

The relationship between the two is symbiotic: without the mass movement, the external organization would have withered; without the outside ANC to provide a banner, the diffuse internal movement might never have coalesced sufficiently to convince the government to negotiate. In practice, however, each has operated autonomously. The ANC's National Executive Committee could not issue a directive from Lusaka and know which civic associations in the townships, if any, would implement the directive. The youths who turn out for rallies wearing ANC T-shirts, waving ANC and South African Communist Party (SACP) flags, and singing Umkhonto songs do not regard themselves as party members subject to party discipline. Yet it is because of the existence of this mass movement that the government is now sitting down at the negotiating table with the ANC.

The external ANC is highly organized, structured, and self-contained, with a clear leadership structure, charts of that structure, a constitution, and party discipline. It would be impossible to draw up an organization chart of the internal mass movement, which is loosely structured, rather anarchic in character, and unclear as to boundaries.

These characteristics have given the mass movement a great deal of flexibility and resilience, making police suppression difficult. But with the unbanning of the ANC, the external and internal organizations have to find a way of merging or at least of coexisting and cooperating in the same sphere without coming into conflict with each other. A great deal of uncertainty exists as of mid-1990 about how this can be done.

The history of the internal movement after 1960 explains both the decentralized structure and some of the complications in its relationship with the external wing. Banned before a strong underground organization had been created, the ANC as a hierarchical structure inside the country virtually disappeared with the arrest of Mandela and his associates. The result was a political lull during most of the 1960s. As Gail Gerhart has phrased it, "Silence pervaded African political life in the 1960s to an extent which had not been known since the years before 1912."

The lull was broken by the rise of Steve Biko's Black Consciousness movement in the late 1960s. Black Consciousness spread quickly during the 1970s, drawing support especially among the youth and leading to a new wave of political agitation beginning in 1976. But police repression led to Biko's death in detention in September 1977 and the banning of all 18 organizations associated with the Black Consciousness movement. This time, however, there was no long lull. Instead, the character of the antiapartheid movement began to change after Biko's death.

The mass movement that developed during the 1980s was an amalgam of student and youth organizations, street committees, township civic associations, and labor unions. Although these organizations looked to the ANC as the symbol of the struggle ("ANC lives, ANC leads," proclaim thousands of T-shirts worn by activists), they operated autonomously.

Whatever coordination exists among these groups was eventually provided by the United Democratic Front, the

Mass Democratic Movement, and the Congress of South African Trade Unions (COSATU). Formally launched in August 1983 as a national umbrella organization of more than 400 groups (some of them umbrella organizations in their turn), the UDF claimed 800 member organizations by 1986, despite recurrent detention of various leaders. COSATU, with 16 affiliated unions, was founded in 1985. In 1987, the Mass Democratic Movement was formed to coordinate more closely the activity of COSATU and the UDF, as well as other groups. (For a list of organizations loosely connected with the MDM, see *The Star* [Johannesburg], August 30, 1989.) When COSATU and the UDF, together with 16 other organizations, were banned in February 1988, the MDM was able to continue operating, although its spokesmen, mostly UDF and COSATU members, were frequently subject to arrest.

This extremely decentralized form of organization, with an intricate network of crisscrossing and overlapping groups, was the strength of the ANC as a mass movement. Periodic detention of leaders and restrictions imposed on specific associations did not destroy the overall network or curb political activity.

As long as the ANC was banned, these internal groups could look at it as a symbol without worrying about the exact nature of the relationship. Once the ANC was unbanned and working to create its own organization inside the country, there was a need to define the relationship. This is complicated by the difference in the character of the external organization, with its hierarchical "democratic centralism," and of the internal mass movement, an amalgam of hundreds of largely autonomous affiliates.

The trends emerging in mid-1990 are contradictory, suggesting a diversity of opinions and trends that could easily lead to conflict. The ANC is highly dependent on the mass movement, which organized Mandela's reception and originally his schedule, provides for his security, marshals crowds, and transports supporters to rallies and demonstrations. But there are ambiguities concerning whether the ANC considers the mass movement as a set of organizations separate from itself. For example, the ANC delegation to the preliminary talks of May 1990 made a point of holding formal consultations with the UDF and COSATU before meeting with government representatives. On the other hand, the UDF members in the delegation were there as individuals, not as UDF representatives. The appointment of UDF members to the regional organizing committees of the ANC also raises questions about the separate identity of the mass organizations.

The provisional ANC constitution of March 1990 appears to assume that South Africa is an organizational tabula rasa. The constitution is that of a unitary party, with membership open only to individuals, not to other organizations. The document simply outlines a classical party structure, with local committees sending delegates to regional councils and so on to the level of the National Executive Committee.

There is nothing notable about such a structure—it is common to parties throughout the continent, no matter what their ideology. Adoption by the ANC, however, is revealing in the implicit failure to acknowledge the existence of the hundreds of internal organizations to which the Congress somehow will have to relate. The question is whether the ANC executive envisages their disappearance once the ANC's own structures are in place, projects their continued existence under party control, or is prepared to accept them as autonomous organizations.

The organizations most directly challenged by the rebirth of the internal ANC are the UDF and SAYCO, whose functions appear to duplicate respectively those of the ANC itself and its Youth League. As a labor federation, COSATU does not face the prospect of disbanding. It does, however, face the issue of autonomy from, rather than subordination to, the ANC. Local committees organized for specific purposes—for example, a rent strike committee in a township—also face the long-term question of how they will relate to ANC cadres.

As of mid-1990, the UDF appears to be vacillating between continued existence and dissolution. At the time of the ANC unbanning, there was talk of dissolution. By late February, the conclusion seemed to have been reached that the UDF should continue existing for tactical reasons. As the UDF's national secretary, Popo Molefe, phrased it: "We are not taking chances. The UDF and the Mass Democratic Movement have no tradition of being involved in the 'armed struggle' and it would be difficult to ban us. We could dismantle our structures, but what will happen if the government again bans the ANC?" Shortly thereafter, however, the UDF announced that the issue of dissolution would be discussed by its national general council in April. But the council meeting was not held. Instead, the UDF held a closed-door workshop. The only decision made public was that the UDF would retain its structures. According to Publicity Secretary Patrick "Terror" Lekota, the UDF will act as a watchdog once the ANC becomes the government and also deal with local issues such as rent and water supplies, to which the ANC, as a national political party, would not be in a position to give adequate attention.

Lekota's statement glossed over the classic problem of the conflict between "state power" and "people's power" in countries where a relatively weak party faces a mobilized population and grass-roots organizations. To be sure, the ANC in 1990 is still an opposition party. It is a party, however, consciously preparing itself to exercise state power. As the UDF Program of Action prepared for the April workshop phrased it, negotiations are a means to the "seizure of state power." In the period leading up to this transition, "Building dual power should be the most important strategic objective of the liberation movement." This would involve depriving the regime of monopoly over the control of all institutions and could be accomplished by developing "organs of people's power" (i.e., grass-roots organizations such as civic associations).

But the UDF recognizes a problem here. Organs of people's power "mushroom when a conducive set of ingredients exist," while the building of a party or trade union "requires years of painstaking work to build the organization increment by increment." It is for this reason, concluded the document, that "serious limits may exist on the ability of the liberation movement to administer in great detail every aspect of the building of dual power" – an implicit reference to the impotence of the ANC in exerting management over grass-roots organizations. The mass movement appears to be the tiger the ANC is riding, not the watchdog making sure it does not stray.

In contrast to the UDF, conscious of the difficult problems ahead and unable to decide whether to disband (the workshop concluded that the issue of disbanding would have to be reexamined in the future), SAYCO decided at its April 1990 congress to dissolve in favor of the ANC Youth League as soon as the ANC entity is reconstituted inside South Africa. SAYCO also called for the dissolution of the UDF in favor of the ANC.

Because the debates at the SAYCO congress were not public, it is not known how controversial the issue was among rank and file delegates. The position clearly suited the top leadership, which is close to the ANC and obviously poised to organize the Youth League's leadership. It is more difficult to know to what extent it also suited the followers. SAYCO has about half a million members, organized into scores of local congresses that do not necessarily follow central directives, as the SAYCO leaders acknowledge. How readily they would submit to integration into a hierarchical structure and would accept party discipline remains an open question.

A final issue, about which rumors abound but concrete information is lacking, is the relationship between the ANC and the SACP. The alliance between the two, Mandela tells his audiences, is strong and long lasting. SACP General Secretary Joe Slovo was a member of the ANC team that began prenegotiations with the government in May. Yet there are rumors concerning the growing strength of the SACP as a separate entity, and above all its influence over COSATU. The ANC-SACP relationship could become an important factor in the future.

The Impact on Negotiations

The challenges faced by the ANC since its unbanning in February 1990 are formidable. The three faces of the organization—as the symbol of the antiapartheid struggle with a broad appeal, as an external organization spread among many countries, and as a loose internal mass organization composed of autonomous groups—must somehow be reconciled with each other. This urgent need for internal coherence arises at the same time the ANC is entering into negotiations with the government and undertaking to change its role from a banned opposition movement into a legitimate party with a role in government. Today's ANC does not have the luxury of tackling one problem at a time.

The outcome of the process of internal reorganization is bound to have an impact on the negotiations, weakening or strengthening the position of the ANC. The government remains anxious to establish that the ANC does not represent the entire black population of South Africa. The original strategy of promoting homeland leaders and traditional authorities to the rank of full participants in the negotiation process ran into major difficulties in April 1990, when all of the homeland leaders, except for KwaZulu's Mangosuthu Buthelezi and Qwaqwa's Kenneth Mopeli, honored Mandela's request and refused to attend a meeting with President de Klerk. In fact, some of the homeland leaders, including Bantu Holomisa of Transkei and Enos Mabuza of KaNgwane, have called openly for the reintegration of the homelands into South Africa. The government does not want to play other political organizations such as the more radical PAC and AZAPO against the ANC, and in any case both have thus far rejected negotiations. The major card left to the government in trying to circumscribe the role of the ANC in the negotiations is the organization's own weaknesses.

Even more important, the political future of South Africa for years to come is bound to be affected by the way in which the ANC handles the challenge of giving itself an integrated identity. The issue of the relationship between the external organization and the internal mass movement is particularly significant. ANC acceptance of the challenge of relating to autonomous grass-roots organizations without seeking to control them directly would provide much greater hope of a democratic future for South Africa than an ANC insisting on control over all organizations seeking a postapartheid destiny.

4

Pretoria's Nuclear Diplomacy

Robert S. Jaster

January 1988

Since August 1977, when the Soviet Union first alerted the United States to what appeared to be a nuclear test site under construction in the Kalahari Desert, South Africa has played a subtle but risky game of nuclear diplomacy. Unlike most aspects of Pretoria's relations with the West, the nuclear strategy has been active rather than reactive, and to a large degree successful. Despite more than a decade of intelligence surveillance and low-key diplomatic negotiations, South Africa's nuclear-weapons capability and intentions remain shrouded in ambiguity. Whether there was an intention to test a nuclear device in 1977, and whether such a test was actually conducted in 1979, are questions still unresolved among Western scientific and intelligence analysts.

The Western powers, particularly the United States, have endeavored since the mid-1970s to dissuade South Africa from testing a weapon or declaring a weapons capability. Western concern has both global and regional elements. Like Argentina and Pakistan, South Africa is seen as a threshold nuclear-weapons state – one of those more likely to break through the fragile nonproliferation barriers. Indeed, South Africa matches in virtually all respects the profile of a likely nuclear-weapons state: (1) it is diplomatically isolated, lacking either membership in an alliance or the security umbrella of a great power; (2) its leaders see the regime's survival under external threat; and (3) it has the materials and technology to produce and deliver a nuclear weapon. Declaration of a nuclear-weapons capability by the white minority regime might encourage other threshold states to do the same, would have a significant impact in the region and on the region's external relations, would intensify pressures within and on the industrial democracies for stiffer sanctions against South Africa, and could generate efforts on the part of Nigeria or South Africa's neighbors to seek nuclear weapons or guarantees from outside powers.

The Basic Strategy

From the South African perspective, the weapons issue is part of a larger nuclear strategy that includes commercial export considerations, the need for reactor fuel, and, more recently, the drive for recognition as a regional superpower and threshold nuclear state.

Because South Africa and Namibia together have within their borders something like a quarter of the non-Communist world's uranium deposits, the initial stage in the nuclear development program was the extraction of ore for export. The first ore-processing plant, built with U.S. and British assistance, opened in 1952. Exports of uranium oxide to the United States alone brought South Africa almost a half-billion dollars in export earnings during the following two decades. During the late 1950s and 1960s Pretoria purchased its first nuclear research reactor and sent nuclear scientists and technicians to Britain and the United States for training.

These earlier developments – the processing of local uranium ores, access to Western nuclear technology, and the acquisition of a research reactor – gave South Africa the necessary technological base for conducting more advanced research on its own. In particular, South Africa was able by 1970 to acquire the means to enrich uranium, the most important step toward achieving an independent nuclear capability.

The decision to develop an indigenous enrichment capability had a plausible commercial basis. In the early 1970s, before the collapse of the world uranium market, South African officials spoke confidently of building a large-scale enrichment plant that would earn $250 million a year from exports of low-enriched uranium for use in nuclear power plants. But uncertain export markets, rising construction costs, and the suspension of U.S. nuclear fuel deliveries in 1978 led Pretoria to opt for a smaller enrichment facility that could be built more quickly, thereby assuring a supply of fuel for its reactor and its Koeberg power station.

There is little doubt, however, that the possibility of developing a nuclear weapon entered the government's calculations from the early stages of the nuclear program. While professing no intention of developing a weapon, South African political and military leaders frequently alluded to the capability to do so. At the inauguration of the first research reactor in 1965, Prime Minister Hendrik Verwoerd noted the government's obligation to "consider" the military aspects of nuclear energy. On the other hand, a statement in 1968 by the army's chief of staff, General H.J. Martin, that South Africa was prepared to produce nuclear arms was repudiated by then-Defense Minister P.W. Botha.

Even declarations of peaceful intent have often been ambiguous. A case in point was a statement by Prime Minister B.J. Vorster to a *Newsweek* correspondent in 1976: "We are only interested in the peaceful application of nuclear power. But we can enrich uranium, and we have the capability. And we did not sign the nuclear nonproliferation treaty." The Vorster comment and others of the same genre over the years suggest, at the very least, that at various decision points along the continuum of nuclear development, South Africa's leaders kept the weapons option alive. By contrast, official statements of noninterest in developing a weapon seem disingenuous in light of strong evidence that South Africa planned to test a nuclear device in 1977 and may have carried out such a test in 1979.

The 1977 "Kalahari Incident"

The facts of the so-called Kalahari incident in 1977 are by now too familiar to warrant more than a brief review here. But recent information on South African enrichment problems and capabilities provides a basis for reassessing both South Africa's intentions at Kalahari and its nuclear diplomacy.

After being alerted by the USSR, U.S. intelligence specialists reviewed high-resolution satellite photography, which revealed a hole in the ground and a cluster of buildings around a prominent tower under construction in the remote Kalahari Desert area of the Western Cape. Several government-connected U.S. think tanks tried but failed to match the site configuration with various nonnuclear activities (e.g., a missile test-range, a diamond mine, etc.). The site design was judged compatible with those of other countries' first nuclear tests of a crude device. Although there were some anomalies, U.S. officials were quoted as being virtually certain that the activities at the site were preparations for a nuclear test.

Intense diplomatic activity followed these findings. Nonproliferation was an issue of high priority in the Carter administration, and the United States and France were contractual suppliers of enriched uranium and nuclear power stations, respectively, to South Africa. Both governments, joined by Britain and West Germany, made strong démarches to Pretoria. South African officials denied that the Kalahari site had anything to do with nuclear weapons, but the explanations they gave U.S. diplomats were both disingenuous and conflicting. Government spokesmen engaged in a sort of mirrors game in denying nuclear intentions: asked for firm denials, officials referred to earlier denials, which on close inspection appeared to have little or no substance.

In spite of this equivocation, President Jimmy Carter told a late August 1977 press conference that "South Africa has informed us that they do not have and do not intend to develop nuclear explosive devices for any purpose, either peaceful or as a weapon; that the Kalahari test site, which has been in question, is not designed for use to test nuclear explosives; and that no nuclear explosive test will be taken in South Africa now or in the future." Prime Minister Vorster later denied on U.S. television that he had made any promises to President Carter, thereby prompting Washington to release the text of a letter from Vorster to Carter stating that South Africa "does not have nor does it intend to develop a nuclear explosive device for any purpose, peaceful or otherwise . . . and there will not be nuclear testing of any kind in South Africa." But that letter, which contains the only categorical denial known to have been given, was dated October 13, 1977 — more than two months after the initial Western démarche to Pretoria.

What were South Africa's intentions? The "hoax" hypothesis — that the Kalahari site was a dummy, constructed simply to gain nuclear concessions from the United States — is the least plausible. South African leaders must have anticipated that discovery of the site would inevitably bring a storm of international condemnation, as well as embarrassment at being caught out. A hoax with such high costs and uncertain benefits would not be worth undertaking. Moreover, an elaborate hoax was not necessary to gain U.S. attention. Discreetly planted official leaks that a test was under consideration, followed by ambiguous denials, would have been enough.

U.S. officials believed that South Africa was, in fact, preparing for a weapons test. U.S. intelligence is reported to have later received independent confirmation that this was the case. Construction activity continued until at least December 1977 — more than four months after the site had been discovered and talks with Washington had begun. Vorster thus allowed preparations for a test to go forward even while his government was under intense external pressure (including a British threat to sever diplomatic relations) and while South African officials were issuing patently misleading statements about the purpose of the site.

How is this behavior to be explained? And why was the test finally called off? Subsequent analysis has focused on South African enrichment capabilities. Although the Valindaba enrichment facility was said to be "fully operational" in early 1977, outside experts now believe that it may have encountered technical problems that held production to 3 percent enriched uranium at that time, so that by mid-1977 it could have produced at most 20 kilograms of weapons-grade uranium — barely enough for a highly sophisticated weapon and not enough for the crude designs typical of previous first-test weapons.

One hypothesis, based on this analysis, suggests that test preparations were allowed to go ahead in the expectation that the problems at Valindaba would be quickly resolved and that the necessary highly enriched uranium would be available by mid-1977. Then, as it became clear that the delay would be much longer than anticipated, the test was called off and the site dismantled. This explanation is consistent with the calculated ambiguity of South African officials about their intentions prior to Vorster's October 1977 letter to Carter.

Vorster may have weighed the risk of discovery of the test site and concluded that a test was worth that risk. He may well have been led to believe that the chances of detection were small; indeed, the Soviet-U.S. discovery of the site appears to have been accidental and by no means inevitable. The disordered and inconsistent responses by

South African officials to the Western démarches, however, were probably due less to Vorster's surprise at being
discovered than to a widespread ignorance of the test preparations among officials outside a very small inner circle
of Vorster advisers.

At the height of the Kalahari crisis, an August 24,
1977, editorial in the authoritative Afrikaans-language newspaper *Beeld* reflected official testiness on the issue:

> The great powers which have nuclear weapons have
> adopted an odd attitude. *One would have thought that
> it would have been tactically more profitable for them
> to draw closer a potential member of the nuclear club,
> which South Africa is. Their bullying attitude could
> result in making us a maverick bull in the nuclear herd*,
> and that is surely not a sound situation from their
> point of view. South Africa will go its own way and its
> own interests will be decisive. [Italics added.]

When the Carter administration pressed South Africa
to sign the Nuclear Non-Proliferation Treaty (NPT), Vorster responded in person, saying South Africa would "consider" signing, but required guarantees of future U.S. deliveries of enriched uranium for its reactors. South African
demands were elaborated in negotiations with Carter's special ambassador, Gerald Smith. They included resumption
of U.S. deliveries of highly enriched uranium (HEU) for
the research reactor, guaranteed supplies of low-enriched
uranium (LEU) for the Koeberg power station, relaxation
of U.S. export restrictions on nonsensitive technology for
the uranium enrichment plant, and U.S. support for the
reinstatement of South Africa on the Board of Governors
of the International Atomic Energy Agency (IAEA), the
watchdog on nuclear proliferation.

Negotiations broke down in late 1978 because South
Africa was unwilling to open its enrichment plant at Valindaba to IAEA inspection as required by the NPT. (South
African officials say their refusal was based on a concern
to protect what they claim is a unique enrichment process.)

By then the United States had enacted its own Nuclear Non-Proliferation Act (1978), prohibiting the sale of any enriched fuel to countries not applying IAEA safeguards to *all* their nuclear facilities.

On balance, the decision to prepare for a nuclear test at Kalahari was a costly one for South Africa. Detection of the site resulted in a U.S. decision to cancel fuel deliveries for the Koeberg nuclear power station, thereby delaying the station's start-up. Kalahari also reinforced suspicions about South African military intentions in the region, contributing to the UN Security Council's enactment in November 1977 of a mandatory arms embargo against South Africa. But the episode, and particularly South Africa's success in maintaining a calculated ambiguity about nuclear test plans, also brought anxious Western diplomats to Pretoria to seek an accommodation, and provided the Western powers with a plausible basis for accepting Pretoria's assurances that South Africa would not test a nuclear weapon. As one observer noted, the Kalahari contretemps demonstrated to South Africa "the value of the nuclear threat as diplomatic leverage, an option to be foregone *in exchange* for reciprocal favors."

The "Vela" Mystery

The issue of South Africa's nuclear capability reemerged a year after Defense Minister P.W. Botha took office as prime minister in 1978. In September 1979, a U.S. intelligence satellite, the Vela, recorded a double flash of light – a signature unique to nuclear explosions – as it passed over a remote expanse of ocean between South Africa and Antarctica.

As in the Kalahari affair, the "Vela incident" has been extensively analyzed. In 41 previous cases where the Vela had registered a double pulse, independent sources confirmed the event as a nuclear explosion. But in this instance the usual corroborating evidence was either missing or subject to conflicting interpretation. A panel of scien-

tific experts assembled by the White House, after review-
ing the evidence for two months, concluded that the case
for a nuclear explosion remained unproven. But it could
find no other plausible explanation.

This finding was vigorously challenged within both
the scientific and intelligence communities in the United
States. Several major pieces of evidence suggested that a
nuclear test had occurred: (1) An ionospheric disturbance
for which there was no natural explanation was recorded
by a radio telescope in Puerto Rico at the same time and in
the same general area as the Vela incident. (2) A hydro-
acoustic signal, the strongest ever monitored by the U.S.
Naval Research Laboratory, originated in the Indian Ocean
near South Africa's remote Prince Edward Islands at the
same time as the Vela flash. (3) A costly study of the detection of seismic disturbances prepared by the U.S. Technical
Information Service had only one purchaser: South Africa's defense and naval attaché. (4) A secret South African
naval exercise was reported to have occurred on the night
of the Vela incident.

The White House panel found problems with much of
this evidence, and a member of President Carter's Office of
Science and Technology Policy later acknowledged that the
technical data did not produce an airtight case. In short,
an administration that placed high priority on nonproliferation needed a smoking gun to reach a verdict that South
Africa had detonated a nuclear weapon. And even those
among U.S. scientific and intelligence specialists who
thought they detected a smoking gun saw it variously in
the hands of India, Israel, South Africa, and the latter two
in collusion.

South African officials issued brief denials that a test
had been conducted. In light of the Botha government's
worsening relations with Washington by 1979 and the suspension of nuclear negotiations, Pretoria apparently saw
no reason to engage in detailed discussion of the charges.
Indeed, four days after the event the *Rand Daily Mail*
quoted Prime Minister Botha as having told a National

Party meeting that South Africa had the conventional capability to counter any guerrilla incursion, and further, "if there are people who are thinking of doing something else, I suggest they think twice about it. *They might find out we have military weapons they do not know about.*" [Italics added.]

If the September 1979 event was, as suspected, a South African test, it appears to have followed logically from the Kalahari incident. That is, based on global reactions to the 1977 test preparations, Botha would have realized that detection of a test could have serious consequences, including the possibility of massive sanctions against South Africa. Elaborate precautions would be required so that a policy of plausible denial would stand up. South Africa' Prince Edward Islands, some 1,200 miles southeast of Cape Town and roughly midway between South Africa and Antarctica, would offer the remotest practicable site. A test carried out at night would reduce the chances of inadvertent sighting. Finally, an explosion close to the surface of the sea would prevent fallout from reaching the upper atmosphere, where detection would be almost certain.

As in the Kalahari instance, however, later evidence casts some doubt on South Africa's capability to produce a nuclear weapon at the time in question. According to U.S. intelligence estimates, the Valindaba facility might have been able to produce as much as 40 kilograms of HEU by 1979. This is less than the estimated 48 kilograms needed for successful detonation of the crude fission devices used in other countries' first tests. It might have been sufficient, however, for a weapon of highly advanced design. In other words, only if South Africa had been able to duplicate or acquire more recent techniques in warhead design would it have had enough enriched material for a weapon. This has led some scientists to believe that the 1979 event was either an Israeli test conducted with South African cooperation, or a joint Israeli-South African endeavor. Other analysts say the issue remains unresolved.

By 1981, when South Africa announced that its Valindaba facility had produced 45 percent enriched uranium for the Safari research reactor, the question of South Africa's nuclear weapons *capability* was no longer in doubt. If a facility can enrich to 45 percent, it can enrich to 90 percent.

From Carter to Reagan

With the advent of the Reagan administration in 1981, South African diplomats pressed their case for an easing of U.S. restrictions on nuclear-related exports. In May 1981, the South African embassy sent a four-page note to then-Secretary of State Alexander M. Haig, Jr., arguing that signing the NPT would leave South Africa at the mercy of the USSR and other hostile powers and urging relaxation of the ban on enriched fuel exports. A few weeks later, U.S. uranium brokers arranged a complicated swap in which France fabricated fuel rods for the Koeberg reactor.

This move violated the spirit, though not the letter, of a French commitment to the Carter administration not to supply enriched fuel to South Africa. But it was consistent with the new U.S. policy, as summarized in testimony by a State Department official: "We feel that we can achieve our objectives better, nonproliferation objectives, with South Africa by not engaging in unnecessary activities which would produce a deteriorating relationship." (Hearings on U.S. export policy with respect to South Africa, Subcommittees on Africa and on International Economic Policy and Trade of the U.S. House of Representatives Foreign Affairs Committee, December 2, 1982.)

Despite South African success in acquiring fuel rods from France, the commissioning of the first Koeberg power station was delayed for an additional year by ANC sabotage of the installation in December 1982. But French-delivered fuel enabled South Africa to start up the two Koeberg power stations, one in 1984 and the other a year later, and to keep them operating at least until late 1987, the scheduled completion date for a semicommercial enrichment plant in South Africa. Once in operation, that plant is expected to supply all the fuel needed for the power stations and the research reactor.

The Reagan administration also authorized the sale of several major pieces of nuclear-related equipment with dual end-uses. These included vibration test equipment, which could be used to test the reliability of nuclear warheads; multichannel analyzers, capable of analyzing complex data at a test site; a Cyber 170-750 computer, powerful enough to model a nuclear explosion; and a supply of helium-3, from which tritium, an element used in thermonuclear weapons, could be derived.

In January 1984 the chairman of South Africa's state-run Atomic Energy Corporation announced that South Africa would conduct its external nuclear affairs—i.e., the transfer of nuclear material, equipment, and technology—in accord with "the spirit, principles, and goals" of the NPT. In the same statement, the AEC chairman said South Africa was ready to resume talks with Washington about nuclear matters and also indicated his government's willingness to talk with the IAEA about allowing the semicommercial enrichment plant now nearing completion to be placed under international safeguards. The existing pilot enrichment plant would be excluded, however.

Negotiations with the IAEA began in 1985, apparently as a result of U.S. pressure on Pretoria. The talks collapsed in August 1986 because South African negotiators demanded the explicit right to withdraw some enriched uranium in the future for possible use in nuclear submarines. They also sought the right to terminate the safeguards agreement without penalty if the IAEA applied sanctions for political reasons or if South Africa's "supreme national interests were jeopardized."

The United States continued to seek Pretoria's agreement to sign the NPT. Unlike IAEA safeguards, which would apply only to those installations designated by South Africa, signing the NPT would require that *all* South

African nuclear facilities be placed under international safeguards. In early 1987, senior U.S. diplomats confirmed privately that South Africa was showing little interest in subscribing to the NPT, because it no longer needed U.S. enriched fuel. About all Washington could offer South Africa as an inducement was support within the IAEA.

In September 1987, Botha (whose title had changed from prime minister to state president by virtue of a new constitution that became effective in 1984) made a surprise announcement that his government was now prepared to open talks with the nuclear states about signing the NPT. The timing of President Botha's announcement—on the eve of the IAEA's annual conference where Third World states were expected to press for the expulsion of South Africa—was clearly aimed at giving the United States and other IAEA members a basis for voting against the expulsion. Indeed, a few days later, when both the U.S. and Soviet IAEA delegates opposed the move against South Africa, the Third World states' initiative collapsed. If Pretoria is serious about signing the NPT, it presumably is ready to shut down the pilot enrichment plant; such a shutdown, in turn, would mean giving up the option to produce weapons-grade uranium. But whether it already has a stockpile of weapons is uncertain.

The Question of Nuclear Targets

Whether or not South Africa has nuclear weapons, the development of such a capability is at least consistent with the view held, especially among senior military officials in government, that a "total national strategy" is required to deal with what they perceive as Soviet-orchestrated regional pressures. It is also consistent with President Botha's perception that South Africa's security situation is analogous to Israel's—a small, technologically advanced state forced to fight alone for its national survival against an array of hostile but weak neighbors armed by the

USSR. A number of credible independent analyses have concluded that Israel already has a nuclear arsenal and a sophisticated delivery system. Moreover, South Africa, like Israel, may have deemed it psychologically useful to foster a suspicion among its neighbors that it possesses a nuclear-weapons capability.

From a military standpoint, South Africa would seem to have little need and few if any potential targets for nuclear weapons. Such weapons would be virtually useless against guerrillas, as either defense or deterrent. To the extent that small bands of ANC or SWAPO operatives, or any existing or future bases in neighboring states, can be located and identified, South Africa's conventional forces are capable of dealing with them effectively. For the foreseeable future, neither the ANC nor Namibia's SWAPO appears capable of moving from sporadic, hit-and-run attacks into the sort of classic guerrilla offensive waged against the Ian Smith government in Rhodesia in the 1970s. The ANC itself foresees no likelihood of such a development.

As for the notion that the threat of nuclear attack might pressure neighboring states into denying the guerrillas sanctuary, South Africa's conventional and unconventional warfare methods have already accomplished that objective, except in the case of Angola. And as long as the threat posed by SWAPO can be contained by standard counterinsurgency measures, any South African threat to move the Namibian-Angolan conflict to a nuclear level would be rash indeed.

Nor would a nuclear weapon be thinkable for use against the major security threat to the regime—revolt in the black townships. Although the ghetto communities are in most cases physically separate from South Africa's cities, they are integrated economically into the rest of the country. Nuclear destruction of the black townships would bring economic chaos, since continued operation of the country's railways, mines, and factories is dependent on the labor of 6 million black employees. Moreover, most black townships are within a few miles of major cities and white residential areas, so that radioactive fallout would inevitably cross the color line.

In the view of South African military planners, the worst-case scenario would be an internal black uprising combined with a massive cross-border attack by African forces backed by Soviet and Cuban troops. Government leaders, despite their past warnings of a "total onslaught" orchestrated by Moscow, now acknowledge that such a development is most unlikely. They continue to express concern, however, over the buildup of heavy armaments in Angola and the Cuban troop presence there. This appears to be more than a politically inspired alarm to win larger defense budgets. Unlikely as a massive invasion may be, military policymakers argue that it remains a worst-case scenario for which the South African Defense Force (SADF) must be prepared. Indeed, the Armaments Development and Production Corporation of South Africa (Armscor) has shifted its focus during the past few years from counterinsurgency weapons to conventional arms. Similarly, major military exercises in recent years have involved defense against a large-scale conventional assault from across the border.

A role for nuclear weapons could be foreseen in such a contingency. They might be used to destroy massed enemy forces about to move against vulnerable civilian targets (e.g., population centers or industrial plants), or as tactical weapons in a conventional battle. Or if hostile armies were seen to be massing along the border, a nuclear device might be detonated in a remote area as a warning against invasion. In 1980 a senior naval officer was quoted in the government's *South African Digest* as having stated that the SADF had the capability to "ward off a combined onslaught by African states, even if this involved *limited* intervention by outside powers." [Italics added.] He further warned that South Africa reserved the right to put its nuclear expertise to practical use.

No hostile forces have invaded South Africa since the Boer War. Indeed, the only recent involvement in conventional warfare occurred inside Angola, a nation that shares no border with the Republic. The SADF acknowledged in November 1987 that its forces were taking higher-than-usual casualties as they helped UNITA guerrillas survive a major ground-and-air offensive by Angolan government troops who, SADF spokesmen alleged, were joined by "Russians and Cubans." Official South African concern over rising SADF casualties in Angola suggests that there are limits to Pretoria's commitment to the survival of UNITA as a military force. These limits would almost certainly preclude the use of nuclear weapons inside Angola given the hostile world reaction that would follow.

In sum, the only remotely feasible use of a nuclear weapon by South Africa would seem to be as a last resort against an invading army – a most unlikely eventuality.

Conclusions

South Africa's nuclear diplomacy has involved the pursuit of three objectives, not all mutually compatible. Access to Western nuclear technology and, until recently, enriched fuel have been priorities. A second goal has been to gain global recognition as a potential nuclear-weapons state and, hence, acknowledgment as the regional superpower in southern Africa. Finally, South Africa has tried to maintain some basis for plausible denial of any weapons intent even while almost certainly pursuing the development of a nuclear-weapons capability.

During the late 1970s the first and third objectives came into conflict. Prime Minister Vorster sought to deal with this conflict by assuring the Carter administration that South Africa had no plans to produce or test a weapon. But Pretoria's dissembling over the Kalahari site, together with its refusal to sign the NPT, led to a cutoff in supplies of U.S. enriched uranium for three critical years, 1978–1980 – a period when South Africa was heavily dependent on U.S. fuel to start up its Koeberg power plant. Evidence of movement toward testing of a nuclear device also contributed to the decision of the UN Security Council to impose a mandatory arms embargo against South Africa in late 1977.

In the early 1980s, however, a successful appeal was made to the Reagan administration for help in acquiring fuel for South Africa's reactors and to refrain from demanding signature of the NPT as a quid pro quo. South Africa also has enjoyed support from both the United States and the Soviet Union in blocking efforts to expel it from the IAEA, although it has so far failed to win back its seat on the prestigious IAEA board.

It was clear by 1981, if not before, that South Africa had all the necessary ingredients to produce nuclear weapons. Whether it had them in 1979, and whether it had tested a weapon, remained issues in dispute. Although South Africa thus achieved its goal of recognition as a potential nuclear-weapons state, this in itself has not figured significantly in its bid for regional superpower status. The concessions wrung from neighboring states were extracted through armed attacks and economic pressure and had nothing to do with its nuclear potential. Nor has the possibility of nuclear reprisal led nearby states to agree to diplomatic recognition or military alliance with the Republic.

Finally, South Africa's military power, including its nuclear potential, has not induced the West to support Pretoria's long-pursued bid for political and economic hegemony in the region. Almost all the Western powers, including the United States under both Presidents Reagan and Carter, have supported the efforts of South Africa's neighbors to develop regional economic cooperation independently of South Africa and thereby to reduce their economic dependence on the Republic.

5

The South African Military Reassesses Its Priorities

Robert S. Jaster

September 1989

South Africa's senior military strategists are still taking stock of the implications of the end of the P.W. Botha era, of Namibia's imminent change from a South African-controlled buffer zone to another unpredictable sovereign neighbor, of the contradictions between Gorbachev's *glasnost* and the dogma of "total onslaught," and of the as yet undefined domestic and regional political agendas of newly elected State President F.W. de Klerk.

An Independent Namibia

In December 1988, the governments of South Africa, Cuba, and Angola agreed upon a process that is scheduled to lead to internationally recognized independence for Namibia by April 1990. This development contains some clear pluses for Pretoria. The imminent departure of the 40,000 Cuban troops from Angola will remove what South African Defense Force (SADF) analysts have viewed as the most significant military threat to the Republic and will remove any doubts about South Africa's status as the dominant military power in the region. The end of the SWAPO insurgency, and the closing down of camps in Angola operated by Umkhonto we Sizwe (the military wing of the African National Congress [ANC]), eliminates one guerrilla threat and weakens another.

South Africa's military planners also see the accords as involving a number of costs and new risks:

1. The end of 74 years of South African rule in Namibia means the loss of a buffer region some 800 miles deep that has separated the Republic from Angola. Apparently with few exceptions, South Africa's military strategists would prefer the present defense line along the Cunene River separating northern Namibia from Angola to one along the Orange River separating southern Namibia from South Africa. Despite the much longer supply route required for the Cunene line, planners drew comfort from the fact that this line kept "the enemy" (or at least the latter's regular military forces) far away from South Africa proper. Some strategists argue that the desert landscape of the Orange River valley is far less defensible than the Cunene area against a conventional attack.

2. Above all, the leadership is concerned that both dissident South Africans and foreign observers might see the Namibia deal as a sign of weakness, especially military weakness – the fall of the penultimate domino following the collapse of white minority rule in Mozambique, Angola, and Zimbabwe, leaving South Africa as the final, isolated white redoubt to be toppled.

3. Paradoxically, there is also apprehension in the SADF about the possibility that the settlement may lead to premature euphoria on the part of some whites inclined to see the departure of the Cuban troops as marking the end of any real security threat. This worry was summed up by Major General P.J. Pienaar, the army's chief of staff for personnel, in the May 1989 edition of *Paratus*, the official journal of the SADF: "[The settlement] has lulled many people into a false sense of security. They are convinced

that peace is in the air with the result that military service can be shortened and the Defence Budget pruned."

4. Some senior members of the military have privately expressed reservations about Pretoria's commitment to terminate support for its longtime ally and client, UNITA's Jonas Savimbi. It would have been useful, it is argued, to retain UNITA in southern Angola after Namibian independence to serve as a trip-wire to alert South Africa to any threatening moves by Angola's armed forces.

Beyond "Total Onslaught"

The military is considerably less certain (or unanimous) than it was a decade ago about just what external threats face the country, but some general observations can be made about the SADF's current outlook.

Military planners now reject the notion of a "total onslaught," a term which they say "is no longer used." They now define the threat as "multidimensional," which is taken to include the dangers of (1) military attack, (2) sanctions and secondary sanctions (i.e., pressure on country B by country A to adopt tougher measures against South Africa), and (3) "revolutionary attack" in fields ranging from sports, entertainment, and official exchanges to trade and finance.

The specific military threat is seen as having two interrelated elements: the presence of a substantial stock of advanced weaponry in nearby states (and the prospect that more may be acquired); and the supposedly unfriendly attitude of these states toward South Africa, particularly with regard to supporting or at least tolerating cross-border ANC operations against the Pretoria government.

Senior military officials acknowledge that the closure of the ANC camps in Angola under the terms of the 1988 accords and the expulsion of ANC guerrillas from other neighboring states in recent years have dealt a serious blow to the ANC's infiltration capability, but they remain apprehensive about the countries that still provide material assistance and/or allow the ANC safe passage. They allege that Zambia and Zimbabwe continue to assist armed ANC contingents en route to South Africa and that Botswana turns a blind eye to ANC cross-border movements. Zimbabwe is viewed as the most hostile neighboring country – the "center for southern African propaganda and militancy directed against the Republic" in the words of one official interviewed in April 1989.

Worst-case scenarios, however, focus more on future military capabilities and action options of neighboring states than on the ANC per se. Any sizable upsurge in cross-border guerrilla attacks during the next decade, it is reasoned, would force South Africa to revert to the recently suspended policy of carrying out preemptive and retaliatory strikes against guerrilla sanctuaries in nearby countries. This response would, in turn, raise the prospect that the affected countries would either upgrade their defense capabilities or seek intervention by external military forces.

Indeed, SADF planners believe that some neighboring states may have already contemplated (but not acted on) such moves. They cite reports that Zimbabwe has considered the purchase of Soviet MiG-29s, advanced fighter aircraft that "would change the whole strategic balance" in the region. They also allege that in early 1989 Zambia, Zimbabwe, and Nigeria were offered substantial numbers of Cuban troops (10,000 in the case of Zambia), presumably to be drawn from those scheduled to leave Angola. Although SADF intelligence officials say the offers were declined, they remain convinced that surrogate forces would be readily available to any regional state requesting them. U.S. intelligence sources report that they have seen no evidence of Cuban troop offers to other African states and express strong doubts that Castro made such an offer.

The 1989–1990 Defense Budget

Although the situation a few years hence may be different (see "Longer-Term Implications" on page 74), the Namibia accords did not result in an immediate reduction in the defense budget. Indeed, the defense budget approved for FY 1989-1990 totaled $3.6 billion—more than 20 percent above the previous year's figure.

Military leaders point out that this sum represents less than 16 percent of total state spending and only 4.4 percent of GDP and offer several reasons why defense spending should not be slashed. For example: (1) The financial costs of military operations in Namibia and Angola accounted for a relatively small share of the defense budget. SADF sources put the figure at $50-55 million a year, or less than 2 percent of defense outlays in 1988-1989. Independent military analysts have estimated the *overall* costs of the war as high as a million rand (roughly $360,000) a day. Assuming that this higher figure is correct and that it includes only those costs normally falling within the SADF budget, it would still amount to less than 5 percent of SADF outlays in 1988-1989. (2) The peace accords themselves have resulted in added expenses for the SADF over the short run—$6 million in 1989-1990 "to implement UN Security Council Resolution 435," and $54 million to remove South African troops and equipment from Namibia and relocate them at home.

A more significant budgetary area not greatly affected by the Namibia accords is the development, production, and importation of new weapons. Some $2.2 billion (about 60 percent of the total projected 1989-1990 defense budget and an increase of more than 20 percent over the previous year's figure) is earmarked for the Special Defense Account, used primarily for clandestine acquisition of foreign weapons.

Armscor's Role

South Africa's strategic military planners acknowledge that uncertainty about future external security threats makes it difficult to assess priorities regarding the procurement of new weapons systems. Planning is further complicated by the effects of a mandatory global embargo on the supply of weapons, weapons technology, and related materials invoked by a unanimous vote of the UN Security Council in November 1977.

The most dramatic of the country's "sanctions-busting" initiatives has been the phenomenal growth of an indigenous arms industry (led by the state-owned Armaments Development and Production Corporation of South Africa Ltd., known as Armscor). South Africa is widely believed to be among the world's 10 major arms producers. With exports to at least a score of countries estimated to be on the order of several hundred million dollars annually, Armscor is the Republic's largest exporter of manufactured goods. Although Armscor's successful development has made possible a drastic reduction in the proportion of arms that must be imported, the embargo is still a serious problem with regard to certain crucial arms categories such as aircraft.

The bulk of investment in arms over the past few years has been targeted on filling this aircraft gap. In 1986, Armscor and the SADF unveiled a locally crafted refurbishment of the country's existing French-made Mirage III fighters (irreplaceable because of the UN embargo). The upgrade is intended to extend the operational life of the plane (renamed the Cheetah) by 10–15 years. This stopgap solution does not, however, eliminate the perceived long-term need to acquire a new generation of combat aircraft to replace the aging Mirages. A March 20 article by Gavin Bell in *The Times* (London) outlined some options:

> "We can't buy a new aircraft, so we have to build one," an informed source said. "The airframe and most of the electronics can be produced locally, but the problem is the engine." One option would be a version of the Israeli-made Kfir which is similar to the Cheetah, but the Israelis would be unable to provide its American engines without incurring America's wrath. An answer might be a discreet transfer of technology. "South Africa buys less equipment from Israel than you might imagine, but there is a lot of know-how flowing both

ways," the source said. Another possibility could be to copy a twin-engine, single-fin fighter which came into production in Taiwan last year. The engines were developed in the [United States], but are now being manufactured locally. . . .

Besides the Cheetah upgrade, South Africa in recent years has produced a small combat helicopter, upgraded its Puma helicopter gunships, and acquired two tanker aircraft from Israel. According to *The Star* (Johannesburg), the SADF was (as of March 1989) equipping its Cheetahs with a new engine to extend their operational range and possibly developing a troop-carrying helicopter.

The *Washington Times* (June 20, 1989) cited anonymous "U.S. intelligence officials" as having said that South Africa would soon test an intermediate-range ballistic missile developed with Israeli assistance that could theoretically be used to deliver a nuclear weapon to a target 900 miles away. (Whether or not South Africa has a nuclear capability remains unconfirmed.) Such a missile could also be used to deliver nonnuclear warheads or to put a photographic reconnaissance satellite into orbit.

The army's stock of tanks consists of 250 Centurion/ Olifants, some of which were purchased in the mid-1950s. Although the SADF has made some upgrades (e.g., fitting them with late-model gunsights), their armor and firepower are inferior to those of Soviet-made T-62 tanks (with which Angola's forces are equipped). A priority SADF goal is to develop a domestically made tank to replace the Centurion/Olifant and match the T-62. This appears feasible, but if over the next decade any neighboring country should acquire tanks more advanced than the T-62, South Africa could find it difficult to keep pace.

An Expanded Role for the Navy?

In the May 1989 issue of *Strategic Review for Southern Africa* (Institute for Strategic Studies, Pretoria), the SADF's senior naval planner, Captain E.P. Groenewald, raised the possibility that unfriendly neighboring countries might attempt small-scale attacks on key South African maritime installations. He expressed particular concern about actions against the deep-water port and naval base at Walvis Bay, a South African exclave on the coast of Namibia.

Groenewald also saw an important offensive role for the navy beyond its more limited traditional function of protecting the Cape of Good Hope sea route and keeping the country's ports open. Reasoning that SADF ground operations will become more difficult given the increasingly sophisticated air defenses of neighboring states, he noted that many of the major cities of nearby coastal countries, as well as much of their economic infrastructure, are concentrated along the coast, a fact that makes it both feasible and necessary for the navy to develop "the capability to project power ashore."

Since 1986 a number of reports have surfaced that Armscor is engaged in constructing submarines modeled after Germany's U-209, using German blueprints and engineers, to replace its three aging French-built Daphne-class craft by the mid-1990s. Meanwhile, the navy launched its first six amphibious landing craft, the locally designed Delta 80, in late 1988.

Manpower

As of mid-1988, the SADF had some 103,000 active personnel (75,000 army, 7,500 navy, 13,000 air force, 8,000 medical service), backed by 455,000 reservists. The military relies on approximately 68,000 white male conscripts for the bulk of its active duty force. Some 25,000–30,000 a year are called up for an initial two-year "national service" stint, followed by up to 720 days of service in Citizen Force "camps" spread over 12 years.

Besides being a massive intrusion into the lives of the country's youth, this system has a negative impact on the economy. Because the draftees are drawn from what is at once the smallest and the best educated ethnic group in the country, the SADF is siphoning off skills badly needed by the private sector.

The draft is also coming under pressure from an End Conscription Campaign (ECC) sparked by the unwillingness of prospective draftees to serve as enforcers of apartheid in the domestic black townships. The ECC has recently been gaining adherents despite stiff jail terms imposed on a number of conscientious objectors.

Given this tug-of-war over young whites, it is not surprising that one of the first major changes in SADF procedures following the December 1988 Angola-Namibia accords was a de facto cut in military service. On April 20, Minister of Defense (General) Magnus Malan announced that although the country's draft law would remain unaltered, after July 1989 annual camps should last no longer than 30 days. More recently, General Jannie Geldenhuys, chief of the SADF, suggested that further reductions in national service might be in the offing.

The SADF has attempted to alleviate the manpower bottleneck by making increasing use of nonwhite volunteers, of whom there are more than the military is willing to accept. (In May 1989, Malan told Parliament that the SADF took 3,511 of the 7,011 nonwhites who volunteered for national service in 1988.) Military officials dismiss the suggestion that they are worried about the political reliability of nonwhite soldiers and claim that the major constraint on their recruitment is the shortage of available training personnel.

Longer-Term Implications

Any large bureaucracy requires time to adjust to major change. The process of trying to understand the nature of what has happened and determine its implications for the organization is seldom orderly or quick. Elements within the bureaucracy will offer differing assessments, while normal bureaucratic inertia and resistance to innovation will slow the process of adjustment.

South Africa's military establishment is no exception to this rule. Responses to the changed situation have been rapid and substantial in such areas as redeployment of troops and weapons, demobilization of the South West Africa Territory Force, and reduction of national service obligations—in part due to deadlines imposed by the peace accords. In other areas, especially assessment of the next decade's military threat and formulation of a new strategy to meet it, the pace has been much slower. In part, of course, this reflects the sudden changes that have occurred in the region, which is in a state of transition and will remain so throughout the 1990s as the Namibia accords are implemented, the ANC debates new strategies, and Angola and Mozambique lurch toward some resolution of their internal conflicts.

Nor have SADF planners yet fully digested the implications of the dramatic shifts under way in U.S.-Soviet relations and in Soviet policy toward Third World conflicts, particularly those in which Moscow has no clear strategic interests at stake. Although some officials have expressed optimism over the possibility that a reduced Soviet willingness to meddle in conflicts of marginal importance may be forcing the ANC to consider a shift from guerrilla war toward negotiations, others in the military see the Gorbachev phenomenon as a "giant hoax perpetrated on the West."

South Africa's strategic planners also appear to have ignored the signs of a waning ideological fervor in the governments of neighboring states in the face of worsening domestic problems. The aggressive deployment of 15,000 heavily armed Cuban troops on the Namibian border in mid-1988 may have so traumatized SADF leaders that they are as yet unable to look beyond that episode toward what seems likely to be a less threatening regional environment in the 1990s.

Such attitudes may be starting to change, however. In

April 1989, Defense Minister Malan told Parliament that South Africa must revise its strategy in light of the shifting relationship between East and West—a development that called for "new thinking, preparation, and a new attitude to the problems, opportunities, and challenges" it presents. He noted the possibility of "an entirely new order in the last decade of this century" with "far-reaching implications [not spelled out] for South Africa."

The military leadership is already sensitive to the likely impact of domestic political and economic constraints on future defense budgets. The departure of the Cuban combat brigade and the end of SWAPO's insurgency, in particular, will make it difficult for the SADF to convince whites of the need for large weapons outlays. Serious economic problems, and especially the critical need to repay several billion dollars of commercial debt to Western banks over the next two to three years, will also exert pressure on military spending. The SADF's strategic planners say that they do not expect further hefty budget increases, but will be content if future defense spending keeps pace with inflation, which in late 1989 was running at 15 to 16 percent.

Another development that will involve some rethinking within the SADF is the departure from the political scene of P.W. Botha, a longtime friend of the military. During the 14 years he served as minister of defense (1966 to 1980), Botha was a strong advocate of the military's agenda and helped push through a sequence of budgetary increases for the SADF. After becoming prime minister in 1978, and carrying through his five years as state president from 1984 to 1989, he restructured the executive branch of his government in ways that assigned a primary role to a State Security Council in which military involvement in overall governmental decision making was greatly increased.

F.W. de Klerk, who was sworn in as Botha's elected successor on September 20, is by comparison a question mark in the eyes of the military. The first signals from the new state president were mixed. Although several cabinet and other organizational changes in the upper levels of government indicated a trimming back of the influence of the "securocrats" of the military and police in the making of national policy, the unexpected retention of General Malan as minister of defense suggests that de Klerk wants to retain an experienced military leader in that post.

6

The SADF Revisited

Herbert M. Howe

July 1991

One point on which all relevant political elements in South Africa agree is that whatever government emerges from the tortuous transition now under way will need for its survival a loyal and competent military. Toward this end, President F.W. de Klerk has set in motion some reforms of the ideology, structure, and personnel of the South African Defense Force (SADF).

For the SADF to become the reconciling force envisaged by de Klerk, it must assuage black fears and suspicions, while at the same time calming white fears about the transition to a postapartheid government. A crucial test of this homogenizing ability will come as it joins—either as the result of the creation of a new military or through an integration of existing forces—with the African National Congress (ANC) military wing, Umkhonto we Sizwe ("Spear of the Nation").

The Botha Legacy

Based on its historical record, the SADF was not viewed at the turn of the decade as a likely agent of racial conciliation. Throughout the 1980s, it played a key administrative and decision-making role in P.W. Botha's "total strategy," which marshaled all the nation's political, economic, and coercive tools to combat what the government's leadership perceived as a Soviet-orchestrated "total onslaught." The "total strategy" involved a multifaceted campaign to destabilize neighboring countries believed to be supporting the ANC or Namibia's SWAPO. In addition, the SADF aided the police in quashing township unrest during the mid-1980s and may have engaged in domestic spying operations.

By 1990, the ANC's elderly senior leadership was uncomfortably aware that SADF and police repression of blacks had generated opposition among many younger ANC members to formal contacts with the government, let alone a full-fledged negotiation process. Moreover, there was the risk that elements of the security establishment could undermine talks or negotiations by isolated local actions. Prior to his release from prison in February 1990, Nelson Mandela may have discussed these concerns with de Klerk; he may even have conditioned acceptance of his own release and of subsequent government-ANC talks on a de Klerk commitment to security reform.

De Klerk faced relatively little opposition from the country's whites on making at least some cuts in the SADF's strength. The decay of communism in Eastern Europe and even the Soviet Union, along with the withdrawal of Cuban troops from Angola under the terms of the December 1988 Namibia accords, virtually eliminated the credibility of the "total onslaught" notion. And South Africa's military campaigns in Namibia and Angola were never popular among whites, who had accepted the costly war only as a necessary defensive action. The two-year conscription, with few loopholes, was inducing increasing numbers of well-educated whites to leave South Africa.

Therefore, a pragmatic de Klerk had a strong incentive (persuading Mandela to accept release and then to work for negotiations) and no real disincentives for his military cutbacks.

De Klerk's Changes

Ideology

A contemporary South African anecdote tells of a teacher at the Police Training College returning a stack of ungraded examination books on February 3, 1990. Referring to a question regarding South Africa's enemies, the instructor intoned: "Gentlemen, everyone must rewrite the question. Yesterday, your answers [about the ANC] were correct. Today, they're mightily wrong."

De Klerk's unbanning of the ANC and other groups on February 2, 1990, his subsequent release of Mandela, and his granting of indemnity to exiles signaled that he did not necessarily view the ANC as an enemy. Indeed, there has been ANC-government coordination in the security area since that time. Pursuant to the Pretoria Minute signed by the ANC and the government in August 1990, Umkhonto and the South African Police (SAP), once archenemies, now openly cooperate on a limited range of matters.

Among other developments, the security establishment has distanced itself from the rigidly anti-ANC "total strategy." Late in 1989, Minister of Defense Magnus Malan stated publicly that South Africa would no longer engage in cross-border operations. Although a cynic could be excused for questioning General Malan's sincerity, South Africa has not renewed its military involvement in Angola or Namibia and apparently has ceased any significant assistance to Mozambique's Renamo. According to some security analysts, the SADF has shifted emphasis from its counterinsurgency capabilities (which were to a considerable extent aimed at the ANC) to its conventional and border defense systems.

De Klerk has singled out as South Africa's primary "enemy" the apartheid-created socioeconomic morass entrapping the country's blacks. The 1990 budget reflected the shift from military to economic priorities. Defense spending declined in real terms by about 15 percent, whereas spending to meet the needs of blacks rose, albeit modestly.

The changes in military policy were due in part to the previously noted reduction in the perceived external threat, the country's financial plight, and de Klerk's desire to encourage the ANC to enter into negotiations. An additional factor is that de Klerk has never been close to the security establishment. Unlike P.W. Botha, who had served as minister of defense for more than a decade before becoming prime minister, de Klerk comes from a civilian background (his last post was minister of national education) and faced informal opposition from the military as a choice for state president.

Structure

During the 1980s, P.W. Botha and his fellow "total strategy" adherents effectively placed South Africa under quasi-military, or "securocrat," rule. The military-dominated State Security Council (SSC) became the center of all national decision making and official power. By the mid-1980s, the National Security Management System (NSMS) and its 500 local Joint Management Centers (JMCs) – accountable to no elected body – had deepened the security establishment's rule of South Africa to the point where the cabinet usually rubber-stamped their decisions.

In his first cabinet shuffle, only two months after assuming office, de Klerk shifted the NSMS director, Deputy Minister Leon Wessels, from the Ministry of Law and Order over to Foreign Affairs and replaced the NSMS with a National Coordinating Mechanism (NCM), which is said to emphasize welfare over security. The NCM is under the control of the state president's office; it is staffed by civilian officials rather than military officers. Annette Seegers, a respected South African expert on security affairs, wrote in mid-1990 that "50 percent of the NSMS posts have been frozen and are to be phased out by the end of 1990."

De Klerk downgraded the State Security Council, reducing its bureaucratic resources and relegating it to its original status as one of four standing cabinet committees.

The cabinet, reasserting its role as the highest decision-making body, now has veto power over SSC decisions. All SSC members must be elected officials.

De Klerk further limited military influence by pointedly excluding all SADF and Ministry of Defense personnel from the government team at the key Groote Schuur and Pretoria meetings with the ANC. He has also imposed strict controls on the military's domestic covert activities, which had particularly outraged the ANC. And in August 1990, de Klerk announced the abolition of the controversial SADF-created Civil Cooperation Bureau (CCB), whose hit squads are rumored to have killed such resistance leaders as Griffiths Mxenge, David Webster, Dulcie September, and Anton Lubowski.

Some critics believe that these changes amount to mere tactical reshuffling and note, for example, that Special Forces personnel from the CCB remain within the army, that the NCM has acquired some functions of the NSMS, and that General Malan may have disregarded de Klerk's decision to terminate the CCB. In fact, however, de Klerk's structural reforms, though incomplete, are significant.

Personnel

On December 7, 1989, de Klerk announced that the period of initial service for South Africa's conscripts would be reduced from two years to one. This has resulted in a reduction in the size of the active military from some 75,000 to about 55,000. Analysts have suggested that Pretoria could now put into action on short notice no more than one to two full-strength combat brigades (of 5,000 troops each). Moreover, the new policy has lowered the SADF's cost-benefit ratio per draftee. Individuals conscripted for "national service" still undergo 10 months of training, but perform only 2 rather than the former 14 months of subsequent operational service. Another significant (albeit intangible) effect of the draft liberalization is a reduction of the siege mentality that worsened race relations and nurtured the "total strategy."

De Klerk has made several other changes involving manpower, some of them symbolic. In mid-1990, the State President Guard Unit was disbanded. In at least five conservative rural areas, there has been limited disarming of "commando" (local defense) units, presumably to reduce potential support for white vigilantism. Black recruitment and promotions have increased, but probably not much more rapidly than before. Nonwhites, who are not subject to conscription, comprise about 12 percent of the SADF's manpower.

Restraints on Reform

The changes in ideology, structure, and personnel that have taken place thus far indicate that de Klerk's limited demilitarization effort is sincere but is still more a set of intentions than an accomplished fact. Even the envisaged cutbacks have their limits. The government has held firm on certain permanent defense needs, in part because of concern that an overly hasty reduction in defense capabilities would provide political ammunition to the country's right wing. Observers predict, therefore, that the standing force will not drop much below the present 55,000 troops.

De Klerk and his defense planners believe that it is possible to meet core security needs without endangering future negotiations. The ANC, which has an increasingly vested interest in stability, agrees on many of these needs. The essentials include border defense and patrolling as well as maintaining enough capability to deal with domestic contingencies.

De Klerk's desire to maintain order while implementing reforms helps explain why he has not replaced all of Botha's securocrats with negotiation-minded technocrats. Still present are such holdovers as Minister of Defense Malan and Minister of Law and Order Adriaan Vlok. In mid-

1990 de Klerk appointed General "Kat" Liebenberg, an acknowledged hawk and an architect of regional destabilization, as head of the SADF. The continuing violence in Natal and in Johannesburg-Pretoria area townships, Umkhonto's militant posturing, and the ANC's talk of self-defense units have probably stabilized the securocrats' role, albeit at a lower level than under P.W. Botha.

The continued tenure of General Malan as minister of defense has surprised many observers who anticipated that his connection with the "total strategy" and the ill-reputed Civil Cooperation Bureau would lead to his forced resignation. De Klerk may still feel a need to consolidate his power in relation to the military, where he had no established constituency when he entered office, and so may have agreed to retain top security personnel, including Malan, in exchange for the military's toleration of his reforms.

Other possible explanations are that de Klerk values Malan's military abilities, that whites would interpret Malan's departure as indicative of "softness" toward black unrest, that "Good Soldier" Malan will follow any orders from de Klerk just as he followed orders from Botha, that Malan represents the National Party's wealthiest constituency (Modderfontein), and perhaps that he possesses politically embarrassing information about high civilian officials.

Attitudinal Trends within the SADF

How is the SADF itself responding to the military reforms? The de Klerk government has reason to worry about officer morale. In an April 1991 article in the *Weekly Mail*, Phillip van Niekerk estimated Conservative Party strength at "50 [percent] at the level of senior military officers and 60 [percent] at junior officer level." In a March 1991 interview with the author, a SADF spokesman acknowledged that "strong uncertainty" developed, especially at the junior officer level, following de Klerk's initial changes (limiting the NSMS/SSC system and slashing conscription time). Permanent Force (PF) officers privately complain about de Klerk's legitimation of the ANC, as well as the conscription and budget cuts. The use of security forces against whites in defense of de Klerk's political reforms, as recently occurred at Ventersdorp when police and soldiers fired on white farmers protesting the presence of black squatters, almost certainly affected army morale.

De Klerk's political position could be weakened if there were a significant number of early SADF retirements or if elements of the SADF have undertaken to provide covert aid to white vigilantes or Inkatha. Some embittered whites who have chosen to remain in the SADF might use unnecessary force in a manner sufficiently flagrant to make the ANC rethink its present preference for negotiations.

In addition, covert units (even ones such as the CCB that have officially been disbanded) may have quasi-independent structures and funding sources as well as some hardened individuals determined to prevent the ANC from gaining power. Personal aggrandizement also could come into play. It has been suggested (though never proven) that certain special units outside of the normally tight chain of command have profited from sales of ivory, diamonds, and hardwoods.

Despite the above concerns, a military coup appears unlikely. Civilian control of the security establishment has been given new emphasis in SADF indoctrination and training. Posters in army barracks featuring a large picture of de Klerk carry his message requiring obedience to the nation's laws. And as far as behavior is concerned, the SADF has apparently continued to exhibit unquestioning loyalty to the country's chief executive.

In this connection, it is significant that the SADF has a strong "citizen" (conscript) character. The Permanent Force numbers only about 12,000 full-time combat soldiers (out of a standing force of some 55,000). In addition, the reservists, who constitute an overwhelming majority of the total force complement, rarely owe their primary allegiance to the military and thus would feel less angered by any threats to the SADF's corporate identity than would full-time soldiers. Meanwhile, the bark of the civilian reactionary vigilantes who might sympathize with a coup attempt has not been accompanied by much of a bite, in part because of internal personal and philosophical feuds.

In sum, any coup planners would face serious obstacles. Even assuming the full secrecy and cooperation of career Permanent Force personnel, their limited numbers relative to the rest of the SADF would make a coup hard to carry out. And overthrowing a government would solve only half a problem. The perpetrators would have to rule and police a South Africa confronted with (1) unprecedented internal opposition across the racial spectrum, (2) outrage on the part of most other nations, which would probably be expressed in the form of tough renewed sanctions, and therefore (3) a free-falling economy bereft of domestic and foreign investment.

In evaluating coup possibilities, it is also noteworthy that significant elements of the SADF's top echelons welcome de Klerk's regional retrenchment and the lessening of the military's political role. In the final years of the wars in Angola and Namibia, both the SADF leadership and P.W. Botha became increasingly concerned about the domestic political implications of rising white casualties. Dispatching white army personnel to help patrol the townships in the late 1980s caused serious drops in army morale and strengthened the End Conscription Campaign.

Despite its image in many quarters as a repressive force, the South African military has long accepted the need for limited economic and political reform. Firsthand knowledge of black socioeconomic grievances gained during the 1980s in the Joint Management Centers and in township patrolling increased the SADF's preference for controlled reform. As Annette Seegers puts it, the SADF hopes for a "'purification of military function,' meaning that the military should not prop up poorly-run civilian departments."

Some of de Klerk's actions since the start of his restructuring campaign have placated officers who had feared for their nation's security when P.W. Botha stepped down. He supported a pay raise for the SADF that ended two years of frozen salaries, substantially increased the police budget, reduced the SADF's uncomfortable presence in the townships, and has often publicly expressed friendliness and appreciation for the military.

Military pension benefits also have improved under de Klerk. Although age 60 is the usual mandatory retirement age, on at least one occasion colonels and brigadiers between ages 45 and 50 have been allowed to apply for full pensions and "golden handshakes." De Klerk has also given his support to lifetime pension and medical benefits for all marine corps personnel not reabsorbed by the Defense Force.

Amalgamation Options

Given present trends in the political arena, the SADF will soon face the challenge of combining forces with Umkhonto (as well as, perhaps, with Buthelezi's Inkatha and the Azanian People's Liberation Army). Some sort of melding of SADF and Umkhonto forces is necessary to reassure South Africa's two major constituencies that the new national military will not act against the interests of either group. Although Minister of Defense Malan has expressed skepticism about such a merger, his statement is viewed as a short-term reaction. Some SADF officers have privately said that either Malan or his successor will negotiate specific integration issues with Umkhonto.

Amalgamation raises a range of potentially divisive ideological, structural, and personnel issues. Can two competitors, historically and sometimes violently identified with opposing views and oriented toward markedly different military methodologies, support a government answerable to all South Africans?

The army will be the focus of concern, because the

ANC has few personnel trained in air and naval operations. A black-dominated government would understandably be concerned about an enemy within the gates – such as dissident officers at the operational level who might stage mutinies, commit sabotage, or simply slow down the bureaucratic process. And former Umkhonto members might find it psychologically difficult to cooperate with and take orders from former SADF personnel.

A central issue of structure is whether the much smaller Umkhonto should be integrated into the existing SADF or a totally new force should be formed (as in Namibia, where the postindependence government headed by President Sam Nujoma ordered members of both the SWAPO military wing and the South West Africa Territory Force to disband and then apply to join the country's new defense force as raw recruits).

The first option, that of integration, would imply a junior, minority status for the smaller and less-experienced Umkhonto despite majority public support for the ANC. The training process might be headed by a mix of SADF, Umkhonto, and homeland (notably Ciskei and Transkei) army personnel. Many of the latter have received SADF training in conventional and nonconventional tactics and weaponry and would probably exhibit more cultural sensitivity than some white SADF officers. Some of the homelands – especially Transkei – have moved politically closer to the ANC, which could help their officers gain the respect of ex-Umkhonto members.

The other approach, that of forming a new army, would have the advantage of a clean break with the controversies and traditions surrounding the SADF. All members would (at least in principle) receive the same treatment, training, and indoctrination. As occurred in Namibia and Zimbabwe, and has been proposed for Angola, a British Military Advisory Training Team [BMATT] might be called upon to manage the training phase.

Whether tomorrow's military is a totally new force or an integration of Umkhonto with the present force, SADF officers wonder whether the army might become a bloated employer of last resort. Peace could unleash job expectations, especially among ex-Umkhonto members, that the economy cannot meet in the short term even with the lifting of sanctions. General Malan reflected this concern when he cautioned during a 1990 parliamentary debate on the defense budget that "we are not on the road to using the army to keep unemployment off the street."

But not all of today's estimated 9,000 Umkhonto members will necessarily want to join the new military. As Stephen Davis points out, many blacks joined Umkhonto simply to leave South Africa or to receive an education. Tired of the long guerrilla struggle, many now hope to enter civilian life. Others are likely to join the growing police force, whose permanent body of manpower is now larger than the SADF's. By the same token, many present SADF members may leave following the establishment of a new government.

Some SADF officers, otherwise supportive of integration, worry (despite recent ANC assurances) that political considerations will force "a lowering of standards." They predict a dramatic drop in morale among both black and white personnel if Umkhonto members—especially in the command and control positions—are exempted from the entry and promotion requirements of SADF officers.

Umkhonto addressed some of the white concerns at a May 1990 conference in Lusaka (Zambia) sponsored by the Institute for a Democratic Alternative for South Africa (IDASA) that brought together Umkhonto and mostly liberal ex-SADF personnel. The consensus at the Lusaka meeting was that South Africa should have a smaller (totally professional) army than at present (a 50 percent reduction in force levels, a phaseout of conscription, and elimination of the commando system), that merit should play a major role in promotion, and that members of the defense force "should not belong to any political party."

Although the envisaged merger would be difficult, steps can be taken to make it more workable. In the area of ideology, a vigorous in-service education program could help "deracialize" attitudes and strengthen loyalty to the new government. The fact that some Umkhonto members are receiving conventional military training in Nigeria and other countries should narrow the philosophical and operational differences between Umkhonto and the SADF and thus increase acceptance of the new recruits. The absence of clear "winners" and "losers" in the SADF-ANC conflict may – or may not – lessen future animosities.

Elimination of South Africa's more controversial units (e.g., the notorious "32 Battalion") would lessen ANC fears and increase the legitimacy of the new force. External training, possibly by British BMATT teams, would place ex-SADF and Umkhonto soldiers on a more equal basis. The predictably negative reactions of some Afrikaners to a British presence might be assuaged by the opportunity such an association would provide to learn how to use the new weapons systems available in a post-sanctions period.

Despite the cited caveats, creation of a new force, or integration of existing forces, could proceed surprisingly smoothly. The transitions in Zimbabwe and Namibia – both following on wars bloodier than the SADF-ANC conflict – were marked by adaptability on the part of many former officers and combatants.

The Balance Sheet as of Mid-1991

Security and political reforms are inextricably linked. Reciprocal reduction of government and ANC military power facilitates political conciliation. The changes that have already taken place in the government's military ideology, structure, and personnel have helped encourage the ANC to suspend its protracted guerrilla struggle and enter a political process expected to culminate in ANC participation in a future South African government. The prenegotiation process and the ANC's relatively conciliatory stance have freed de Klerk from the policies of his predecessor, have demonstrated to security-concerned whites that their president is dealing with reasonable men, and have increased the likelihood of National Party influence in future South African governments.

Despite the increased evidence of genuine communication, as exemplified by the Groote Schuur agreement and the Pretoria Minute, security-related tensions will continue as the government and the ANC prepare for negotiations. They are currently both allies and adversaries in this area, cooperating on such matters as coordinating security for political events and quarreling on others, such as the government's curfews.

Some of the tension results from efforts by both sides (and Inkatha) to use physical force to maximize future bargaining positions. Despite President de Klerk's legalization of the ANC in 1990 as a prelude to political negotiations, some of his security measures – curfews and arms seizures, refusal (at least until May 1991) to ban "cultural weapons," and continued use of Askaris (former Umkhonto members) to identify and monitor ANC officials and locate arms caches – have circumscribed the ANC's political options. Some National Party officials may believe that direct repression of the ANC or assistance to Inkatha could force political compromises from a weakened ANC. In fact, such steps would be more likely to shift black support away from a negotiated settlement and toward resumption of the armed struggle.

Although the military reductions implemented to date by the government and the ANC have furthered political conciliation, the future is less certain. Perhaps because of the need to avoid an exodus of skilled personnel during the initial stages, de Klerk's security reforms have not yet fully assuaged black fears. No top officers have been removed; most controversial units remain intact. The reforms have proven relatively pain-free thus far to the army and the larger white community. The real test will come with military amalgamation (in particular the appointment of senior ex-Umkhonto officers to replace some present white officers and the disbanding of controversial operational

units) and with the entry of the National Party into an
interim government with widely respected black leaders.
Significant inclusion of the SADF-trained black homeland
forces in the future military, along with some Umkhonto
forces, may help satisfy white demands for a competent
and neutral force.

Restructuring of the police will also affect white attitudes toward the coming changes in the military. A police
force that remains white-influenced, or a newly minted one
that is seen as impartial, would temper white concerns
about military changes.

De Klerk's security reforms, although incomplete, have
introduced a new sense of change and acceptance. The security reforms entail compromises by, and risks to, both
partners. The government has reduced its military capabilities. The ANC, by suspending armed struggle and recruiting, has done the same. These compromises have caused
both the government and the ANC to lose some support,
but as of mid-1991 the losses appear manageable.

7

Reconstructing Education for a New South Africa

Bruce McKenney

December 1991

One of the many striking changes taking place in South Africa is that township youth are beginning to view education as a fundamental need that should not be used as a political tool. "Inkululeko ngoku, i-degree ngomso!"—the Xhosa slogan calling for "liberation now, education later" that inspired school boycotts in the 1980s—is rarely heard in 1991.

Although the African National Congress (ANC) formally rejected the 1980s concept of liberation before education, it gave tacit support to the student boycotts of that era by designating schools as a "primary site of struggle." In early 1991, in contrast, the ANC joined with the Pan-Africanist Congress (PAC), the Azanian People's Organization (AZAPO), and the Inkatha Freedom Party (IFP) in calling for all children to make this year "a memorable one for serious learning free of disruptions and school boycotts." The organizations were largely reacting to the worst-ever results for blacks on the matriculation examinations that secondary school students must pass in order to qualify for university entrance. Although the overall number of matric certificates issued to blacks has continued to grow over the years (from 20,562 in 1980 to 175,963 in 1990) due to a high population growth rate and increased access to schooling, only 40.7 percent of black students managed to pass the matric examination in 1990, as compared to a pass rate of 51 percent a decade earlier.

Thousands of pupils heeded the political organizations' unified call for a return to the classroom. Indeed, the appeal was so successful that numbers in black secondary schools rose by almost 20 percent. This turnaround created a new crisis. Already bursting at the seams, the overcrowded township schools could not accommodate the tremendous influx of new pupils. The result has been more disruptions, student boycotts, and teacher strikes. At a primary school in Khayelitsha, a township of Cape Town, pupils began the 1991 year with no books or desks and practiced their writing in a thin layer of sand spread out on the concrete floor. These developments warrant an attempt to assess longer-term trends and prospects.

The Legacy of Apartheid Education

In the decades that South Africa's learning tree has been entangled with the politics of apartheid, the Bantu education system has de-emphasized English, mathematics, and science in favor of an ethnic cultural focus. In effect, the racially compartmentalized system offered black South Africans an inferior, pretechnological education that worked all too successfully to keep them out of skilled employment fields. It is estimated that approximately 16 percent of black pupils who entered primary school in 1991 may be expected to reach their final year of secondary school, while the corresponding figure for white pupils is 82 percent. According to educationists across the political spectrum, including the government ministers in charge of the stratified education system, the crisis caused by apartheid education will take at least a generation to redress.

The education crisis may have reached nightmarish

proportions, but there is reason for guarded optimism. The release of Nelson Mandela, the unbanning of political organizations, and the scrapping of most of the legal pillars of apartheid have resulted in an unprecedented atmosphere of genuine negotiation. Rhetoric is being replaced by pragmatism among all the major interest groups. Instead of continuing to treat education as a political football, almost everyone involved is working to depoliticize the issue in order to encourage a return to schools and disciplined learning.

The Cost Factor

Although political organizations and educationists maintain their pressure on the government to equalize spending for black and white schooling, all sides recognize that it will take more than a budget increase to solve the pervasive problems left by the legacy of Bantu education. John Samuels, the ANC's education director, acknowledges that there will be "no miraculous transformation; restoring the learning culture takes time." Equal funding would require annual expenditures amounting to 40 percent of the current central budget.

In 1986, then-Minister of National Education (and now State President) F.W. de Klerk launched a 10-year plan aimed at providing parity in education funding, but it had to be canceled three years later due to a lack of funds. In 1990–1991, government expenditure on education rose 16.1 percent, just ahead of the 15 percent inflation rate, and education accounted for 17.5 percent of the total budget. The budget for the Department of Education and Training, which controls funding for black schools (excluding the four "independent national states" and six "self-governing territories") was increased by 21.9 percent. For 1991–1992, spending on education will take up 18.5 percent of the budget, the largest single item. Although black and white education remain grossly unequal, steady progress is being made. In 1990–1991, 3.8 times as much was spent on each white pupil as on each black pupil, whereas a decade ago the disparity was 10 to 1.

The Bureaucratic Complexities

The administrative structure of South Africa's education system has been dubbed a bureaucratic monster for good reason. There are 19 separate departments of education— 5 for white education, 1 each for so-called Coloured and Indian education, 11 for black education (in South Africa proper and each of the 10 "homelands"), and an umbrella department to control the purse strings and set the norms and standards for the other 18.

For years the ANC and other antiapartheid organizations have been demanding that these bureaucratic structures based on ethnic divisions be scrapped. The Anglo American Corporation mining conglomerate has recently joined in the call for a unitary, nonracial education system. The government has agreed in principle that a single nonracial education system is necessary, but it continues to speak in terms of an educational model that allows for classroom composition to "accommodate cultural and language diversity."

In sum, broad consensus seems to have developed on the need to shift to a single education system, but there is not yet agreement on how to get there. In the short term, the government would prefer to continue to address the imbalances within the existing framework, gradually working toward equal provision of education for all students, irrespective of the particular department under which they fall. Instead of scrapping the existing administrative structures immediately, the plan appears to be to begin by bringing the currently divergent "norms and standards" regarding syllabi, exams, and teacher-pupil ratios in line with each other. Professor Johan Muller of the Education Policy Unit at the University of Cape Town summarizes the dilemma: "The government knows it needs one education department, but there are such different norms for everything—both in terms of facilities and variable financing—and the government knows it will have to have one set of norms in order to have one department."

The philosophy of separate education is cemented in the Republic of South Africa Constitution Act of 1983 (which sets forth the culturally segregating concept of "own affairs" and defines education at all levels as an "own affair"). The current position of the government is that the education system can be radically changed only when agreement is reached on a new constitution. But the reasons for the reluctance to undertake drastic restructuring go beyond a lack of funds or the need to await a future constitution. The National Party government is aware that it stands to lose the support of much of its white constituency if white educational standards are perceived to be eroding due to a move to a unified education system.

The Search for a New Model

In February 1991, President de Klerk, Nelson Mandela, and a group of leading educationists met to discuss the black education situation. Although no clear policy goals came out of the meeting, the parties were in general agreement on the extent of the crisis and the need for a new centralized nonracial system. The makeup of this gathering underscored the government's recognition that no new education system will be considered legitimate unless all sides participate in creating it. The noticeable absence of political rhetoric about the subject since the meeting is one indicator that the search for a new education model has begun in earnest.

One of the major challenges now facing policymakers is how to overcome the inefficiency of the diffuse educational bureaucracy. For decades, the 19 education departments have barely communicated. A surplus in one department cannot readily be transferred to another needier department. Although some black departments are experiencing severe shortages of teachers and facilities, white departments have a relatively stable pupil population and spare capacity. Assuming a pupil-to-teacher ratio of 30 to 1, white departments are reported to have a 37 percent surplus of teachers while black departments function at more than a 50 percent deficit. The government estimates that at the beginning of 1991 there were 164,009 empty places in white primary and secondary schools.

Instead of transferring black students to empty white facilities or opening them up to all races, the government has in the past customarily closed down underutilized schools. In 1990, in an effort to address the underutilization problem, a plan was introduced that allows a white school to open enrollment to all races if a voting majority of 72 percent can be achieved in a poll of at least 80 percent of the students' parents. The plan was criticized by liberal-minded whites for requiring an exceedingly high "yes" vote, while right-wing groups protested the policy as a breach of the constitution undertaken without consulting the (white) electorate.

Thus far, approximately 10 percent of white schools have managed to attain the necessary vote to be declared "open." This surprisingly high number has encouraged the de Klerk government to take some significant steps toward opening up the education system further. White teacher training colleges and technikons (tertiary polytechnic institutions providing job-oriented instruction in applied sciences, technology, and related skills) have now been given the power to open their doors to all races, and parliament has passed a Universities Amendment Bill that formally abolishes the racial quota system for university admissions. (In practice, several universities had been ignoring the quota system for years.)

The most important policy shift came in response to an outcry over the closing (on grounds of their underutilization) of 47 white schools with 12,032 places and five white teacher training colleges. The closings were viewed as a colossal waste of resources and as a slap in the face to black education administrators struggling to cope with enormous backlogs of students. In August a dramatic turnabout occurred when the two cabinet-level education ministers announced that underutilized schools would no longer be closed down. Instead, allowances would be made for "the cost-free and expeditious transfer of underutilized schools to other departments." Although the change in government policy was welcomed as a solid step toward redressing the backlogs in black education, the shifting of schools from one racially defined department to another was criticized as a continuation of an "own affairs" approach.

Some Longer-Term Recommendations

After a year of analysis, a government-commissioned working group released its Education Renewal Strategy (ERS) in June 1991. Although the group was created to investigate short- and medium-term managerial solutions to some of the most pressing problems, the ERS discussion document makes several long-term proposals as well. It recommends nonracial regional authorities, equal educational opportunities for all, free as well as compulsory education for all South Africans up to Standard Five (the equivalent of the seventh grade in the United States), and a single new education department for all races that would make "satisfactory allowances for the accommodation of diversity."

Opponents of the ERS plan argue that the education system needs to be reconstructed, not "renewed." Most of the criticism has been directed at the ambiguous nature of the ERS phrase "accommodation of diversity." Opposition groups worry that the ERS plan, rather than promoting a sensible tolerance of different opinions, may be a subtle maneuver to sidestep meaningful change. They note that the government historically has replaced apartheid policies that came under serious pressure with deceptively repackaged but essentially similar programs, justifying the "new" policies by pointing to South Africa's indisputable cultural and lingual diversity.

The ERS has also been criticized for recommending only that education be free and compulsory through Standard Five. The ANC-aligned National Education Coordinating Committee (NECC) charges that this "reform" would replace formal racial divisions with a kind of de facto economic apartheid, because many blacks would be unable to afford a general education beyond Standard Five.

Education as an Economic Priority

A related criticism of current education reform programs is that they are not yet sufficiently attentive to South Africa's economic needs. As Minister of National (overall) Education Louis Pienaar recently phrased it, "we're producing square pegs for round holes." There is agreement that the number of people receiving technical education is far too small to overcome South Africa's worsening skills shortage. Among the consequences of Bantu education's deemphasis of mathematics and physical science is the fact that less than 1 percent of tertiary-level black students go on to obtain a technical or vocational education. Given the likelihood that the annual GNP growth rate will be around 2 percent, the South African Institute of Race Relations estimates that there will be a shortage of approximately 200,000 workers with a degree, diploma, or comparable skills by the year 2000.

As of 1991, for all races combined, there are seven university students for every two technikon students. Some economists believe that the ratio should be closer to one-to-one if South Africa is to overcome its skills shortage. The Education Renewal Strategy suggests placing a far greater emphasis on vocational education in the primary and secondary school curricula, paying higher salaries to math and science teachers, and making it easier for students to transfer between universities and technikons.

Can the "Lost Generation" Be Reclaimed?

Although encouraging students to follow vocational study programs may help South Africa redress its skills shortage in the future, there is an immediate need to develop strategies for saving the country's "lost generation" – the black students who were of school age during the chaos of the post-Soweto uprising era. Since 1980, open universities and several technikons have sought to help educationally disadvantaged students make the transition from secondary to tertiary education.

One such effort undertaken by several universities is the Academic Support Program (ASP), which facilitates the entry of students who have passed the matric examination required for university admission but have various educational gaps. Some ASP students are required to undertake a pre-university year of bridging courses, while others are provided with supplementary courses during their first year. For example, physical science students are given the opportunity to develop laboratory skills, while humanities students focus on critical reading skills, essay writing, and study methods.

Although the program has been successful at improving the first-year pass rate at universities, there has been little change thus far in the number of black students who graduate. When the support ends in the second year, the pass rate begins to decline. Students criticize the high cost of an extra pre-university year in the ASP and the stigma attached to being selected for remedial academic support. Proponents of academic support believe that the program needs to be expanded to the second and third years of university in order to make a real difference in the number of black graduates, but the resources for this expansion do not exist. Until the Department of National Education acknowledges that academic support is essential, these programs will continue to depend solely upon nongovernmental financial sponsorship.

Although clearly a step in the right direction, the academic support programs do not address the question of the large number of students who do not meet the requirements for university entrance but seek to be brought up to the level of "matric." The ERS has suggested the creation of "edukons," quasi-community colleges that would offer bridging courses to universities and technikons for students who have had inferior schooling. (Whereas about 30 out of 1,000 white students go on to attend university, the figure for black students is approximately 3 per 1,000.)

South African educationists praise the U.S. community college system for its vocationally focused curricula and its well-designed transfer programs that enable disadvantaged students to move from community college to university level. At the same time, however, South African educationists harbor fears that universities might use the community colleges as dumping grounds for ill-prepared students rather than investing more in their own academic support programs, thus perpetuating the underrepresentation of blacks at the university level.

The "People's Education" Pioneers

Access to university education has been a hotly debated issue ever since several of the traditionally white universities, defying government policy, began in 1985 to accept significant numbers of black students. This change in admissions policy created a situation in which universities were flooded with applicants meeting the minimum matriculation requirements for university study. To deal with the crunch, the pioneering white universities raised admission requirements as a means of limiting the number of incoming students to a capacity level. Proponents of "people's education"—the slogan that can be seen on T-shirts on the campuses of universities throughout South Africa—acknowledged that there are good educational arguments for limiting the growth of student numbers by raising the admissions requirements, but rejected the timing of the new admissions policy. Although vaguely defined, "people's education" is an attempt to conceptualize education in a post-apartheid era in terms of the goals of the ANC Freedom Charter. In essence, the call is for traditionally white universities to be reformed and for educational opportunities to be redistributed.

"People's education" institutions, such as the formerly "Coloured" University of the Western Cape (UWC), initially undertook after 1985 to accept any student who met the minimum statutory requirements for admission, despite the enormous strains the policy placed upon the university. Between 1986 and 1990, the UWC student population shot up from just 6,700 to 12,400. By 1988, the open-door admissions policy was causing unmanageable overcrowding and severely straining the university's resources. A new admissions policy is designed to limit student intake while ensuring (through consideration of applicants' matriculation scores, gender, population group classification, geographical origin, and social class) that each incoming class is representative of the general population. Rector Jakes Gerwel admits that the system is not perfect, but he believes it represents the one attempt by a South African university to develop an admissions policy that is both socially and ethically defensible.

The traditionally white universities have adopted policies of growth keyed to the limits of the physical, human, and financial resources of each institution. Despite the raising of admission requirements, the student population at the University of Cape Town (UCT) has increased from 12,393 in 1986 to 14,393 in 1991, and black enrollment has grown during the same period from 16.4 percent to 29.3 percent of the student body. Although admission is primarily based on matriculation results, UCT has established an Alternative Admissions Research Program (AARP) to help devise more effective admissions criteria for disadvantaged students. An independent entrance test offered in many city centers to an increasing number of black Standard 10 pupils is one of the innovations developed thus far. Based upon the independent test scores, AARP recommends some black students who would otherwise not be eligible for admission.

Recent official moves to open some white schools and universities to all races have spurred abrasive debate over standards. The UCT administration bristles at the idea of lowering standards, claiming that its traditionally high standards are essential for South Africa to remain a competitive nation in the world economy. Professor Michael Ashley, dean of the Faculty of Education, summarized the UCT view in an interview published in the *Argus* in October 1990: "If white education standards are reasonably satisfactory, then they should be maintained, and as many other people from historically separate sectors as possible should be brought up to those levels."

The University of the Western Cape's stance on the maintenance of standards is somewhat more ambiguous. As its admissions policy illustrates, UWC is accelerating its efforts to become more representative of the population at large. This does not mean, Rector Gerwel makes clear, that standards will be allowed to erode to a point where the university becomes a "glorified community college."

The political debate over precisely what standards are suitable for each level of education centers on the issue of access. Educationists fear that the maintenance of present standards in a future system would mean the continued exclusion of a disproportionate number of blacks from higher education, but that the alternative of diluting standards would ultimately lead to a mass of poorly qualified, alienated graduates and a nation ill-equipped to compete with the rest of the world.

Looking Ahead

An air of tolerance, reconciliation, and debate pervades campuses. Arguments continue between proponents of "people's education" and those favoring a more traditional academic approach, but there is an increasing acceptance that both concepts have a place in a future education system. Among student organizations, historically a good indicator of political trends in South Africa, the current trend is nonconfrontational. At student protest marches, the tear gas, police charges, and unpredictable violence of the 1980s have been replaced by unprecedented peaceful dialogue between student protest leaders and the police.

In 1991, for the first time in history, the ANC-aligned South African National Students Congress (SANSCO) participated in a University of Cape Town student government election. SANSCO leaders said they believed that their participation in the university election reflected "the mood in the country that people should talk about their differences." The decision by SANSCO, the largest university student organization in South Africa, not to boycott the election gave a major boost to the democratic process. Following the student government election, another milestone was passed when SANSCO and the traditionally white-liberal National Union of South African Students (NUSAS) merged to form the nonaligned South African Students Congress (SASCO), with the stated objective of depoliticizing, unifying, and blurring the color lines of student organizations.

A recent survey found that black South Africans view education as the government's most urgent priority, ahead of housing and health care. As previously noted, the government-sponsored Education Renewal Strategy makes several far-reaching recommendations for the creation of a nonracial education system and illustrates an earnest commitment to address the crisis in this critical nation-building sector. It should be noted, however, that the 68 ERS proposals could only be adopted by making changes in the present constitution. Although the government has thus far put off confronting the bloated education bureaucracy, the opening up of an increasing number of schools, teacher training colleges, and technikons to all races demonstrates marked progress toward removing apartheid from education.

In the search for a nationally acceptable and effective system, a culture of learning is being developed to replace the concept of "liberation before education" with "education for liberation." The crisis in black education will not be remedied quickly, but the openness of discussion among the government, the ANC and other black political parties, the private sector, and student organizations gives hope that the bitter fruits of South Africa's learning tree are beginning to sweeten.

8

Why South Africa's Transition Is Unique

Frederik van Zyl Slabbert

February 1992

To understand the complexity of the transition now under way in South Africa requires, first of all, a recognition that our situation has no historical precedent. Because South Africa's white governing establishment is not, and never was, the instrument of any European colonial power, the techniques of ending white minority rule that were available to other African countries beginning in the late 1950s are not applicable. There is no possibility of massive withdrawal of the white population to some kind of motherland or of external intervention by some internationally recognized agent that can impose a Resolution 435 on us or whatever. We sit with the paradox of colonial rule without the option of resolving it according to the historical precedents by which colonial rule was resolved elsewhere on the African continent.

Legacies

Aside from the fact that negotiating a transition from white domination to democratization in circumstances such as ours is a unique phenomenon, the process is further complicated by the fact that the process of negotiation does not occur in a vacuum in South Africa. Each aspect is influenced by a sequence of legacies from various phases of white rule. The legacies of four of these periods warrant citation:

1. From 1910 to 1948, we had what one might call uncomplicated colonial rule in South Africa. I always identify this as the "bwana" period, during which white domination in South Africa—as in other colonial societies—was regarded as fairly unproblematical. The legacy of the period, of course, was that whites generally became accustomed to a kind of colonial life-style privilege based on race and the black majority became increasingly aware and resentful of their relative deprivation.

The colonial legacy is evident when one talks to a far right-wing person in the rural areas. He will immediately link the concept of majority rule to the consequences for whites of colonial withdrawal in the rest of Africa—decline of living standards, loss of control, loss of self-determination. This fear of the consequences of "colonial" transition predominates in the far right despite the clear reality that the changes taking place in South Africa are not comparable to the typical colonial transition elsewhere in Africa. Among the more militant and younger black people there is also some unrealistic fantasizing about what can be expected in a postapartheid South Africa.

2. Two important legacies of the apartheid/separate development period from 1948 to 1979 also impinge on the process of negotiation now under way. One of these is the dream of partition that informs the hopes or motivations of between 35 and 40 percent, if one wants to be fairly conservative, of the white electorate. The other is the enormous bureaucracy (e.g., 14 departments of health or education, 5 departments of foreign affairs, and 5 departments of defense) that evolved.

It will not be easy to transform a civil service structure that was meticulously created over decades to implement a policy of separate development and adapt that structure to the needs of a nonracial democracy. If one looks at the defense and security establishment as part of the civil service, the implications are even more traumatic. The bureaucracy can be a source of continuity in transition, an obstacle to progress, or a combination of both.

3. The period 1979 to 1989 was the period of both reform and a backlash to reform. Two legacies from that decade bedevil current negotiations. One is the inheritance of a fiercely partisan security structure. There is no question that the 1980s saw the politicization of both the police and the defense forces in South Africa. This politicization flowed from the way in which the struggle was perceived both by the regime and its opponents. It was very much viewed as a matter of us versus them, liberation versus domination, revolution versus repression. This polarized the security apparatus.

In the new transition phase of the 1990s, that same security system has to become a source of impartial stability if a climate conducive to the process of negotiation is to be maintained. And this is a very, very real problem, as questions of past or present complicity and involvement of one element or another of the security forces in dubious activities continue to make headlines.

A second legacy from this period is the dilemma posed by controversial co-optive structures that were created in the name of reform, from the tricameral parliament to regional services councils to indirectly elected bodies.

4. A fourth source of significant legacies is the period of revolutionary transition stretching from 1912 until 1989. Although the term "revolutionary transition" was not on the agenda of the founding meeting in 1912 of what subsequently became the African National Congress (ANC), the concept became over time a basic commitment of the ANC as well as other opposition movements. By 1985, we had a highly polarized society.

One aspect of the "revolutionary transition" period with troublesome implications for the current negotiations is the very strong belief among supporters of the ANC and the Pan-Africanist Congress (PAC) that somehow there should and would be a sudden transfer of power—the flag comes down, a new flag goes up, a new regime takes power, and off we go. That view of transition is still very much alive, particularly among more militant and younger people in South Africa. It is a constant source of anxiety and concern for the leaders of the ANC now engaged in negotiations with the government of President F.W. de Klerk because the moment they get (as they inevitably must) into fairly confidential discussions that they cannot convey to the rank and file, they risk being accused of seeking common cause with the government, selling out to the fat cats, whatever you want to call it.

A second legacy is the link that existed through the 1980s between the South African Communist Party (SACP) and the Soviet Union and the way in which this link influenced strategic thinking and organizational structures. This legacy of vanguardism did not die with the Soviet Union; it feeds into a strategy of mass mobilization and mass protests that runs concurrently with the ANC strategy of engaging the government and negotiating.

Key Players in the Negotiations

It is my view that political organizations and movements are going through a process of drastic restructuring marked by splits and new alliances. Therefore, I would not want to put my head on a block that the National Party we see today will be the National Party we will see in a year's time or that the ANC we talk about today will be the ANC of a year hence.

There is a fundamental shifting taking place, which I view as a realignment between those who will risk managing and sharing responsibility for transition and those who will oppose it (or, phrased slightly differently, those who will try to coalesce into some kind of a center to oversee the process of transition and those who oppose it).

In this context, the National Party has undergone a fundamental change in both its composition and philosophy. In a sense, you could say de Klerk sacrificed the traditional constituency of the National Party by the initiatives he took and is now searching for a new constituency. This search includes an active effort to bring blacks, Coloureds, and Indians into the National Party.

In extending the political arena beyond Parliament, the National Party has no choice but to broaden its base and constituency or enter into alliances in order to participate in the management of transition.

The right is a moving feast, by which I mean that there is a great deal of ideological confusion in its ranks and a great deal of uncertainty about what the right hopes to achieve. Broadly speaking, it is possible to distinguish between what one might identify as greedy partitionists and sacrificial partitionists. The greedy partitionists want a large slice of the country (such as the Boer republics, i.e., the Orange Free State and Transvaal) for themselves, while the sacrificial partitionists would settle for areas along the Orange River and, perhaps, Upington.

It is my view that the right will split in Parliament. The split will be between those who believe it is in their interest to work within the Convention for a Democratic South Africa (CODESA), the forum organized in 1991 to negotiate a framework for transition to a democratic government, and those who do not. I doubt it will be a major split away from Conservative Party leader Andries Treurnicht, but some key figures will go, and this will affect the solidarity of the conservative movement.

There is really no new thinking in the current Conservative Party (CP) about how to solve the problems should it get into power. It would be very much the dilemma of the fox terrier that catches the bus and does not know what to do with it once it has done so. Although CP strategists could be right in their view that the party could win an election, it is becoming increasingly evident that there is not going to be one.

As for the ANC, I doubt that its internal alliance will stay intact until CODESA has completed its work. It is not that I think there is necessarily bad faith, but rather that the ANC, as a SACP-COSATU alliance, is increasingly beginning to appeal to different constituencies and focus on different problems.

Key figures within those black movements choosing not to participate in CODESA—the PAC, the Black Consciousness movement, the Azanian People's Organization (AZAPO)—are coming forward with so many contradictory statements that it is very difficult to say who speaks on whose behalf. One thing is clear, however. They are exploiting a particular vein in the South African body politic—the idea of South Africa being for blacks, and that whites can be part of black South Africa if they are prepared to be Africans in a rather romantic sense of the word that is very difficult to understand. It is a fertile area of discontent to explore, one that cannot be ignored.

Another set of players that, surprisingly, have come to the fore are the homeland governments. Prior to de Klerk's historic speech before Parliament on February 2, 1990, unbanning key black political organizations and calling for negotiations with black leaders, homeland governments were conventionally regarded as entirely dispensable—dismissed by the ANC as being stooges and sellouts and by the government as a marginal constitutional issue. All of a sudden, they turn up at the CODESA talks and demand in strong terms their places at the table. I don't think either the government or the ANC can claim complete loyalty from the homeland governments. There is a shift taking place and one should not underestimate the long-run importance of pensions and patronage.

Homeland governments are significant for another reason. At this stage in the transition, they represent pockets of bureaucratic expertise in maintaining stability, particularly in the rural areas. The ANC, on the other hand, has as yet nothing approaching a civil service in waiting that can simply walk in and take over.

Finally, a special word about Inkatha, which has been squeezed between the regime and its opponents. President P.W. Botha did not like Inkatha leader Chief Mangosuthu Buthelezi and did not consult him. The ANC too increasingly disliked him. Although this alienation from both the government and the ANC created problems of survival, Buthelezi has managed very skillfully to keep himself politically relevant in the current situation. It would be shortsighted to dismiss the role that he can play. The fact remains, however, that Inkatha as a movement or an organization is so personally bound to Buthelezi that it is difficult to predict what would happen to Inkatha if he were no longer there. In this connection, an interesting move on his part with regard to CODESA was his insistence on the presence of the Zulu king and his subsequent explanation that Inkatha is a nonracial, national movement whereas the king reflects the cultural interests of the Zulus. Given the fact that neither the ANC nor any other player took issue with Buthelezi on this point (indeed, Mandela acknowledged the importance of incorporating traditional leadership), one can see down the track the prospect that ethnicity and nationalism may come into the process of negotiation.

Options Available until 1994

Under the terms of the current constitution, there has to be an election in 1994. De Klerk said in the last election in 1989 that blacks would not be excluded from the vote in the next one. That would seem to mean that either a new democratic constitution will have to be in place by 1994 or something else has to happen.

There is nothing happening now that suggests to me that a new constitution is remotely possible in the next two years. So what is the "something else" that can happen before 1994 that would enable the government and its opponents in CODESA to get around this particular constitutional constraint? I use the term "constitutional constraint" quite deliberately to introduce a sense of urgency, for there is a limit to the amount of time that CODESA-style talking can be sustained.

It is my view that there are four options available that can be considered by a combination of various interest groups (the National Party, the ANC, the PAC, Inkatha, sections of the government sympathetic to the right wing) to maintain transitional stability en route to 1994. These are a high-cost clampdown, a low-cost clampdown, and two variants of a government of transitional unity (GOTU). (Here the term "cost" refers to the degree of international isolation and domestic polarization that the exercise of a given option would bring upon South Africa.)

A High-Cost Clampdown

The right, on its own, cannot effect a clampdown. It can attempt it, but not maintain it. The fox-terrier-and-bus dilemma of the right is that a clampdown has to be administered—and how do you administer it if more than 50 percent of the people in the civil service are black?

What kind of circumstances might lead to such an outcome? One scenario might be a failure of CODESA-style negotiations to bring forth a broadly acceptable agreement as the ANC remains hesitant about doing a deal with de Klerk and others, against a background of escalating crime and political violence as well as increasing concern in the international community about the inability of the government and its opponents to manage the transition. People in the security forces begin to advocate stopping the negotiations because of a perceived threat of governmental and economic collapse. They eventually act upon these concerns by implementing a clampdown in the name of preserving whites and other minorities from a bloodbath. The prominent role of the right wing makes this a "high-cost" outcome.

I would say that the sequence of events described in the preceding paragraph is not impossible, but it is highly improbable before 1994 or perhaps even afterward (although one should not underestimate the current concern and anxiety in security and right-wing circles).

A Low-Cost Clampdown

A low-cost clampdown cannot be ruled out. Consider the following scenario. De Klerk and the ANC leadership increasingly agree about how to manage transition, but elements of the ANC go out of CODESA saying this is a sellout and too much of a cozy club. These disaffected elements join up with outside forces and establish a new common front. In the meantime, the government goes ahead with its reforms. There are black judges and a visible deracialization of the civil service. More and more elements (including the homeland governments) are included in CODESA-associated working committees. Programs of social reconstruction and development get under way. But the country remains polarized, with the right continuing militancy in the form of violent destabilization and a new left-wing common front outside the CODESA process appealing increasingly for a more radical transfer of power.

As 1994 approaches, the government and the ANC negotiators look at the situation and agree, together with the security forces, to clamp down temporarily in order to save South Africa in the name of democracy and give the economy a chance to recover. Under these circumstances, a great deal of energy would go into a propaganda initiative aimed at explaining to the international community why this step, though unfortunate, was necessary and unavoidable.

The foregoing outcome is improbable by 1994, but it can't be dismissed altogether if we fail to get some degree of economic recovery.

A High-Cost GOTU

This would be a government of transitional unity that does not feel confident enough to test popular support by referendum. Declaring itself an interim government, it makes use of existing constitutional machinery to get around the provision in the constitution requiring an election, either through the President's Council or by getting the required votes in Parliament. For this to take place would require a significant split in the right, as well as majority support in the (Indian) House of Delegates or the (Coloured) House of Representatives.

Although not impossible, this option is improbable, because it would heighten accusations that the ANC (or whatever black organizations choose to participate) has sold out to tricameralism and the current constitution.

A GOTU That Has Popular Support

This, in my view, is what CODESA is all about. The ANC talks about an election for a constituent assembly. De Klerk talks about a referendum giving a mandate to change the constitution that would make an interim parliament possible. I can see a compromise developing here. By the middle of 1993, assuming progress in CODESA, there could be an agreement to go for a government of transitional unity and to legitimize it through a national referendum. This national referendum would ask for a mandate to stop the violence, to get the economy going, to help with the improvement of the quality of life, and to negotiate a democratic constitution. It would be very difficult to vote no under those circumstances. In fact, I am confident that the government and CODESA would get such a mandate.

The new GOTU now has to deliver the goods. This means creating appropriate interim structures to administer programs of social reconstruction in the areas of health, housing, education, and so forth. And meeting this challenge is directly linked to the performance of the economy.

In Sum

I do not see any possibility of an imminent collapse in South Africa. A fully consolidated, stable democracy within the next two to three or four years is unlikely, but I do see some form of government of transitional unity that can maintain a workable stability. The mandate for such a government of transitional unity will be in the area of coping with violence, stimulating economic growth, helping with the improvement of the quality of life, and going for a democratic constitution.

These may sound like rather platitudinous goals. In the South African context, however, they are very important. If consensus can be reached on the basics of growth and development, it means that agreement will have been reached once and for all on the kind of economic system that will prevail. I see increasingly clear signs of a convergence in this area.

Assuming consensus on these basic points, the major challenge that would face a government of transitional unity over the next three to four years would be how to integrate the politics of negotiation with the politics of administration in a transitional phase.

This is the dilemma that faces the ANC. If it stands aside and allows the regime to administer the transition, all the credit will go to de Klerk. If it becomes an integral part of the transition process, it becomes vulnerable to outbidding from opponents who stay out.

As of now, the PAC takes the position that "whitey" created the mess; "whitey" must fix it up; then we will come in. The ANC realizes that it can't afford to hold back, because if it stays out and the government begins to negotiate with others and manages to administer the transition, then the ANC will become, in effect, redundant to the process.

Administering the transition means, effectively, having access to the civil service, having access to the budget, not only sitting in departments but influencing policy in those departments. Last year, the ANC complained (justifiably) that the budget reflected a lack of democratic involvement. The only way to have "democratic involvement" is to have access to the treasury, to have access to finance, to have access to where the budget is formed.

This assessment leaves us with four imponderables. The first is an unresolved security situation in the sense that the defense force and the police force are still controversial as far as maintaining stability is concerned. This situation has to be resolved. A UN monitoring force similar to the one that was present at Namibia's transition to independence is not an option for South Africa.

A second imponderable is how to get transitional legitimacy. I have suggested a referendum, but holding a referendum has certain implications. It must reflect a fair degree of confidence on the part of those participating in CODESA that they can risk a referendum. Whether separate elections are held for whites or not is really immaterial. There is a need to find out if a majority of whites are going to support a transitional arrangement in order to know whether it is going to work. It is a power shift that has to take place; it is not a morality play. And it is a very serious matter.

A third imponderable is the question of when and to what extent the economy may improve. A fourth imponderable, also in the economic area, is the unrealistic assumption that democracy means development. If the economic forum now being discussed comes off and all parties sit down and talk seriously about this issue, some kind of economic contract could be hammered out within which the problems and options of socioeconomic development can be seriously addressed. There is a tension between the equity and participation demanded by the ANC and the government's insistence on growth and stability.

I am not saying that these priorities are totally irreconcilable. But if somebody figures out a way to have all four at the same time, well, then, we have discovered a way of walking upstairs and downstairs at the same time – and we certainly haven't.

9

The March 1992 Referendum

Marina Ottaway

April 1992

The referendum of March 17, 1992, in which 68.7 percent of the more than 2.3 million white voters casting ballots endorsed the negotiations taking place between the South African government, the African National Congress (ANC), and 17 other organizations, provided a clear sign that the process of change that started more than two years ago is finally irreversible. The single question on the ballot: "Do you support continuation of the reform process which the State President began on February 2, 1990, and which is aimed at a new constitution through negotiations?"

The first milestone was passed on February 2, 1990, when President F.W. de Klerk dramatically accelerated the dismantling of apartheid by announcing the unbanning of all opposition groups, including the ANC. Nine days later, Nelson Mandela walked out of prison after more than 27 years of incarceration. Since then, the government, the ANC, and a broad array of other political and quasi-political organizations have established the Convention for a Democratic South Africa (CODESA), a forum in which the adoption of a democratic, nonracial constitution and the process leading to elections are being negotiated. The

March referendum represented an important second milestone on the path to that objective.

A Crisis of Confidence

The decision to hold a referendum was reached by de Klerk
and his small inner circle of advisers immediately after the
defeat suffered by his governing National Party (NP) in a
by-election in Potchefstroom, in the western Transvaal, on
February 19. With an 11.2 percent swing from the NP to
the Conservative Party (CP), the Potchefstroom results
were much worse than the government had anticipated.
This by-election was one of a series that had recently shown
an unmistakable loss of support for the National Party.
Confronted with the CP claim that he no longer had white
support and must call for a new parliamentary election, de
Klerk believed that he had to go back to the white voters
to obtain a mandate enabling him to continue negotiating
with the ANC from a position of strength.

The conservatives' accusations that de Klerk had
never received an explicit mandate to negotiate with the
ANC were correct. The 1989 election, which returned the
National Party to power with only 48 percent of the popular vote (and with 31 percent going to the Conservative
Party) was run on an ambiguous platform. During the referendum campaign, CP leaders were able to score points
quoting 1989 speeches in which de Klerk had called the
ANC a terrorist organization and had promised to protect
group rights.

Negotiations for a new South Africa had come about
not in response to a swing in popular opinion but as the
result of a decision taken by a small number of individuals
in the government and the ANC. The respective constituencies of the two organizations were not involved. Within the
ANC, discontent over the leadership's tendency to make
major decisions without consulting or even informing the
rank and file manifested itself early; the issue was debated,

and at least partially solved, at the ANC consultative con- ference of December 1990 and at the organization's July 1991 congress. Although tensions persisted, the ANC lead- ers had become aware of the limits of their autonomy and of the necessity to consult with the organization's members in order to maintain their support.

The National Party, on the other hand, did not give priority to instituting a broader process of consultation within its ranks. In 1992 as in 1990, de Klerk has appeared to make decisions after discussing issues with an extraor- dinarily small proportion of individuals even within the party's leadership, and not at all with the constituency. In 1990, he did not even inform the party caucus in advance of his announcement of the unbanning of the ANC in his opening-of-parliament speech. In 1992, he was still playing his cards close to his chest. The NP members of parliament only learned about their party's new proposal for a transi- tional government from a public de Klerk speech. Even the party congresses, held every year in each of the country's four provinces, were not utilized to consult with the con- stituents and debate issues, but simply to announce new policies to be accepted by acclamation.

In the past, this top-down style of rule had not created problems. For over three decades, the National Party main- tained the allegiance of its white constituency by deliver- ing protection and benefits, not by consultation. Its ability to "deliver" was seriously eroded during the 1980s, how- ever, and even more so after the CODESA negotiations be- gan. By the late 1980s, a stagnating economy and the need to devote more money to upgrading services in the town- ships in the hope of winning over some hearts and minds forced the government to curtail spending on whites.

In 1991, attempting to get negotiations under way and sanctions lifted, de Klerk orchestrated the repeal of most major pieces of apartheid legislation, including the Group Areas Act and the Population Registration Act. Although the latter remained in effect for all practical purposes, the writing was on the wall. It was only a matter of time before it would be impossible for whites to isolate themselves from the black majority surrounding them by seeking refuge in their own residential areas, their own schools, hospitals, and public amenities. The government's promises that job security and community rights (the word "group" was struck from the NP vocabulary) would be protected sounded increasingly hollow in the face of the reforms being enacted.

The National Party was slow in taking note of the increasing white discontent and anxiety. Although all by-elections held since 1990 indicated a serious slippage in the level of support for the NP, the leadership dismissed each such result due to special circumstances affecting that particular constituency. After a November 1991 by-election in Virginia (in the Orange Free State) showed a 15 percent swing in favor of the Conservative Party, de Klerk and his colleagues claimed that the vote did not indicate rejection of the reform process, but was simply a reaction to the uncertainty prevailing in a town badly hit by economic recession. Potchefstroom, they argued, was a more typical town and would provide a better barometer of public confidence in de Klerk. When the Potchefstroom results proved almost as poor as Virginia's, de Klerk decided he had little choice but to call the referendum.

How the Economy Fueled Frustration

Although the National Party made serious mistakes in the handling of its constituents during the first two years of the negotiating process, it is not certain that a different set of tactics could have prevented loss of support. Movement toward universal suffrage in South Africa represented a complete reversal of National Party policy and thus was bound to create uncertainty and opposition among whites, especially during a period of economic recession.

Due in part to the effect of sanctions, the South African economy was stagnant through most of the 1980s, and the situation worsened in the early 1990s. Coupled with rapid population growth, this created a crisis. The lifting of sanctions after 1990 did not bring immediate relief, because the political situation remained too uncertain and the economy too depressed to attract substantial foreign investment. Along with blacks, increasing numbers of whites were losing their jobs. The problem of white poverty, which the National Party had solved by creating employment in the civil service and parastatal organizations, was reappearing. The repeal of many apartheid laws also meant that whites would be left to compete for jobs with blacks at a time when the total supply of available positions was shrinking rapidly.

The economic crisis was compounded in 1992 by a severe drought affecting much of southern Africa. Coming on top of a decrease in the level of agricultural subsidies in previous years, the drought threatened to put hundreds of highly indebted farmers out of business. An additional concern was that the abrogation of the Land Acts of 1913 and 1936 opened up the possibility that holdings of defaulting white farmers would be used to resettle blacks. Farmers in the Transvaal and the Orange Free State, traditionally the most conservative segment of the country and also the hardest hit by drought, became increasingly fearful and resentful. It is not surprising that these areas returned the smallest percentage of referendum "yes" votes in all of South Africa, with the majority in the northern Transvaal voting against negotiations.

Among blacks, the unemployment rate was estimated at almost 50 percent of the labor force by 1991. Informal-sector trading and crime were becoming major means of survival for the unemployed. The once-white business districts of many cities, Johannesburg in particular, became beehives of informal activities, changing their character and creating resentment among whites. The crime rate in the suburbs soared, with residents feeling increasingly under siege behind high walls.

The escalating political violence in the townships also

contributed to the growing climate of insecurity, increasing the conviction that the changes favored by de Klerk, notably the easing of police controls and repression, were simply leading to chaos. White conservatives in particular saw the release of Nelson Mandela as the factor triggering an increase in crime and political violence. To them, reform was not a solution to old problems, but the beginning of new ones.

In sum, white discontent had much deeper causes than the perceived arrogance of the National Party leadership. An entire way of life was threatened by the reforms and, until confronted by the referendum, many whites appeared to think that the problems could be solved by turning the clock back.

The Referendum Campaign

Under the existing circumstances of apparently decreasing support, economic recession, drought, and fear of crime and violence, de Klerk's decision to call for a referendum was a gamble. This was not uncharacteristic. Since he succeeded P.W. Botha as head of state in 1989, de Klerk has shown that he is willing to take risks. Moreover, he had two pressing reasons to consult the electorate at this particular time: First, there were clear signals of the need to strengthen his mandate. It was not only the Conservative Party that questioned whether de Klerk still represented a majority of whites. The ANC leadership too was worried about de Klerk's weakening position, wondering whether in the end the president would be able to deliver his constituency if an agreement was reached in the CODESA negotiations. Second, the National Party had a made a commitment in its 1989 electoral platform to submit a new constitution to the white voters for approval. At the opening of Parliament in January 1992, party officials had renewed the pledge. This reaffirmation was met by a chorus of complaints from black organizations across the board that such a consultation amounted to granting whites a veto over the reform process.

By calling for the referendum in March, de Klerk could claim to have fulfilled his pledge to the white voters, while avoiding submitting the constitution to their approval. The early referendum was risky, but probably not as risky as asking white voters to approve a document that revealed how much power they were surrendering in the new South Africa. The National Party made it clear that, if the voters gave de Klerk a mandate to continue negotiating on the basis of the constitutional proposals already announced, a second referendum on the new constitution itself would be redundant. The early consultation was also more acceptable to black organizations, which only expressed perfunctory disapproval without making any serious attempt to stop the process.

In the referendum campaign, the National Party had all the advantages. Television and (in many parts of the country) radio are government-controlled. The business community raised money, and most newspapers helped by giving discount rates to the "yes" advertisements. The left-of-center Democratic Party also supported the NP position on the referendum. The Conservative Party, with no comparable funds and no access to discounts, was effectively locked out of the mass media, relying on posters to get its message across.

Both sides appealed more to emotion than to reason, offering few details about their plans but predicting doomsday if their opponents won. The National Party warned of a return to the failed apartheid system, renewed sanctions, renewed exclusion from international sports, deepening economic crisis, and the anger of the country's black majority if the "no" vote prevailed. Democratic Party leader Zacharias de Beer went so far as to conjure up the specter of foreign warships blockading the Cape. The Conservative Party painted catastrophic images of the fate of South Africa under "a black Communist government" led by Nelson Mandela, a man, it said, whose friends included Fidel

Castro, Mu'ammar al-Qadhafi, and Yasir Arafat. The CP also argued that a "yes" vote was a blank check for de Klerk, who had already shown he was a traitor to his own people.

On the concrete issues, both sides were vague. The National Party stressed above all continuation of the negotiating process, leading to a constitution based on power-sharing without domination. The outlines of such a constitution were contained in a document published by the National Party in September 1991. It is highly doubtful that many voters had a clear idea of what the party was proposing or how much it would have to compromise in order to reach an agreement with the ANC. The Conservative Party, for its part, tried to convince voters that it did not favor a return to the apartheid system but instead advocated the right to self-determination for all ethnic groups. The disintegration of the Soviet Union and Yugoslavia was cited as proof that a multiethnic state could not work. The principle of negotiating the future of South Africa with other groups was not rejected, but any participation in the "Communist-dominated" CODESA was specifically excluded. Acceptable negotiating partners would include all organizations supporting self-determination for their ethnic group within a commonwealth of nations, politically independent but economically interdependent and cooperating on foreign policy, defense, trade, and communications. The CP was vague about the boundaries of these independent nations, however, particularly when it came to the question of how there could be an Afrikaner or white state when blacks made up the majority of the population throughout the country.

The Referendum Scorecard

De Klerk's gamble paid off. The referendum settled many issues at a relatively small cost. The process of change became truly irreversible, not because an agreement was reached, but because the overwhelming majority of whites showed that, though they might be fearful of the future, they were not willing to make a last stand in defense of the past. The question about de Klerk's mandate was also put to rest.

The referendum did entail some costs. The third of the white electorate that voted against the change is bitter and more mobilized than before the campaign. Although whites willing to turn to violence are probably a small minority of the "no" voters, they might feel compelled to act soon to show that they are not a spent force. Right-wing violence in the past has been fairly minor – a few bombs placed at NP offices, post offices, and schools that admitted black pupils, but timed to explode at night when nobody was around. This could now change. An organization resorting to terrorism can do much damage with a small number of participants. The right-wing threat still exists.

Although the referendum created some polarization, it did not divide the society sharply along either geographic or English-Afrikaans linguistic lines. Only one of the 15 referendum districts – Pietersburg in the extreme north of the country – returned a majority of "no" votes, and then only one of 57 percent. Heavily English-speaking areas returned the largest "yes" majorities – about 85 percent in both Durban and Cape Town – but the overall results showed that a majority of Afrikaners also voted for reform. Extreme polarization was by and large avoided.

Where the Negotiations Stand

The decisive victory for the National Party signaled that the CODESA process, suspended for all practical purposes during the campaign, would start again. The second plenary meeting of CODESA was postponed until mid-April, but the working groups resumed functioning immediately. Even more important, private meetings between the government and the ANC continued throughout the period before the referendum.

Although the two parties remained far apart in their

constitutional proposals, they had narrowed the gap on issues of process, and, above all, the formation of an interim or transitional government. In an especially promising development, government and ANC leaders appeared to have agreed by early March to move toward a transitional government fairly quickly, postponing the discussion of the most difficult and controversial issues until later.

When CODESA first convened, the ANC viewed it as a short-lived forum that would reach agreement on basic constitutional principles, form an interim government of national reconciliation, and then cease to exist. With the constitution suspended and Parliament disbanded, the interim government would then both administer the country and organize elections for a unicameral constituent assembly elected on the basis of universal suffrage and proportional representation. This script was unacceptable to the government, since a unicameral constituent assembly would probably be dominated by the ANC, and an interim government (unchecked by a constitution or legislature) could only rule by decree.

The government's plan called instead for the existing administration and Parliament to remain in place until CODESA reached agreement on a new constitution, the white voters had approved it in a referendum, and the constitution had been enacted by Parliament. Elections would then be held, and only at that point would a transfer of power take place. The ANC objected on the grounds that negotiating the constitution at CODESA meant giving disproportionate power to small parties represented at the negotiating table but unlikely to win any seat in an election, and the plan would allow the National Party to govern alone until the lengthy process was completed, which could be many months if not years down the road.

In an attempt to make its plan more acceptable, the government conceded in January 1992 that CODESA would not negotiate a permanent constitution, but only a transitional one, based on the power-sharing model outlined in September 1991. This included a bicameral legislature, with one chamber giving equal representation to all regions and also to the three largest parties within each region; an all-party cabinet that would reach decisions by consensus; and a three-man rotating presidency. This transitional charter would be submitted to a white referendum and then ratified by Parliament. If whites did not approve the constitution, CODESA would have to reopen negotiations. Elections for a new transitional legislature would then be held and a transitional government formed.

This new formula was, in essence, the old plan, except that everything was now transitional. It was also clear that the government hoped the transitional government would become permanent: the transitional constitution could be amended by the new parliament, but did not have to be if it proved satisfactory. Because the completion of CODESA negotiations, approval by Parliament, a referendum, and elections would involve a long span of time before a transitional government could be in place, the ANC was pressing for an interim government appointed by CODESA to be functional by June 1992 and elections for a constituent assembly to be held before the end of the year.

In the weeks following the January 1992 impasse, both the ANC and the National Party started modifying their positions. The NP came to recognize that some form of interim government was needed well before the time one could be formed under the complicated January scenario. For its part, the ANC set forth a detailed new proposal that took into account most of the government's objections. Dropping the idea that CODESA should nominate an interim government to replace existing institutions, it proposed instead that an "interim government council" be formed to supervise these institutions. The tricameral Parliament, the National Party cabinet, and the governments of independent homelands would continue to function, but under the supervision of the new council. In particular, multiparty committees would oversee the security forces, foreign relations, the budget, and local governments. The council would also form two independent commissions, one to supervise elections and one to supervise the media, ensuring equal access to all parties during the election campaigns. Elections for a constituent assembly would be held within six months of the formation of the interim government council. The constituent assembly would legislate as well as enact a constitution by a two-thirds majority within a period of nine months. The government expressed reservations about the plan, but declared it a step forward.

By early March, before the referendum campaign froze the negotiating process, the government and the ANC appeared to be close to an agreement in principle that an interim government of national reconciliation should be set up as soon as possible after Parliament had approved the necessary legislation. This would open the way for an elected constituent assembly that would also act as a legislature in the interim. The discussion of controversial issues would thus be postponed until the constituent assembly was elected. The two sides were clearly negotiating in earnest, each responding to the other's objections and slowly narrowing the gap. If the two parties were still far apart in their vision of a final political system for South Africa, they were reaching an agreement on intermediate steps.

Key Post-Referendum Issues

As negotiations resume after the referendum, the question is whether incremental progress is still feasible or whether changes set in motion during the campaign will force the parties at CODESA to discuss some of the most difficult and controversial issues immediately – in particular the future of the ANC's military wing, Umkhonto we Sizwe (MK), and the reincorporation of the homelands. The homelands issue is tied to what may emerge as the most difficult question of all – that of ethnic representation in the new political system. If these questions are forced on the

CODESA agenda immediately, progress toward an interim government may slow.

Integration of the South African Defense Force (SADF) and the MK is laden with symbolic as well as practical problems. The ANC holds that the MK cannot simply be disbanded, but must be integrated into the SADF in the same way that liberation armies were integrated into the defense forces of Zimbabwe and Namibia. The government, on the other hand, takes the position that the MK is an illegal organization, a private army that has no place in a democratic political system, and thus must be disbanded.

The issue is extremely touchy for both the government and the ANC. It involves the relationship between de Klerk and the generals of the SADF on the one side, and between the ANC and its more militant supporters on the other, making it difficult for either group to back down.

For de Klerk, the security forces are a delicate issue within the existing government. The "securocrats" played a key role under his predecessor, P.W. Botha, but de Klerk has no close links to the military. Minister of Defense Magnus Malan, a carryover from P.W. Botha's time, would not even consider the integration of the MK into the SADF. Roelf Meyer, who replaced Malan as defense minister in July 1991, has long been solidly entrenched in the reformist camp and probably is not as opposed to the integration of the MK, but he has little control over the military. During the referendum campaign, speculation was rife that a military coup engineered by conservative generals could occur, particularly if the vote showed strong white sentiment against the reform. Whether or not such a danger was ever real, the overwhelming white support for reform has made military intervention extremely unlikely.

The ANC cannot easily give in to government pressure on the Umkhonto issue. The problem is not Umkhonto itself, which is generally regarded as an ineffectual organization, but rather the impact its formal disbanding would have on ANC supporters, particularly the youth for whom the symbolism of the armed struggle remains important.

The decision to suspend the armed struggle in August 1990 created discontent within parts of the ANC, and disbanding the MK without obtaining its integration in the SADF would involve new risks.

In sum, although the SADF-MK issue was not created by the referendum, its handling could be a serious obstacle to an early CODESA agreement. The problem is not unsolvable, but it complicates the next phase of the negotiation process, requiring a more comprehensive, and thus more difficult, agreement.

The second issue that may have been made more difficult by its salience in the referendum campaign involves the related questions of the future of the homelands and of ethnic representation in the future political system. Both aspects of this issue seemed to have been marginalized until some homeland leaders brought them up at CODESA and the Conservative Party raised them again during the referendum campaign.

After February 1990, the government conceded that the homelands, including the independent ones, would have to be reincorporated into South Africa. By the time it published its constitutional proposal in September 1991, the National Party had also given up on ethnic-group representation in the political system, relying instead on decentralization and on power-sharing among political parties to prevent the consolidation of a monolithic black majority.

During the first meeting of CODESA in December 1991, Chief Minister Mangosuthu Buthelezi of KwaZulu and President Lucas Mangope of Bophuthatswana demanded representation for the Zulu and Tswana nations. Buthelezi, whose Inkatha Freedom Party (IFP) is participating in CODESA, refused to take part personally in protest over the fact that the Zulu king and the administration of KwaZulu were denied participation. The rules of CODESA stated that only political parties and governments of *independent* homelands could attend. Buthelezi argued that this left the Zulus out of the process because

the IFP was a multiethnic organization and that an agreement reached without the participation of the Zulus would
be unenforceable. For his part, Mangope claimed that Bophuthatswana's reincorporation into South Africa would
leave the Tswana nation unrepresented. Ciskei, too, was
raising difficulties concerning reincorporation. By this
time, the National Party's position had moved so far away
from group representation that it found itself siding with
the ANC against the nationalist homeland leaders.

Buthelezi's and Mangope's claim that their nations
must be represented in politics was echoed during the
referendum campaign by the Conservative Party and all
right-wing white organizations. They demanded self-
determination for whites and all ethnic groups, proposing,
as previously noted, a commonwealth of independent
states as the solution that would guarantee peace in South
Africa. Andries Treurnicht, leader of the Conservative
Party, claimed to have the support of Buthelezi, Mangope,
Brigadier General Joshua Gqozo of Ciskei, and other homeland leaders, hinting that negotiations with them on self-
determination could provide an alternative to CODESA.
Buthelezi, however, denied that such an alliance existed or
that Inkatha might withdraw from CODESA.

The difference between Buthelezi and Treurnicht did
not involve ethnic representation, but rather participation
in CODESA versus the establishment of an alternative forum. The defeat of the Conservative Party in the referendum campaign ruled out the possibility of a new forum
replacing CODESA. It did not, however, eliminate the issue of ethnic representation from the negotiations. Indeed,
the issue may become even more important, particularly if
the Conservative Party faces up to the implications of the
defeat and decides to join CODESA, as part of its leadership now favors. The presence of the Conservative Party
at CODESA could create a bloc of organizations committed to ethnic representation. They would be a minority, but
a bloc of four or five organizations would be problematic

for a process working on the basis of sufficient consensus, forcing discussion of an extremely controversial issue in an early phase of the negotiation process.

In Sum

The March referendum has ensured that negotiations will continue in South Africa, but it has not necessarily made the process easier. De Klerk could become overconfident and harden his position because of the large support he has received. Whatever progress has been made so far is based on a willingness to tackle issues one at a time, rather than aiming for an overall agreement on all issues. Given the complexity of the problems involved in dismantling the apartheid system, this appears a promising approach. The risk now is that the issues injected into the referendum campaign by both the government and the Conservative Party, and into CODESA by some homeland leaders, could slow down the process by overloading it in the early stages.

10

Is Democracy Achievable in Russia and/or South Africa?

Patti Waldmeir

August 1992

Of all the many nations struggling to cast off the burden of an authoritarian past, few face rougher paths to democracy than Russia and South Africa. Neither has the cultural habits, traditions, or history that would predispose it to democracy, and the societies of both countries have been deeply damaged by aberrational experiments in social engineering (communism and apartheid).

Yet both have now set off on the quest for a future in which government rules by consent and not coercion and freedoms are guaranteed by law. Leaders of both nations— whether President Boris Yeltsin in Russia or President F.W. de Klerk and Nelson Mandela in South Africa—profess a commitment to democracy that is absolute (at least at the rhetorical level). The next few years of political transition will sorely test this commitment.

Neither Russia nor South Africa is likely to follow a direct path to a liberal democratic ideal. As Samuel P. Huntington, a leading U.S. democracy theorist, observes in his recent book, *The Third Wave: Democratization in the Late Twentieth Century* (University of Oklahoma Press, 1991): "Historically the first efforts to establish democracy in countries frequently fail; second efforts often succeed." Russia and South Africa may need more than two chances to reach the democratic goal – if indeed they ever do. Both face problems of ethnicity and economic hardship that pose formidable obstacles to democratization. South Africa shoulders an added burden that could prove too much for a fledgling democracy to bear: the problem of gross economic inequalities determined by race. As Huntington phrases it: "Democracy is difficult in a situation of concentrated inequalities in which a large, impoverished majority confronts a small, wealthy oligarchy." This is especially true if that oligarchy is racially defined.

But a return to either totalitarian communism (that most extreme form of authoritarianism) or to apartheid is out of the question. Both ideologies have been permanently discredited. The search is on for a (more or less) democratic form of government that can hold anarchy at bay while protecting at least a decent minimum of civil liberties.

In the near term, both countries could end up concluding that the state cannot be reformed under conditions of democratic freedom, which are perceived in some quarters as fostering chaos, crime, and violence. In both countries, many already yearn for a "strong man" to restore order. Less than a year after the August 1991 "revolution" that brought Yeltsin and his reformist colleagues to power, observers say Russians are gripped by "post-totalitarian depression." In South Africa as well, there is clear evidence among both blacks and whites of what political scientists call "authoritarian nostalgia." It is perhaps not surprising that, in Huntington's words, "memories of repression [fade] and [are] in some measure replaced by images of order, prosperity, and economic growth during the authoritarian period."

As Alexis de Tocqueville pointed out in the early nineteenth century, "it cannot be doubted that the moment at which political rights are granted to a people that had before been without them is a critical one." Russia and South Africa are living that dangerous moment now; whether they will survive it as democracies is impossible to predict.

But they are struggling on, and there are lessons to be learned from the struggle–especially for South Africa, which, isolated at the tip of a distant continent, tends to view its problem as historically unique. For years the African National Congress (ANC), which was closely allied to the South African Communist Party, looked to the Soviet Union as a political model for a future South Africa; ANC leaders would do well to look for pointers now from the USSR's most powerful successor state, Russia.

Any comparison of prospects for democratization in Russia and South Africa must address four critical components:

• South Africa's postapartheid government will inherit at least one crucial element that Russian democrats are struggling to create against desperate odds: a functioning market economy.

• While Russians battle to establish political parties, independent courts, and the other institutions of parliamentary democracy, South Africans can draw on a long parliamentary tradition, which, though it has largely been limited to whites, can provide models for the future.

• The vibrant "civil society" so utterly lacking in Russia–the community associations, church groups, trade unions, and business organizations that are the fabric of democratic society–exists in both black and white South Africa to varying degrees.

• The South Africa bureaucracy, bloated and inefficient as it is, provides a functioning state apparatus, which Russia does not have. Pretoria may have lost control over black local government and black education, but the crisis of administrative and executive power is far more pervasive in Russia.

The Economic Scorecard

The South African economy, like that of Russia, has suffered the effects of excessive state intervention over 44 years of National Party rule. The party (and its governments) pursued a kind of "Afrikaner socialism," using state capital to set up nationalized industries dominated by Afrikaners and packing the bureaucracy with members of the "white tribe of Africa." But the extent of state control over economic production never approached Russian levels. A vigorous private sector was active throughout, and a large property-owning white middle class (both English-speaking and Afrikaner) had evolved by the 1980s. Since then, a fledgling black property-owning class has also begun to develop. In recent years, government has privatized and deregulated a number of industries, leaving an economy that is still constrained but no longer stifled by the state.

The ANC also professes its commitment to "the market," but with the crucial caveat that, if the market does not deliver "economic empowerment" to blacks, it will be made to do so by the state. ANC leaders are now restraining their earlier rhetoric on the issue of nationalization, but their instincts remain overwhelmingly statist. They make the point that they seek political power in order to improve the standard of living of the disenfranchised. That priority could still entice them into the eventual use of "commandist" methods.

Before ANC leaders decide to tamper with the market, however, they should first consider the ways in which a mixed economy could underpin the democratic system that they profess to be their goal. A vigorous private sector can function as an important "check and balance" on the power of governmental authority. Moreover, only a market economy can provide the prosperity that, in the long run, will bolster democracy from below. As de Tocqueville observed: "General prosperity is favorable to the stability of all governments, but more particularly of a democratic one, which depends upon the will of the majority, and especially upon the will of that portion of the community which is most exposed to want. . . . When the people rule, they must be rendered happy or they will overturn the state."

Admittedly, the structure of the South African economy needs adjustment to correct its flaws of low growth, low productivity, high unemployment, and inflation. As Frederik van Zyl Slabbert (a South African political scientist, former member of Parliament, and founder of the influential Institute for a Democratic Alternative for South Africa [IDASA]) points out, "it is inconceivable that there can be any serious progress towards a democratic constitution" under sluggish economic conditions marked by an inexorable rise in both unemployment and the cost of living.

Rather than repairing an existing flawed structure, Russian leaders must build that very structure itself, and from scratch. They lack the institutional supports for capitalism—the active financial markets, the detailed body of company law that South Africa inherits from the apartheid era. ANC leaders should (and some do) recognize this legacy as an advantage.

Institutional Building Blocks Compared

Paradoxically, leaders of the new South Africa will also inherit other potentially democratic institutions from the apartheid era. Although apartheid violated the first principle of democracy, the right to elected representation for all, the white state operated as a parliamentary democracy within the racial limits prescribed by apartheid. A variety of political parties have been formed over the years, giving whites (at least) decades of experience in party politics—something that Russian politicians lack.

There are currently three parties in the (white) House of Assembly in South Africa's tricameral Parliament—the ruling National Party, the ultraright Conservative Party, and the liberal Democratic Party, each with a significant bloc of seats. And despite the fact that the National Party has been dominant since it won power in 1948, its success has not done much more to stifle parliamentary democracy among whites than has the dominance of the Liberal Democratic Party in the case of Japan. This has been especially true since the early 1980s, when President P.W. Botha's political reforms prompted a number of National Party MPs to break away and form the Conservative Party. The Democratic Party (formerly the Progressive Federal Party) has also gained many more seats over the past decade.

So, at least in the white community (and to a lesser extent among Coloureds [mixed race] and Indians, who have their own elected token houses of Parliament under the terms of the new constitution that went into effect in 1984), parliamentary procedure is understood and the tradition of party formation is established. White parties have efficient grass-roots organizations and could form the nucleus of a strong opposition to the ANC, which has yet to transform itself from a liberation movement to a political party. Both the National Party and the Democratic Party hope to attract moderate blacks, Coloureds, and Indians as members; these parties could prove a powerful check on the activities of any radically oriented government.

For Russian politicians, on the other hand, party formation is a far more difficult challenge. The dominance of the Communist Party, which invaded every aspect of personal and public life, has deeply discredited the very notion of "party." As one U.S. diplomat phrased it, "Politics is a dirty word in Russia." Although limited political reforms were introduced under the Czar during the brief 1905–1917 window and political parties began to form, aspirations to multiparty politics were crushed after the November 1917 Bolshevik coup, when the elected Constituent Assembly – dominated by the Bolsheviks' opponents, the Social Revolutionaries – was simply dissolved by Lenin.

Given these circumstances, it is no surprise that true political parties are slow to develop in today's Russia. Western commentators quip that most Russian parties as of 1992 are really only "three men and a fax machine," groups that rely heavily on the personality of their leader, with little or no grass-roots organization. Larger groups have formed and re-formed, but they splinter rather than coalesce. Even President Yeltsin is something of a one-man band: he lacks a political party that can disseminate his ideas, and he commands no faction in the Congress of People's Deputies upon which he can count to pursue his legislative program. If the essence of democracy is political choice, exercised through regular elections, it is difficult to see how this could operate in Russia as long as there are no coherent party alternatives to Yeltsin himself.

Perhaps more important even than parties – certainly from the point of view of protecting civil liberties – is the question of that quintessential liberal democratic institution, the independent judiciary. Here, too, South Africa's new leaders will inherit an institution that they destroy at their great peril. (This is not to suggest that the ANC opposes the notion of an independent judiciary. Constitutional principles published by the organization stress the need for independent courts of justice. But the real test will come only when a future court frustrates the will of a new government – especially if that government is convinced that it is acting in the national interest. The independent judiciary has scarcely been noted for its flourishing good health elsewhere in Africa.)

One significant disadvantage the South African judiciary carries as the new multiracial era begins is that it is almost all white. Despite this racial imbalance, however, the courts managed to preserve a tradition of independence even in the worst days of apartheid abuse. Antiapartheid lawyers have challenged state repression through the courts (often successfully), establishing a tradition that augurs well for protecting the much-extended civil liberties promised by both the ANC and the government under the anticipated new constitution.

Russia has no such tradition of challenging state power through the courts – certainly not under communism, when challenging party decisions by any means at all was effectively forbidden. The establishment of Russia's new Constitutional Court is clearly a milestone on the path to democracy. Valery Zorkin, the court's chairman, has defined his mission as that of creating "an expanse governed by the rule of law." Graham Allison, director of the

Strengthening Democratic Institutions project at Harvard University's John F. Kennedy School of Government, points out that the new court has already tested its power as a check against the executive, ruling unconstitutional President Yeltsin's decree merging the KGB with the Internal Ministry for Security of the Russian Federation: "It had been previously unimaginable to challenge a decree by the head of state, let alone expect the executive powers to concede. . . . But the court's decision held, marking a decisive step in its institutional empowerment."

Although this is surely a vital first step toward a fully independent judicial system, the fact remains that Russia lacks the institutions and the practitioners (courts, judges, and lawyers schooled in the exercise of independence) that exist in South Africa. The South African legal system is far from perfect (the bench has handed down some shockingly racist judgments in its time, refusing to convict or imposing trivial sentences on whites who kill blacks), but it is a crucial building block of a democratic South Africa.

Indeed, the ruling National Party, which has embraced the virtues of liberal multiracial democracy now that it sees its interests threatened by a black government, cherishes the hope that the democratic institutions used in the past to protect whites against whites can now be used to protect whites against blacks. President de Klerk is not advocating changing the system in South Africa. He simply wants to include blacks as full members, and to add checks and balances to ensure that no black government can ever exercise the power white presidents have wielded.

Contrasts in Civil Society

As Shirley Williams, former British politician and now director of Harvard University's Project Liberty, points out:

> Democracy is much more than the holding of free, multiparty elections at regular intervals. . . . Fundamen-

tal to democracy is civil society, the structure that underlies the political system, a structure fashioned from innumerable relationships among friends and colleagues. . . .

Democracy requires more than political parties and even elections to sustain it. A vigorous civil society must underpin the political system. This includes everything from independent trade unions to women's organizations, from churches to chambers of commerce, from independent universities to local community associations, all of them providing a check on would-be tyrants. De Tocqueville made much the same point about U.S. democracy over 150 years ago: "In the American townships, power has been disseminated with admirable skill, for the purpose of interesting the greatest possible number of persons in the common weal."

Although South Africa falls far short of de Tocqueville's ideal, civil infrastructure is well developed in both white and black society. Liberal lawyers have formed a wide range of organizations to protect prisoners' rights, protest against the death penalty, and provide defense teams in human rights cases. Professional associations, charities, think tanks, liberal universities, church groups, and, most important, business organizations and trade unions also thrive. Business organizations provide the most potent white antidote to state power, and trade unions (with a membership probably approaching 2 million) the strongest black challenge to the state. The largest union federation, the Congress of South African Trade Unions (COSATU), is now affiliated to the ANC but has served notice it intends to pursue independence under a postapartheid government.

Business and labor represent crucial building blocks for democracy in the new South Africa. To achieve the kind of social accord that alone can deliver long-term peace and stability, these two key players must work together in the national interest. Recent negotiations between COSATU and the South African Employers' Consultative Committee on Labour Affairs (SACCOLA), representing major employers, failed to produce a pact aimed at jointly pressuring the white government to accelerate the transition to democracy. But the groundwork may have been laid for a future deal that would have important implications for the achievement of democracy in South Africa.

The extensive range of civic associations in black townships have acted as perhaps the most important agents of the liberation struggle. Although these organizations (which are overwhelmingly dominated by the ANC) found it much easier to organize boycotts of council rents and utility payments than to persuade residents they should resume payments as part of a deal with neighboring white cities to develop township facilities, they could in the future provide a far more effective network for articulating community grievances than exists in other African countries.

Church groups could also prove crucial. Census figures show that three-fourths of the South African population is actively religious, belonging to one of the country's many Christian and non-Christian sects. Church leaders have often intervened in the past to ease conflict; their mediating skills may be called for often in the future.

The media, too, will have an active role to play in protecting democracy in the new South Africa. It is far from clear, however, whether it is as yet up to the task. The broadcast media, dominated by the state-owned South African Broadcasting Corporation (SABC), seldom shows a flicker of independent spirit and is demonstrably negatively biased in its reporting of the ANC. The board of directors will be changed under an interim government, but it is a moot point whether the news staff, dominated by conservative Afrikaners, will quickly develop the habits suited to independent reporting.

Perhaps conditioned by past decades of censorship, the mainstream press also seems to lack initiative in its reporting—with the notable exception of the weekly *Sunday*

Times and its outspoken editor-columnist Ken Owen. But recently the "alternative" press—small antiapartheid publications such as the *Weekly Mail* and the Afrikaans-language *Vrye Weekblad*—have played a courageous role in exposing scandals such as the use of state funds to finance Chief Mangosuthu Buthelezi's Inkatha Freedom Party and the existence of security-force assassination squads. It is reasonable to hope these publications will apply the same critical spirit to apartheid's successors as to its perpetrators.

The Russian press, on the other hand, seems to have taken on enthusiastically the role of guarantor of democracy. Readership has declined since the heady early days of *glasnost*, when Russians flocked to buy publications that aired (for the first time in decades) criticism of the regime. Nevertheless, the print media continues to operate freely and in a relatively independent spirit—although with most printing facilities state-owned and most newspapers subsidized by the state, total independence of the press has yet to be achieved, and informal political pressure on editors is not unknown.

While today's Russian civil society can boast an energetic press, the same cannot be said of its other institutions. *Glasnost* spurred the formation in 1987 and 1988 of thousands of informal clubs and associations, from conservation societies to associations for the preservation of historical monuments to political debating groups, but this blossoming of civil society proved short-lived. As the economic revolution took hold, Russians were left struggling so hard to survive that they gave up such luxuries.

Community spirit has survived much more nearly intact in South Africa, despite apartheid repression. Although it seldom crosses the color line—most members of each community (white, black, Indian, Coloured) feel an obligation only to its own members—the damage done to the overall society is probably less in South Africa than in Russia.

How Functional Is the State?

South Africa's new leaders will inherit a state machine that actually works, albeit inefficiently in many areas and with the qualification that the departments administering black affairs are permeated with corruption and lack legitimacy in the black community. In Russia, as Alexander Motyl of Columbia University's Harriman Institute phrases it, "the collapse of totalitarianism has not yielded democracy but instead a complete and total void, a vacuum." Because party and state were practically indivisible in Russia, the demise of the one has destroyed the other as well.

A new South African government could face a crisis of executive power, but of much lesser intensity than the one Russia is experiencing. Although many senior bureaucrats are Afrikaners, and some are staunch conservatives, they are unlikely to be either keen or able to form a united front against a postapartheid executive (especially if, as expected, that executive includes prominent Afrikaner politicians). And unless events take a dramatic turn for the worse, South Africa will never face a situation of state collapse comparable to Russia's.

Thus, the triple challenge facing Russia is to create a modern state, a modern market economy, and democratic political institutions and to do so simultaneously under conditions of great economic hardship. Whatever other problems South Africa will face—and these are huge—Russia's democrats face a breathtaking task of institution-building that is likely to prove far more difficult than South Africa's.

Cultural Constraints

The Russians, no less than the Afrikaners and the Africans, have long been autocrats by nature and are democrats only by recent persuasion (if at all). Some observers believe a new authoritarian Yeltsin could emerge under pressure to replace this year's democratic Yeltsin. On the other hand, there is considerable evidence that Russians have adjusted to greater political freedom more easily than South Africans (white or black). At least the Russians tolerate different points of view (as evidenced by the new vigor of their press) without murdering each other in the numbers now being slain in South Africa.

Although the Afrikaners have in the past observed the democratic niceties in dealing with their own people (with the exception of left-wing whites), they have not found it easy to achieve a spirit of democratic tolerance toward blacks. A striking example is the evidence that right-wing whites in the police force, through callous omission or simple incompetence, have exacerbated the violence in black townships that has left some 14,000 people dead since 1984.

Africans, too, have a weak record in the area of sustained democracy. In the 35 years since Ghana gained independence from Britain in 1957, only a few sub-Saharan African nations have managed to sustain multiparty governments for any significant period. Botswana, Namibia, Mauritius, and Gambia are the most convincing examples in 1992.

The ANC and its main black opposition, the Zulu Inkatha Freedom Party, profess to be different; they both support multiparty democracy in principle. But it would be difficult to imagine a more hierarchical, tribalistic, and intolerant party than Inkatha, and the ANC's professed commitment to internal party democracy has always clashed with the Stalinist model adopted by its close ally, the South African Communist Party, some of whose members occupy senior leadership positions within the ANC. In this interim period, the ANC's commitment to democracy can only be taken at face value. As Huntington points out, "Political leaders out of office have good reason to advocate democracy. The test of their democratic commitment comes when they are in office." The ANC's desire for democratic elections is only exceeded by its desire to win them.

Another factor that must be taken into account is that the Western-style democracy advocated by the ANC – with its emphasis on the individual – may take root only with difficulty in the soil of communally oriented tribal Africa. Although South Africa has the most highly urbanized population on the continent, rural Africans bring their beliefs and political principles with them to the city and abandon them only slowly.

Despite the willingness of both major black parties to make major concessions to whites (the ANC's offer to allow a one-third minority to block constitutional changes could mean an effective white veto), neither will give an inch to its black opponent. As a result, thousands have died as politicians jockey for power and as the white government looks on, unwilling or unable to stop the carnage.

In the final analysis, however, the weight of history and culture alone will probably not sink South Africa's democratic experiment. Nations can change their political habits if it is sufficiently in their interest to do so. Otherwise, democracy would not exist on earth. There are few nations that seem to be naturally born to it. Under the influence of Western television, which feeds audiences capitalist and more-or-less democratic values along with all the pap, habits can change; some commentators believe TV was a major factor in feeding Russian opposition to communism.

Paradoxically, Russia's recent history of totalitarian communism could actually work to its advantage in the quest for democracy. If nothing else, that experience has taught Russia what it does *not* want from a political system. A period of strong, even authoritarian rule from the center is a near-term possibility, but a return to totalitarianism – authoritarian rule at its most chillingly brutal – is out of the question.

In South Africa, on the other hand, what has been discredited is domination by race, not authoritarianism per se. This was demonstrated during the (currently suspended) constitutional negotiations of the Convention for a

Democratic South Africa (CODESA), when the ANC and the government agreed that a multiracial interim government would reimpose detention without trial and a state of emergency — the very measures used by whites in the 1980s to crush black opposition to apartheid.

The Two Major Threats

In the end, ethnicity and economic hardship probably pose the gravest threats to democracy in both Russia and South Africa.

South Africa's ethnicity problem becomes more obvious by the day, as ethnic tensions fuel quasi-political struggles in the townships. This is scarcely surprising, when one recalls that ethnic division was the guiding principle of apartheid, which sought to confine South Africa's races and ethnic groups to geographically separate neighborhoods and homelands on the principle that mixing them was both dangerous and theologically forbidden.

Millions of blacks were forced to live in ethnically segregated rural homelands, and those who were "lucky" enough to dwell in Soweto, the largest black township, were segregated by neighborhood (though intermarriage between ethnic groups later blurred the barriers). The Afrikaners' obsession with ethnicity led to absurdities of race classification and has left a legacy of division that will be hard to overcome. Although daily relations between whites and blacks are remarkably cordial, the political transition has put these relations under increasing strain, and relations among the various nonwhite racial categories and ethnic groups are if anything worse.

Russia also has ethnic problems, but probably less severe than those of South Africa. It faces a dual threat, from non-Russians living within what is now the Russian Federation, and, more important, from the millions of ethnic Russians living outside Russia in the other republics of the former Soviet Union. Commentators disagree over the seriousness of the threat posed by non-Russians in the Russian Federation. They point out that some 82 percent of the Federation's population is ethnically Russian, and the next-largest group, the Tatars, represent only a little more than 3 percent. That scarcely compares with South Africa, with its 5 million whites, 3 million Coloureds, 1 million Indians, as well as 7 to 9 million Zulus (census figures are unreliable), 6 million Xhosas, and hosts of other black ethnic groups.

The problem of the many millions of ethnic Russians left marooned in outposts of the former Communist empire is potentially more serious. The three Baltic states of Latvia, Lithuania, and Estonia, home to as many as 2 million ethnic Russians, have all drafted constitutions that would bar many ethnic Russians from citizenship and force them to use the local language. Ethnic Russians have declared part of Moldova an independent republic. Aided by troops from the Russian Federation, they have fought against the Moldovan army. Numerous other potential conflicts are brewing. Indeed, some commentators believe there is a risk that right-wing nationalist sentiment might be exploited as the basis for a coup that could topple President Yeltsin himself, ushering in a hard-line Russian chauvinist dictatorship.

Nationalism on its own is difficult enough to combat, but economic hardship makes the task tougher still. And there is no sign that Russia's hardships will ease in the near term. Lives that were hard enough have become immeasurably harder since Russia first began stumbling down the path to a modern market economy. Real wages have fallen, in some cases sharply, or are paid in kind, not cash; standards of living have sunk; Russians have been left exhausted and apathetic by the daily struggle to survive. There is no shortage of those willing to claim that life was better under Brezhnev – or of those who call for authoritarian methods to force through economic reform (what Martin Wolf, Moscow correspondent of the *Financial Times*, has called the "despotic route to the market"), à la Chile under General Pinochet.

But it is in South Africa that the potent cocktail of ethnicity and poverty is likely to prove the most serious challenge to democracy, because of the correlation between wealth and race in that country. Russians struggle (more or less) equally to survive; in South Africa, on the other hand, race largely dictates the degree of hardship one experiences.

History provides no apparent solution to this problem. Democracy invites the individual to use his vote to obtain a fairer share of wealth. But any South African government that seeks to close this wealth gap rapidly, through redistribution, will seriously jeopardize economic growth by alienating (white) skills and capital. So successive governments are probably doomed to frustrate the immediate expectations of blacks and to suffer for it at the ballot box. One must wonder whether a new government would take its democratic chances under these circumstances or instead seek other means to perpetuate its rule.

It is worth remembering that whatever kind of post-apartheid government emerges will inherit one of the globe's most radicalized populations. Although the battle cry "liberation now, education later" has largely given way in the 1990s to a view that education is a fundamental need that should not be used as a political tool, the millions of young blacks who spent most of the 1980s boycotting or burning down their schools in the struggle for liberation can hardly be expected to be transformed overnight into responsible and patient citizens. It is also possible that the long-suffering black majority — who have known great privation under apartheid, especially during the past decade, when per capita incomes have fallen steeply in real terms — may be converted to greater militancy by the acquisition of political rights. They may find intolerable what had previously seemed a bearable burden.

Options

Frederik van Zyl Slabbert concludes his recent book, *The Quest for Democracy: South Africa in Transition* (Penguin, 1992), with this assessment of South Africa's options:

"There is nothing inevitable about a democratic outcome to transition in South Africa. The dynamics of its transition may precipitate undemocratic outcomes . . . they may even mix or alternate until South Africa becomes a democracy (if indeed it does at all)." The most he can say is that "the prospects of South Africa becoming a democracy are daunting and challenging but not out of the question."

Slabbert explores possible short-term results of the current transition. If negotiations fail to yield a new deal by the next general election, due in 1994 or early 1995, the National Party might postpone elections or even hold them under the apartheid constitution, which excludes blacks. He dismisses these options as unlikely. Two other broad scenarios seem more plausible. The white government could impose a new security clampdown, either with or without the cooperation of moderate blacks. Slabbert's description of the latter option: "A new modernizing nonracial oligarchy, together with the security forces, effect a clampdown, pleading that it had 'no choice' to restore stability to South Africa and save it for a 'future democracy' and a 'vibrant market economy'" (the Chilean option). Or an unelected multiracial "government of transitional unity" could be installed, with or without a referendum to test its legitimacy. He concludes: "South Africa has the capacity to become democratic, but it is going to be much more difficult to achieve than remaining undemocratic in any one of [these ways]."

For four months earlier this year, black and white South Africans met almost daily at the CODESA negotiating forum in an effort to agree on a postapartheid constitution. The process is currently halted, but when it resumes (and there is a broad consensus that it will), the debate will be the same: whether majority rule or power-sharing is best for a country of such enormous diversity.

The government favors a complicated solution known to the cognoscenti as "consociational democracy," which involves power-sharing among various groups at the executive level (rigidly enforced or voluntary); maximum devolution of power in a federal state; and a minority veto in Parliament. An advocate is Berkeley political scientist Arend Lijphart, who argues: "Majoritarian democracy may be preferable in terms of democratic quality, but because the probability that it will work in a plural society is very low or nil, it is not a realistic option. Practically speaking, the only choice is between consociational democracy or no democracy."

Huntington partially concurs:

> In most cases of communal pluralism, democracy can operate only on a consociational rather than a majoritarian basis. . . . [But] it will often break down because of social mobilization that undermines the power of elites; the only way it can be stable is if it becomes consociational oligarchy.

The latter is also one of Slabbert's options. Pretoria often cites Switzerland, with its cantonal system of government, as a model for South Africa. But Switzerland's language divisions are surely nowhere near as deep as South Africa's ethnic and racial ones, and they are minimized by prosperity. Not surprisingly, the government seldom cites Lebanon—a striking example of consociational government gone wrong.

Still, some elements of consociationalism obviously make sense in South Africa—especially the principle of federalism (though this is an element of many other systems as well). Many of the thorniest problems of governing a multicultural society can only be dealt with at the local level. When the country is both large and divided, as is true of South Africa, federalism makes a lot of sense.

Although the ANC now seems willing to accept a degree of devolution of power to regions, most ANC leaders continue to believe a strong central state is necessary to direct the process of overcoming economic inequalities. In general, the ANC favors a majority-rule constitution, albeit with large majorities required for changing its provi-

sions. President Nelson Mandela and Secretary General
Cyril Ramaphosa have said that the ANC will voluntarily
share power with whites in the first executive government
of the new era (not just in the transition to a new constitution, but after the first postapartheid elections have been
held). It is not clear, however, how much power they have
in mind. Whichever form of constitution is eventually chosen will have to include a significant amount of power-
sharing, or the white government will simply not agree to
it. And without white support, the ANC knows that the
economy would collapse and political power would be
meaningless.

A constitution that imposes a white veto in perpetuity
would obviously be unacceptable to blacks. Sooner or later,
there will have to be a major reallocation of political power
in South Africa. There will have to be majority rule. But
the prospects for successful majoritarian *democracy* appear doubtful unless power-sharing governments can solve
the economic inequality problem more rapidly than seems
feasible at the moment.

In Russia, a fragile democracy is already in place. The
country's leader has been chosen legitimately through the
ballot box for the first time in a millennium; the press is
free and active; government respects all the democratic
freedoms of speech, association, protest, and so forth.
Many worry that a right-wing nationalist coup could dis-
place all of this, or even that Yeltsin himself could decide
to put democracy aside for the moment, dissolving the legislature and ruling entirely by decree (with or without protecting civil liberties). Stephen Sestanovich, director of the
Russian and Eurasian Studies Program at CSIS, doubts
this outcome. "Russia is *very* pluralistic. There's been a
dissolution of power and it would be very difficult to rees-
tablish central control," he argues, adding that it would be
harder to put an authoritarian regime in place than to deal
with Russia's problems by more democratic means.

The prospects for democracy in Russia — although they
may look bleak at this time of economic, political, and so-

cial chaos – are probably better than in South Africa over the long run. As Dimitri Simes of the Carnegie Endowment for International Peace in Washington, D.C. argues: "Russia's problems are horrible but they're temporary. There are no structural reasons why they can't muddle through to democracy and prosperity." He adds, however, that this "muddling through" is likely to be a long process.

No Going Back for Either Country

Even if both Russia and South Africa revert temporarily to some form of authoritarian rule, there can be no returning to the specific abominations of the past. Totalitarianism and apartheid are ruled out forever. The Russian and South African peoples can only hope that the system chosen to govern them next time is at least more humane, responsive, and representative than the last one.

11

Postapartheid South Africa: Steps Taken, the Path Ahead

Witney W. Schneidman

January 1994

White domination formally ended in South Africa on December 7, 1993, when the multiparty Transitional Executive Council (TEC) was established to oversee government until all-race elections are held in the last week of April 1994. Two weeks later, on December 22, the country's tricameral Parliament (which comprised one house each for whites, Coloureds [mixed race], and Asians but excluded blacks) voted itself out of power by passing an interim constitution that provides the overarching legal and institutional framework for the TEC and a government of national unity that will rule for five years after the elections. With Parliament's demise, apartheid's entire organizational, legislative, and administrative underpinnings no longer exist.

These developments are the product of nearly four years of dialogue among parties that seemingly had no capacity for carrying out a negotiated political revolution—an extraordinary triumph of pragmatism over extremism. As the South African government, the African National Congress (ANC), and the other actors worked to frame the new constitution, the country's transition has evolved from one driven by mass mobilization and confrontation (even armed struggle) to a process that is defined primarily by negotiation. The process has been strengthened by the relatively spontaneous formation, beginning in 1991, of more than 400 negotiating forums around the country. These forums have convened at all levels, from the national to the local, to address virtually every significant issue (e.g., the economy, the health care system, education, housing). In the process, they have helped to empower many black South Africans who previously had no vehicle for expressing their concerns and had little connection to the constitutional talks. They have also eroded many of the divisions and enmities created by generations of apartheid rule, thus enabling politics based on embryonic interest groups to counter the influence of race and ethnicity.

Underpinning the emerging culture of negotiation and compromise is a civil society that has coalesced over the last several years to form a rather durable political center. In addition to the various forums, the center includes the corporate sector, which provides the managerial backbone for an economy whose GDP is three-quarters that of all southern Africa's. Equally important is the 1.2 million-strong Congress of South African Trade Unions (COSATU), which has honed its skills at flexing its political muscle while making pragmatic compromises. The 1.2 million mostly Afrikaner bureaucrats and administrators, including a majority of those in the South African Defense Force (SADF) and police, have reason to be supportive of the transition process because multiparty negotiators have opted to guarantee the jobs and pensions of all civil servants, including those who served in the homeland administrations. (Pensions will also be paid to individuals "who have served the public interest" in helping to establish democracy, such as antiapartheid activists, ANC leaders, guerrillas, and their dependents.) The influential township civic associations ("civics") are also likely to play a constructive role in ensuring that the new government is responsive to the needs and expectations of a large segment of the black urban population.

Does this mean that the ongoing process of political transition and reentry into the global economy will go more smoothly and quickly than it has over the last four years? The answer is that it probably will not. Political and criminal violence, continuing uncertainty over what the future holds, and the inevitable tensions involved in establishing a democratic government make it all but inevitable that future progress will be characterized by setbacks as well as breakthroughs. Nevertheless, the seeds of South Africa's political future have been planted, and there is reason to believe the new culture of negotiation will ultimately overcome the culture of violence and extremism that appears so threatening. This chapter will examine the steps that have brought South Africa to a scenario that would have seemed almost unbelievable even five years ago.

Talks about Talks: 1984–September 1991

The government and the ANC took a tentative step toward dialogue in July 1984 when Nelson Mandela, serving the twenty-first year of a life prison sentence, was visited by Minister of Justice Hendrik "Kobie" Coetsee. There were no further overtures until May 1986, when Mandela received a Commonwealth "Eminent Persons" delegation (accompanied by Coetsee) in his cell. In response to Mandela's plea for the government to initiate talks between the country's estranged white and black leaders, Coetsee's visits became more regular as domestic unrest and international pressure intensified.

It was not until May 1988, however, that the government of President P.W. Botha formalized these secret visits by establishing a four-person committee to handle contacts with Mandela and the exiled ANC leadership. By then, Mandela had realized an opportunity existed to win through negotiation what three decades of "people's war" had failed to achieve, and influential officials in the government were beginning to understand that a settlement with the ANC would not necessarily lead to an intolerable future for South Africa's whites. The government therefore used the dialogue with Mandela to determine whether he believed a peaceful political settlement was possible, to explore his vision of what a settlement might entail, and to assess the degree of his personal commitment to communism. Mandela's objective was to arrange a meeting with President Botha to press for formal negotiations. (See David Ottaway, *Chained Together* [New York: Random House, 1993] for an informed overview of this period.)

On July 5, 1989, President Botha arranged for Mandela to be brought to his official Cape Town residence next to Parliament. Oddly enough, the ANC leader would later describe the encounter as one of the warmest meetings he has had with another politician, commenting in an October 1993 interview with the London *Guardian* that "the thing that impressed me was that he poured the tea." Botha unexpectedly publicized the visit, which stunned the nation and underscored the inevitability of face-to-face negotiations between the government and the banned and demonized ANC. Six weeks later, Botha resigned from public life — not, ironically, for reasons related to the meeting with Mandela, but rather because of failing health.

Throughout this early period of dialogue with senior government officials, Mandela refused offers of formal negotiations in return for pledges by the ANC to renounce violence, end its alliance with the South African Communist Party (SACP), and forgo its demand for black majority rule. Nevertheless, it was clear that he was prepared to make concessions. In a 10-page document prepared by the ANC leader for his session with Botha and discussed at length with President F.W. de Klerk at their first meeting on December 13, 1989, Mandela put forward a "road map" outlining a course for negotiations. A key compromise he offered, once "a proper climate for negotiations" existed, was a willingness to suspend the armed struggle in return for a government commitment to negotiate directly with the country's "acknowledged black leaders." Mandela's repeated willingness to address white fears, "however irrational they might be," also suggested his openness to some form of power-sharing. Thus, when de Klerk made his historic February 1990 speech legalizing the ANC and 30 other black opposition parties and Mandela walked out of prison nine days later, both the government and the ANC leadership had already recognized their mutual dependence and need for cooperation if South Africa was to end more than a generation of economic decline and political paralysis.

Over the next 12 months, the South African government and the ANC began the process of transforming their adversarial relationship, in part by reaching agreement on three accords—the Groote Schuur Minute (May 1990), the Pretoria Minute (August 1990), and the D.F. Malan Accord (February 1991). These agreements, which included commitments from the ANC to "suspend" the armed struggle and from the government to release all political prisoners, removed key obstacles to constitutional talks.

The first formal multiparty agreement was not reached, however, until September 14, 1991, when representatives of 50 political parties, business organizations, and public interest groups met to sign the National Peace Accord at a conference in Johannesburg. Although the accord had no impact on the country's escalating violence, the meeting was an important confidence-building measure and afforded an opportunity for the first face-to-face meeting of Mandela, de Klerk, and Chief Mangosuthu Buthelezi, leader of the powerful Zulu-based Inkatha Freedom Party (IFP, often referred to simply as Inkatha). Several weeks later, the ANC's national executive committee officially endorsed an all-party conference and noted that it had already met several times with the government to plan such a meeting.

CODESA I: December 1991

On December 20, 1991, delegations from 18 organizations and the government gathered at the World Trade Center outside Johannesburg for the first session of the Convention for a Democratic South Africa (CODESA). The meeting constituted the broadest cross section of the country's political leadership ever to meet, even though the IFP was not represented at the senior (Buthelezi) level and the black nationalist Pan-Africanist Congress (PAC), which viewed the proceedings as a "sellout" of black South Africans, opted not to participate. The session's primary accomplishment was the signing of a Declaration of Intent that committed participants to an undivided South Africa, peaceful constitutional change, a multiparty democracy with universal suffrage, a separation of powers, and a bill of rights. There was also general agreement that there should be some form of interim government until a democratically elected body could draw up a new constitution.

Major differences remained between the ANC and its allies and the government despite the declaration signed at CODESA I. Even though both sides agreed on the importance of a democratically elected body to draw up a new constitution, the government and the ANC came away with quite different perceptions of what negotiations, and CODESA, would achieve. De Klerk – and the National Party's presumed allies (notably Inkatha) – assumed a transition of at least 10 years, and the government did not envisage relinquishing its power to an elected assembly until guarantees on power-sharing were in hand. From Pretoria's perspective, CODESA was to be used primarily to limit the powers of an elected assembly.

The ANC, on the other hand, envisaged CODESA as a vehicle for organizing a swift transition from minority rule to a new order shaped and ruled by elected representatives of the majority. This meant that the existing order must give way as quickly as possible to an interim government and an elected constitution-making body and that CODESA's lifetime should be brief, with few formal agreements, to allow the elected representatives freedom to shape the new government.

Not unexpectedly, CODESA I ended in a deadlock over these conflicting visions of a political settlement. Moreover, it was apparent that the CODESA session was essentially a media platform for the ANC and the government to gain public endorsement from their respective allies for their positions on the creation of a transitional government. All these nuances were overshadowed, however, when de Klerk, in his closing speech (on December 21, 1991), accused the ANC of violating the September 14, 1991, peace accord by maintaining a "private army" and questioned the ANC's right to participate in the future constitution-making body. In an angry response that stunned the convention into silence and astounded listeners across the country, Mandela launched the most searing public attack on a South African president ever made by a black South African. Although the two publicly shook hands the following day, the acrimonious exchange left the CODESA delegates, and the entire nation, uncertain about the next step in the process of constitutional negotiations.

CODESA II: May 1992

De Klerk and Mandela did not meet again for nearly five months. Instead, CODESA's agenda was delegated to five working groups (on the creation of a free political climate; constitutional principles and the composition of a constitution-making body; a transitional or interim government; the reincorporation of the "independent" homelands of Transkei, Bophuthatswana, Venda, and Ciskei; and time frames for the implementation of the agreements), which began their consultations in February 1992.

Growing public disillusionment with CODESA created pressures on the negotiators to "show results" whether or not they had been achieved. Repeated leaks to journalists from participants in the World Trade Center talks about nonexistent "breakthroughs" raised extraordinarily high expectations (among the participants as well as throughout the country) for a settlement. Under this considerable pressure, delegates to CODESA agreed to convene a second plenary session in the hope of finalizing the transitional process.

Although it had appeared from the media coverage that the multiparty forum was on the verge of an agreement on a transitional government, it was evident when the second full gathering opened on May 15, 1992, that the major parties in fact were still divided by many complex issues. Pressed to resolve conflicts that it had only partly addressed, CODESA II collapsed, a development that further diminished public understanding of the negotiations and respect for the participants. (See Steven Friedman, *The Long Journey: South Africa's Quest for a Negotiated Settlement* [Johannesburg: Ravan Press, 1993].) The talks fell apart over a seemingly arcane dispute about the size of the "special majority" that would be required for the constituent assembly to decide on issues such as changes in the constitution or the powers of future regional bodies. The ANC had been insisting on 66 percent and the government (in the hope of protecting its minority veto) 75 percent.

The underlying problems at CODESA II, however, were an enduring lack of trust between the government and the ANC and deep differences over federalism and power-sharing. Moreover, de Klerk's resounding victory in a March 1992 referendum among whites on his reform policies and his newly found international credibility imbued National Party leaders with a false sense of confidence about their ability to control the pace and outcome of the negotiation process. The ANC, on the other hand, needed concrete results to justify to its supporters involvement in talks with the government and to deflect mounting pressure from the South African Communist Party and other militants among its allies to take power as quickly as possible.

Equally troubling was the unabated political violence, especially in the townships on the East Rand outside Johannesburg and in Natal, which exacerbated doubts among all South Africans, particularly blacks, about the viability and relevance of constitutional negotiations. A major crisis erupted on June 17, 1992, when 46 township dwellers were massacred by a group of Inkatha supporters in the township of Boipatong. The ANC immediately suspended all contacts with the government, ostensibly to protest the police's handling of the attack, further weakening the CODESA process.

The Record of Understanding: September 1992

Frustrated by the failure of CODESA II and the overall pace of negotiations, the ANC's more militant members persuaded the organization's leadership to launch a "rolling mass action" campaign. The campaign ended tragically on September 7, 1992, on the outskirts of Bisho, the capital of the Ciskei homeland, when Ciskei troops and police opened fire on 70,000 ANC marchers, killing at least 28 and wounding some 200 others.

The disaster at Bisho had the effect of discrediting the radicals in the ANC-SACP alliance and strengthened the hand of those who supported a power-sharing arrangement with the government. Paradoxically, SACP chairman Joe Slovo was the most influential of those advocating a negotiated, incrementalist approach to the constitutional transition. Slovo and his allies recognized that the ANC was likely to win a democratic election but would not be able to take effective control of state power until it had trained and appointed its own bureaucrats, a process requiring several years at least. They argued, therefore, that the ANC would have to share power with the National Party for a substantial transitional period in order to consolidate its control over government operations.

The Mandela-de Klerk summitry, strengthened by continuing deliberations in the five CODESA working groups, resumed after the Bisho tragedy, and on September 26 the two leaders agreed to what was called a "Record of Understanding." This formally committed the National Party to accepting an interim government that would prepare for the election of a transitional Parliament charged with drafting and adopting a new constitution. The accord also signaled the implicit acceptance by the ANC leadership of the proposition that it would have to share state power with the National Party during the transitional period.

The accord provoked a bitter reaction from Buthelezi because it implicitly served final notice that his special relationship with the government, so carefully nurtured by both sides during the Botha years, no longer existed. Buthelezi was also personally incensed by the unilateral decision reached by the ANC and the government in the course of finalizing their Record of Understanding to prohibit his followers from carrying "traditional weapons" in public and to have Inkatha-dominated hostels around Johannesburg fenced in and surrounded by police.

The accord also had the effect of transforming the negotiations from a dialogue between two parties in basic agreement on a set of common objectives (the ANC and the National Party government) into a three-sided process. The third side crystallized in early October 1992 when Inkatha formed an alliance (the Concerned South Africans Group [COSAG]) with the (white) Conservative Party (CP) and the homeland governments of Ciskei and Bophuthatswana. COSAG opposed ANC-NP "deal-making" and demanded maximum decentralization of power to regional governments.

Despite the Record of Understanding, many South Africans (black and white) continued to have serious doubts about the viability of the negotiation process. Doubts were exacerbated by the ANC's efforts to define itself as an organization and revelations of widespread government graft and allegations that government security forces were fomenting township violence. Nevertheless, the Record of Understanding helped to revive negotiations, and in February 1993 the ANC and the government announced agreement that a government of national unity – consisting of a multiparty cabinet, governmental bureaucracy, and Parliament – would share power for five years on the basis of a democratic election, to be held in early 1994. The negotiators further concurred that each party would be represented in Parliament according to the percentage of the vote it won, and in the cabinet if it won 5 percent of the vote. Accord was also reached on the concept of a Transitional Executive Council on which all parties would be represented during the period leading up to elections.

The Multiparty Negotiating Forum: April 1993

With broad agreement having been reached between the National Party and the ANC on the TEC and a number of subcouncils that would effectively assume joint responsibility with the government for administration during the transition, multiparty negotiators agreed in early March 1993 to convene a third CODESA-type plenary session. When 26 political entities gathered in plenary session, the agenda included such issues as the election date and the role of the security forces in the transition. At the insistence of those (including the Conservative Party, Inkatha, and the Pan-Africanist Congress) absent or without senior-level representation at previous CODESA sessions but at the table on April 1, the name of the process was changed from CODESA to "Multiparty Negotiating Forum."

The tenacity of the negotiators became apparent on April 10, when negotiations continued despite the assassination (by a white right-winger with ties to the Conservative Party) of Chris Hani, the general secretary of the SACP and the country's most popular leader among blacks next to Nelson Mandela. The fact that Hani's death, the most significant crisis since February 1990, resulted in relatively little retributive violence was a striking affirmation of the commitment to negotiating peace and a new constitution. The fallout from the assassination led to a visible shift in the balance of power from the government to the ANC. Whereas President de Klerk issued a statement through his press secretary, Mandela was the one who went on national television to appeal for calm. By asserting his authority, Mandela demonstrated his influence among black South Africans and made it clear to white South Africans that the country could not be ruled without the ANC.

The "Freedom Alliance" Challenge

As prospects for a genuine and workable settlement increased, so did opposition from those parties with the most to lose, primarily Inkatha and white groups on the far right. The resumption of multiparty talks sparked the formation on May 7, 1993, of the Afrikaner Volksfront (AVF), an umbrella group of more than 18 far-right organizations under the chairmanship of retired General Constand Viljoen, former chief of the South African Defense Force, to press demands for an "independent" Afrikaner state within a confederation.

When the Multiparty Negotiating Forum in early July 1993 ratified April 27, 1994, as the date for elections, the Conservative Party and the IFP walked out of the talks, setting the stage for the formation of a "rejectionist" front, with the Concerned South Africans Group at its core. In September, COSAG formalized its association with the AVF and renamed itself the Freedom Alliance. In addition to the Conservative Party and Inkatha, the Freedom Alliance initially included the AVF and the homeland governments of Ciskei, KwaZulu, and Bophuthatswana. (In January 1994, Ciskei joined the TEC.) This incongruous grouping of black homeland leaders and conservative whites forged an effective union on the principle that regional governments should be able to exercise wide-ranging powers within a federal state. The Freedom Alliance also opposed the April 1994 election date because the member groups realized they would exert more influence in the multiparty talks than in an elected constituent assembly. While cloaking their demands simultaneously in threats to resort to violence and appeals to federalist sensibilities, the Freedom Alliance highlighted the most significant constitutional conundrum facing South Africa: how to reconcile the power of the majority with the fears of the minority.

In an effort to stave off a permanent fragmenting of the political center, the ANC and the government opened a second track of negotiations in August 1993 by holding bilateral meetings with members of the Freedom Alliance. Ironically, the dialogue between the ANC and the AVF (which included a secret August 16 meeting between Nelson Mandela and General Viljoen) developed the most momentum. ANC-AVF discussions have centered on finding a formula under which right-wing parties could take part in the April elections in exchange for a gerrymandered province in which Afrikaners would form the majority. Mandela's involvement underscores the ANC's belief in the importance of including the far right in the process—not only to minimize the potential for violence and increase the prospects for a successful transition but also to isolate Buthelezi.

On December 21, 1993, the ANC and AVF announced they had reached a strategic interim agreement that would enable the Volksfront to participate in the Transitional Executive Council and elections in return for the ANC's willingness "to seek ways to address the desire of many Afrikaners for self-determination in a *volkstaat* [Afrikaner homeland]." The agreement collapsed the following day, however, over resistance by the Freedom Alliance to the idea of committing itself in writing to an eventual constitutional settlement as a precondition to negotiations on possible amendments to the interim constitution that would increase regional autonomy. Although General Viljoen seemed to offer hope that an agreement could still be reached before the February 12 cutoff date for political organizations to register for the April polls, the AVF and Inkatha appear to be holding out for greater ANC and government concessions. In fact, their position has hardened in recent weeks. Inkatha insists that regions be granted "exclusive" powers that could not be overruled by the central government, while the AVF, on January 30, declared symbolic independence from South Africa by electing its own interim government to rival the TEC and called on Afrikaners to hold their own separate elections at the same time as national elections.

The Transitional Executive Council: December 1993

Despite the opposition of the Freedom Alliance and the Pan-Africanist Congress, the 21 parties negotiating at the World Trade Center continued to make significant progress on the details of transition. On September 7, 1993, negotiators reached final agreement on the creation of the Transitional Executive Council in which black South Africans for the first time would share a governing role with the white minority regime. The mandate of the TEC is to "level the playing field" by creating a climate for free political participation and a free and fair election.

The Transitional Executive Council, which met for the first time on December 7, 1993, is essentially a continuation of the Multiparty Negotiating Forum, with added power (i.e., each of the 21 parties that endorsed the TEC bill has a representative on the council). Much of the council's activity, however, is occurring in the seven subcouncils overseeing policy developments in finance, defense, law and order, intelligence, foreign affairs, regional and local government, and the status of women. Council decisions will be made by consensus or, on disputed issues, by a 75 percent majority for policing, defense, and intelligence matters, and a two-thirds majority in the other subcouncils.

Along with the Independent Electoral Commission, the Media Commission, and the Broadcasting Authority, established at the same time, the Transitional Executive Council has considerable power to ensure that no party is unfairly disadvantaged in the run-up to elections. It is empowered to order the government, any self-governing homeland administration, and/or any political party or organization (including those parties not participating in the council) not to proceed with planned legislation or other actions that the council has "reason to believe" would undermine its authority. For instance, the Transitional Executive Council in its first days forced the suspension of a loan from the Development Bank of Southern Africa to the homeland government of Bophuthatswana on the grounds that all such loans needed prior TEC approval.

Throughout the TEC's lifetime (it is scheduled to be disbanded at the first sitting of the government of national unity), there will be tension between the government, which wants to limit its powers, and an ANC seeking to use the council to assert as much influence as possible. In fact, within the first week, the ANC provoked a showdown in the council by urging the deployment of police in northern Natal—something that the TEC is technically not empowered to undertake. The government balked because of its concern that such a step could lead to a clash with the KwaZulu government, which rejects the TEC's authority. The ANC, on the other hand, insisted that the deployment was necessary for the TEC to demonstrate its policing powers in order to ensure fair and free elections. The ANC redoubled its pressures for deployment in northern Natal in late December after the South African police commissioner acknowledged that some members of the KwaZulu police had embarked on a campaign to drive ANC members from some Inkatha-dominated areas.

There has been considerably less acrimony on the TEC's finance subcouncil. This is due in part to the significant degree of consensus that exists between Minister of Finance Derek Keys and Director of the ANC Department of Economic Policy Trevor Manuel. The emergence of a policy consensus has also been shaped by nearly two years of discussions within the National Economic Forum (a working group made up of government, labor, and business representatives).

Primary among the many problems confronting the TEC in the months before the elections will be relations

with the homeland governments of KwaZulu and Bophuthatswana, which have threatened to impede free political
activity and campaigning in their territories. A number of
white conservative town councils are also likely to thwart
campaigning. It will be virtually impossible to hold free
elections in parts of KwaZulu and on the East Rand if
violence continues (as seems likely) at existing or higher
levels. Plans to establish a 10,000-strong multiparty National Peacekeeping Force, under the control of the defense
subcouncil, are moving forward, but the force will have at
best a marginal impact before the elections.

These challenges notwithstanding, there is a growing
confidence that the TEC will succeed in fulfilling its mandate of preparing for elections.

The Elections: April 1994

All South Africans at least 18 years of age – which includes
approximately 16 million blacks, 3 million whites, 2 million
Coloureds, and 750,000 Asians – can vote for members of a
National Assembly and nine provincial legislatures in the
elections now scheduled for April 26–28, 1994. (The ANC
eventually agreed to a Freedom Alliance demand that voters be able to cast two ballots – one each for the National
Assembly and provincial legislature.) The 400 National Assembly members will be elected via a proportional representation system with equal division between national and
provincial party lists. The provincial legislatures – to be
elected on a proportional basis – will be between 30 and
100 seats, depending on the size of the local electorate.
There will also be a 90-member Senate – 10 elected by each
of the nine provincial legislatures. It will be headed by a
Senate president and will have to agree by special majorities on specified categories of legislation relating to the
provinces, such as changes to their boundaries.

According to a *Sunday Times* (Johannesburg) poll released January 16, and corroborated by recent polls con-

ducted by the authoritative Human Sciences Research Center of South Africa, the ANC would win 65 percent of the seats in Parliament if the elections were held now. In fact, the larger the turnout of black voters, the larger the potential for the ANC winning the two-thirds majority needed to rewrite the interim constitution with minimal opposition. The ANC is also predicted to win large majorities in at least five of the nine provincial legislatures. The National Party, which could win the Western Cape region, consistently polls around 15 percent; its support on election day will be influenced by whether members of the Freedom Alliance compete as an alliance, separately, or not at all. In evaluating these predictions, it should be noted that the category of "undecided" voters has fluctuated from 4 to 30 percent in recent polls.

Inkatha's support is believed to have slumped to about 5 percent nationally and in Natal to about 18 percent, largely because of disillusionment among both white and black voters with Buthelezi's leadership and the IFP's boycott politics. The white right-wing parties (the CP and AVF) together are expected to get about 4 percent of the vote. Other parties attract minimal support. For example, the Democratic Party and the Pan-Africanist Congress won the backing of only 2.6 percent and 1.7 percent respectively of prospective voters in the *Sunday Times* poll. The South African Communist Party is expected to attract support from less than 1 percent of the voters, since most of its members will vote ANC, but SACP members have a strong presence on the ANC national lists.

The fairness of South Africa's voting will be determined by the Independent Electoral Commission, which will include five international members. This body, accountable to no other branch of government, is authorized to devise an electoral code of conduct that will have statutory force. The code will be instrumental in helping to level the electoral playing field. Nevertheless, intimidation and political violence are likely to intensify as April approaches, and many voters, especially blacks, have reason to fear for their safety if they go to the voting stations. Another problem is the suspicion raised by a secret ballot among some African voters who equate secrecy with the apartheid era and perceive it as contradictory to the notion of democracy and openness. There are also concerns about whether eligible voters will be registered in time. Registration is a particularly sensitive issue given that a large turnout would favor the ANC whereas a low one would work to the NP's advantage.

On the other hand, the Independent Electoral Commission will benefit from the extensive voter education training and violence-mitigation programs that have been implemented over the last year by both international and domestic organizations. Indeed, it is estimated that the donor community will spend about $50 to $60 million helping South Africans prepare to vote. There are likely to be more than 30,000 polling observers and monitors, domestic and foreign, providing oversight to the process, as well as a corp of domestic and international journalists scrutinizing procedures. The United Nations is expected to send the largest delegation of foreign observers (about 2,800).

In short, the run-up to the April elections will not be smooth. Nevertheless, given the importance accorded by the majority of South Africans to these elections, the voting is likely to be fair enough to produce a credible outcome despite all the apparent difficulties.

The Government of National Unity: May 1994

In early May 1994, once the results of the election are certified, a government of national unity is to be sworn in. The locus of power and the mandated unity will be in the 27-member cabinet. It will be headed by a president (probably Nelson Mandela), and two deputy presidents (most likely ANC National Chairman Thabo Mbeki and F.W. de Klerk). The second deputy president will be drawn from the party with the second largest majority. Despite their designation as "executive" officers, deputy presidents will not have veto powers, although Mandela has offered verbal assurances that critical decisions will not be taken without de Klerk's approval. The National Party, which from the beginning of the negotiations had been holding out for the right to exercise a minority veto in the cabinet, settled well below its bottom line on this crucial issue, probably because it had no choice as its perceived power diminished steadily in the course of negotiations.

It is impossible to forecast the cabinet's makeup because it is uncertain whether (and in what sort of alliance) the right-wing and homeland leaders will participate in the election. But indications are that the National Party will hold at least several portfolios, probably including finance, agriculture, and perhaps a security department. Cabinet decisions will be reached "in a consensus-seeking spirit," with no predefined fixed majorities.

The character of the new South Africa will be largely determined by the interim constitution, especially by the charter of "fundamental rights" entrenched in the document. In creating a Western-style separation of powers, the interim and "final" constitutions will be protected by an 11-member constitutional court whose members are to hold office for a maximum of seven years. There will also be a separate supreme court, headed by a chief justice, that will be independent from the executive apart from appointment by the president after a complex series of consultations.

The interim constitution (which is to remain in force until the final constitution is ratified) guarantees multiparty democracy, equality before the law, fundamental human rights and freedoms, an independent judiciary, and a free press. There is also a formula for equitable allocation of state revenue to the provinces. Other safeguards against the abuse of power include a second legislative chamber (the Senate) and agreement that a final constitution must be passed by at least a 60 percent majority (see below). In short, it is not, as some critics contend, a majority-rule or winner-take-all constitution.

At the same time, the new constitution falls short of being the "federal" document, assiduously demanded by Inkatha and others, that the National Party initially promised to deliver. The NP's 1991 constitutional proposals called for political power to be divided among three tiers of government (central, regional, and local), with each tier to have "original and entrenched authority with which other tiers of government may not interfere." The constitution as finally approved provides for the delegation of certain powers (in such areas as education, health, and policing), but Pretoria will retain broad powers of intervention to impose "uniform national standards" or to protect national security or the national economy. And with regions barred from imposing taxes without central government approval, federalism seems likely to be limited from the beginning.

At the local level of government, the National Party won agreement on what amounts to a minority veto in order to placate many conservative white town councils. When local elections are held in two years, white voters in existing municipalities will elect 30 percent of the seats on new, multiracial town and city councils. All tax and rent payers will get another 30 percent. The remainder will be elected on a nonracial basis. Municipal budgets will require a two-thirds majority for passage.

A constitutional assembly consisting of a joint sitting of the National Assembly and the Senate will draw up the final constitution observing guidelines laid out in a "solemn pact" of 32 "principles." These guarantee such elements as multiparty democracy, entrenched clauses, provincial "integrity," and the independence of the reserve bank. The final constitution, scheduled to be drafted by May 1996, must be approved by a two-thirds majority in the constitutional assembly. If it fails to pass, the document will have to be subjected to a referendum, with 60 percent popular approval required for passage. If this in turn does not occur, the final constitution must wait until the next general election (1999). Then the new constitutional assembly can try again, this time subject to a reduced 60 percent majority.

The Violence Factor

Political violence has intensified since the reform process accelerated in February 1990. In the overwhelming majority of cases, both the perpetrators and the victims have been black. According to independent monitors, political violence claimed the lives of more than 4,200 people (including a record 250-plus policemen) in 1993. This turmoil is largely restricted to a small portion of the country—parts of rural Natal and several townships on the East Rand outside Johannesburg.

In assigning blame for the current situation, the de Klerk administration and many whites single out the guerrilla armies of the ANC and the PAC. These groups, in turn, point their fingers at the South African Defense Force and the South African Police as well as a shadowy "third force"—conservative elements at least nominally aligned with the security forces—that foments strife among blacks for political ends. Buthelezi, on the other hand, accuses a Xhosa-dominated ANC of waging a campaign of "ethnic cleansing" against his Zulu loyalists. The ANC and Inkatha have been engaged in an intense and violent rivalry since the mid-1980s (primarily for political influence in Natal province) that has been responsible for thousands of deaths. In short, all parties bear some responsibility for the country's extraordinary levels of political violence.

Criminal violence is actually more pervasive in South Africa than the political variety. Its randomness and the anxiety it generates among all South Africans, especially those living in urban areas, is the most significant source of pessimism about the country's future. An unemployment rate of about 46 percent, an influx of automatic weapons into many black townships with the winding down of the war in neighboring Mozambique, and grass-roots hostility in the townships toward the government police have combined to create a local culture of arbitrary street justice that sustains the lethal activities of criminal gangs, local warlords, and self-defense units.

The level of political violence is likely to drop in the postelection period, especially if conservative whites and Inkatha participate in the campaign. Even if these groups decide to boycott the poll or resort to violence to promote their agendas, they will be confronted – for the first time in the country's history – by a superior security force employed by a government with unprecedented popular legitimacy. Thus, for left and right alike the "civil war option" has little chance of success. Moreover, there is broad sentiment among all South Africans for effective government action to curtail violence. Nonpolitical criminal violence, on the other hand, will be more difficult to root out because of its social and economic origins; this will depend on long-term factors such as economic growth, job creation, and skills training.

Military Restructuring

The South African Defense Force consists of 49,900 army, 4,500 navy, 10,000 air force, and 8,000 medical corps personnel, plus 235,000 reservists. Until recently, white male conscription provided the SADF with many of its active-duty personnel (only about one-third of the permanent force is black), but this practice was abolished in August 1993 and the army is now being staffed on a volunteer basis. One of Africa's most militarily powerful countries, South Africa was reported to be developing a nuclear capability as early as 1977. In March 1993, the government (which acceded to the Nuclear Non-Proliferation Treaty in

1991) acknowledged that it had possessed six nuclear devices in 1989, all subsequently dismantled.

The SADF is not the whole story, however. South Africa's military mosaic also includes the armies of the four "independent" homelands plus at least three nongovernmental militaries (the military wings of the ANC and the PAC as well as the paramilitary forces of the Afrikaner Weerstandsbeweging [Afrikaner Resistance Movement]).

The first step to be taken toward replacing this ad hoc mix of organizations with a single integrated national defense force is the creation of the National Peacekeeping Force, which will be composed of elements drawn from the SADF, the South African Police, Umkhonto we Sizwe (the ANC's military wing), and several homeland armies. The former head of the Venda military has been selected to head the force, and General Bantu Holomisa, leader of the Transkei homeland and a nemesis of the Pretoria government, is likely to play an influential role on defense issues in the postelection government.

Although government and ANC military leaders on the Transitional Executive Council have created a panel to oversee the training of the peacekeeping force, plans to deploy it in place of existing military and police units by the end of March 1994 are, in the view of Washington military analysts, overly ambitious. The primary responsibility for security and stability in the run-up to elections will rest with the government's security force. The peacekeeping force will play a supplemental role at best, but could make a significant psychological contribution to lowering tensions when present at trouble spots. The TEC has created a second panel, the Joint Military Command Council, that will lay the groundwork for combining South Africa's various military components—from the government, the black homelands, and opposition groups—into a new National Defense Force after the election.

One of the most difficult challenges in creating an effective security force centers on the restructuring of the 114,000-strong national police force and the integration of

20,000 members from the 10 homeland police forces. Although the national force is more than 50 percent black, there are few black commanders – a factor that contributes to ineffectiveness and lack of credibility of the police in black areas. (Nelson Mandela, for example, has repeatedly called for the withdrawal of white South African security forces from townships where violence is most intense.)

Despite these tensions, senior government and ANC leaders have begun work on a plan, likely to be launched by February 1994, for a massive security crackdown and the introduction of socioeconomic upliftment programs in the most strife-torn areas. Other measures designed to improve police accountability include the TEC's supervisory role over police operations throughout the country, investigations by the Goldstone Commission into sources of political violence, and the presence of foreign observers, from the United Nations and elsewhere, whose numbers will increase in advance of elections.

Signs of Economic Recovery

South Africa's four-year recession appears to be over, and economic prospects are better now than at any time in the last decade. As Chairman of the Standard Bank Investment Corporation Conrad Strauss has phrased it, "the buds are on the branch." He does not appear to be alone in this judgment. According to the South African Chamber of Business, business confidence is at its highest level since the start of the recession in late 1989. Renewed confidence is based on a range of signals, including a drop in the inflation rate to single digits, projections of an economic growth rate of over 2 percent in 1994 and possibly double that in 1995, a booming stock exchange, and a 4.5 percent increase in gross domestic fixed investment. Corporate taxes have been cut, and real wages and real interest rates have started to fall.

The economy's turnaround is attributable to several

factors, including expectations that the April elections will go smoothly and that the government of national unity will be friendly to investors. South Africa has also benefited from high levels of liquidity in world financial markets, a firming gold price, and the country's newly fashionable status as a relatively dynamic emerging market. (The *Economist* [London] recently ranked South Africa eleventh out of 24 emerging markets it surveyed.) Confidence has also been buoyed by the lifting of virtually all financial and oil sanctions (the UN arms embargo is the only major sanction still in place), sustained improvements in exports, normalization of relations with the International Monetary Fund (IMF), the World Bank, and other international financial institutions, and a final agreement with foreign creditor banks on South Africa's outstanding debt. A substantial improvement in the agricultural sector followed the drought of 1991–1992 has also contributed to the economy's recovery.

These positive trends will help South Africa deal with a number of critical issues in the domestic economy, particularly high unemployment. A related concern is the need to increase workers' skills in order, for example, to supply the estimated 75,000 senior managers needed by the year 2000. The balance of payments remains a problem as heavy capital outflows continue, and Pretoria is committed to repaying more than $1 billion annually for the next eight years. This will generate pressure to retain the dual exchange-rate system and exchange controls at least for the next 12 to 18 months, which inhibits the ability of South African corporations to realize their full potential in the global marketplace. Another pivotal question is whether the nascent economic turnaround will lead to significant amounts of new foreign investment. According to a recent World Bank econometric study, a strong resurgence of private investment will be essential to the new government's ability to respond to the needs – and expectations – of black South Africans.

The climate for foreign investment is improving. Over

the last two years, 124 new non-U.S. multinationals have invested in South Africa, an increase of about 27 percent. These firms have been primarily British, German, and French, but other major corporations such as Daewoo of Korea have entered into joint ventures. In contrast, many U.S. businesses have been cautious about investing, in part because of sanctions still on the books at the U.S. state and local level as well as uncertainties about violence and the transition in general. Nearly 200 U.S. firms gained entry to the market by establishing licensing or distribution agreements over the last year (an approach that limits their risk and exposure), whereas only some 35 U.S. firms invested in South Africa in 1993 (bringing the total to about 139, which, ironically, was the number of U.S. firms present in 1988).

With Nelson Mandela's September 24, 1993, call for the lifting of all economic and financial sanctions, and the prospect of successful elections, U.S. firms and financial institutions have begun to view South Africa's market potential with a more active interest. The repeal of 121 of 180 state and local sanctions within 90 days of Mandela's call has enabled several U.S. financial firms to develop mutual funds that will invest primarily in South African stocks and begin positioning themselves for corporate restructuring opportunities as the country's major conglomerates face pressure from black South Africans seeking more opportunity in the formal sector to "unbundle" their webs of holdings. Finally, many consumer product firms are interested not only in the potential of South Africa's domestic market and the southern African regional market but also in South Africa's proximity to, and capability to service, markets throughout the Indian Ocean basin, the Middle East, and Asia.

U.S. business interest in South Africa was further spurred by President Clinton's signature on November 23, 1993, of the "South Africa Democratic Transition Support Act of 1993." This legislation, which officially ended U.S. federal sanctions, contributed significantly to the success of the trade mission led by Secretary of Commerce Ronald Brown in December 1993. Brown's visit resulted in the signature of an investment incentive scheme involving the Overseas Private Investment Corporation and laid the basis for significant expansion of bilateral economic relations. Indeed, the Clinton administration's policy toward South Africa, and southern Africa in general, is likely to be measured by the degree to which it can facilitate trade and investment and promote sustainable economic growth and development throughout the region.

The "Nationalization" Issue

South Africa's economic policy debate essentially revolves around one fundamental issue: how to enhance the capacity of the region's strongest economy while rapidly redistributing skills, opportunities, and resources to the black majority. For the last several generations, the ANC has been concerned primarily with the redistribution aspect of this dilemma. Until its unbanning in 1990, the organization adhered closely to the 1955 Freedom Charter, which advocated the nationalization of the mining, industrial, and financial sectors. Over the last four years, however, the ANC leadership has come to realize that it cannot improve the conditions of blacks in the absence of economic expansion. ANC leaders also accept that economic growth will require a vibrant private sector, foreign capital, technological and managerial know-how, and an investor-friendly regulatory environment.

In short, ANC leaders have turned their backs on nationalization as a basis for economic policy and Mandela has frequently assured investors that their property will not be confiscated, while affirming their right to repatriate profits and dividends. Moreover, the ANC's draft Reconstruction and Development Program, endorsed by its allies over the January 22–23 weekend, sets ambitious goals – including the building of 1 million homes and electrifying 2.5 million others in the next five years – but also conveys

caution about the speed of implementation and a commitment to fiscal discipline and macroeconomic balance.

Some skepticism over the ANC's rejection of nationalization lingers, however, for several reasons. Many blacks
at the grass roots, who equate apartheid with capitalism,
still believe that nationalization is a viable policy option.
Many whites will not be convinced of the ANC's conversion
until they actually see an ANC government implement its
economic policies. Finally, ANC economic policy, which is
still evolving, is predicated on redressing the glaring dis-
parities bequeathed by decades of apartheid. Thus contentious proposals, such as a reconstruction levy (or wealth
tax), and efforts to prescribe investments in support of
black interests will be part of South Africa's investment
environment for the foreseeable future.

On balance, however, it is apparent that an initial economic policy consensus has emerged among South Africa's
business leaders, trade unionists, government officials, and
black opposition leaders. Leaders of these constituencies
basically agree that a vigorous private sector must coexist
with a degree, although still unspecified, of state intervention. Many corporations, until recently ambivalent about
black advancement in the workplace and for much of the
apartheid era restricted from giving blacks positions of
skill and responsibility, have begun to embrace black empowerment programs such as affirmative action. Indeed, it
has become apparent to many business leaders that, as
Executive Chairman of the Independent Development Trust
Wiseman Nkuhlu commented at a recent meeting of the
CSIS Working Group on South Africa, "the way to deal
with black expectations is to treat them seriously and acknowledge them as legitimate."

In Sum

Most political transitions in Africa have been marred by
the suddenness with which they occurred. From the independence era of the early 1960s to the democratic reform

movement that began in the late 1980s, African opposition parties have not had the opportunity to think through structures of democratic governance, to foster the emergence of a durable civil society, or to stimulate at least a small measure of sustainable economic growth before acquiring political power. Despite delays and frustrations, South Africa is an exception in that nearly four years of reform have created a relatively broad-based political center, a viable framework for democratic government, and a macroeconomic policy environment that could lead to meaningful growth. Moreover, these successes have been achieved largely without external mediation.

As a result, many South African leaders who formerly were implacable foes have developed a measure of mutual trust – a precondition for the success of democratic government. Secession or sustained warfare is not a genuine option for extremists on the right or left and it seems safe to say that even random violence, such as assassination, will not derail the transition process. If, however, the new government finds it necessary to resort to authoritarian and coercive measures to maintain stability and security, this inevitably would have ramifications for civil society and the functioning of a democratic order. The country's future as a nation will be determined not by the outcome of the April 1994 election but by the ability of former adversaries to govern together and enshrine in practice what was achieved in the context of political trade-offs.

12

Southern Africa in the Year 2000: An Optimistic Scenario

Millard W. Arnold

March 1991

Preoccupation with developments in the Gulf, concern over the possible resurgence of hard-liners in the Soviet Union, and the priority being given to the reconstruction of eastern Europe have all but obscured a range of fundamental political and economic changes taking place in southern Africa that are reshaping the future prospects of the region, and over time of the continent as a whole. The consequences of apartheid in South Africa and various levels of conflict and unrest in other countries have suppressed the capacity of this third of the continent to generate long-term, sustainable economic growth. Now, however, a genuinely representative political order in South Africa is a realistic prospect, and negotiations are under way that could end the protracted civil wars in Angola and Mozambique. If these goals are realized, the major impediments to integrated regional development would be eliminated. Although the road ahead is filled with unpredictable twists and turns, the time has come to assess the promise of a postapartheid southern Africa and to offer an optimistic "what if" scenario.

An Overview of Regional Resources

More than 100 million people–a quarter of sub-Saharan
Africa's population–reside in the southern states of An-
gola, Botswana, Lesotho, Malawi, Mozambique, Namibia,
Tanzania, South Africa, Swaziland, Zambia, and Zimbabwe.
The World Bank's categorization of nations according to
per capita income supports the generalization that this is
sub-Saharan Africa's most economically productive region.
Six of the countries–South Africa, Zimbabwe, Swaziland,
Botswana, Angola, and Namibia–are among sub-Saharan
Africa's 15 strongest economies.

Moreover, unlike any other region of sub-Saharan Africa, the countries in the south are remarkably compatible
in their judicial, financial, and institutional infrastruc-
tures. With the exception of Portuguese-colonized Angola
and Mozambique (which are only gradually building closer
ties with the local commercial network), all have similar
tax structures, commercial codes, property laws, judicial
processes, accounting systems and business styles, as well
as a common language. Although a common currency does
not exist, in practical terms the freely convertible South
African rand serves a similar purpose in most of these
countries.

With several excellent deep-water ports, redeemable
rail systems capable of further integration, and major air
links with most of the European capitals, southern Africa
has the makings of a substantial integrated transportation
and telecommunications network. In South Africa and
Zimbabwe the region has the beginnings of a major money
center, because the continent's most sophisticated and active stock markets and financial institutions are in these
two countries. Most important, the region's mineral, oil,
and agricultural potential has barely been tapped. Approximately 60 percent of the world's gold reserves, 75 percent
of its rare earths, 75 percent of its manganese, 65 percent
of its phosphate, 55 percent of its cobalt, 90 percent of its

chromium, and 60 percent of its diamonds are located in Africa, the vast majority in southern Africa.

The case of Angola warrants special attention. Although virtually the sole source of its current income is the approximately 500,000 barrels per day of oil produced in the northern enclave of Cabinda and offshore wells, known reserves are at least 2 billion barrels. Moreover, exploration has yet to begin on the estimated 51 billion cubic meters of natural gas associated with the oil deposits. Before decades of anticolonial and subsequent civil war took their toll, Angola was the world's third largest producer of coffee and a net exporter of agricultural products. Other resources include diamond reserves conservatively estimated at 180 million carats, extensive timber areas, iron ore, coastal fishing areas, and hydroelectric power.

Mozambique presents significant opportunities as well. Only some 5 percent of the country's arable land is currently cultivated – land that in preindependence days produced a range of exportable cash crops including cashew nuts, sugarcane, cotton, tea, and sisal. Eventually, the Cahora Bassa dam (constructed by a consortium of South African, German, and French firms) can be the basis for what is planned to be Africa's top hydroelectric complex. Known mineral resources include coal, tantalite, ilmenite, iron ore, bauxite, graphite, diamonds, uranium, platinum, natural gas, and gold. The government has recently approved a $100 million mineral sands project with Johannesburg Consolidated Investment Company that could generate $44 million of annual revenue. Trans-Natal Coal Corporation of South Africa, the British multinational Lonrho, and the Brazilian state-controlled mining firm Companhia Vale do Rio Doce have signed a contract to develop a major coal deposit that could produce 7 million tons a year. Lonrho has also indicated interest in Mozambique's gold and platinum potential and Namibia's diamonds and gold.

Zimbabwe probably has more mines than any other

country on the continent except South Africa. Although mining represents only some 7 percent of Zimbabwe's GDP, it generates 43 percent of the country's foreign exchange. Current development of the $200 million Hartley Platinum Project (by the Australian company Delta Gold) will give Zimbabwe 3 percent of the world's annual production of platinum.

When Mozambique's railways and roads again become functional, the ports of Maputo, Beira, and Nacala, with a combined potential handling capacity of between 7 and 12 million tons per year, will play an important role as outlets to the sea for the landlocked neighboring states of Zimbabwe, Zambia, Malawi, Botswana, and Swaziland. In addition, because of its close proximity to the Johannesburg-Pretoria industrial complex, Maputo is an economically attractive alternative to South Africa's own port of Durban. On the west coast of the region, Angola's Luanda and Lobito are logical ports for the transshipment of goods to and from Zambia. Another outlet to the sea for Zambia is the Tazara railway linking the country to the port of Dar es Salaam in Tanzania. After years of problems, this Chinese-built railway is now regarded as a significant element in the regional transportation grid. Eleven countries and organizations have indicated their confidence in its future by undertaking to supply Tazara with $140 million for the refurbishment of engines, rolling stock, and other machinery.

Also noteworthy is the growing recognition by countries of the region that policy reform is as important as infrastructure when it comes to achieving economic growth. Within the past five years, Mozambique and Tanzania have scrapped the socialist models of the early postindependence period and opted for market economies. Angola is moving in that direction. Zimbabwe, despite a lingering allegiance to socialist rhetoric, is steadily giving greater freedom to the private sector. Subsidies are being removed, government regulations revoked, the civil service trimmed, price and labor controls lifted, and import restrictions relaxed. Virtually every government in the region has drafted a new investment code in an attempt to attract foreign capital. Indeed, some comparative studies indicate that Mozambique and Zambia may have two of the most liberal investment codes on the continent. With the exception of Zambia, the region is not unduly burdened with debt, nor does it have the drought, famine, and systemic refugee problems that characterize much of the rest of the continent.

The "Destabilization" Interlude

Although Portuguese colonial rule left Angola and Mozambique ill prepared for self-rule and the economic policies that both countries pursued after independence were not oriented toward growth, the major constraints on economic development throughout southern Africa have been political.

A sequence of regional developments beginning in the mid-1970s set off alarms in the halls of government in Pretoria. These included the establishment of Marxist-oriented regimes in Angola and Mozambique when these nations suddenly achieved independence following the collapse of the Caetano regime in Lisbon; the unexpected emergence of Robert Mugabe, a perceived Marxist, as the elected prime minister in newly independent Zimbabwe in 1980; and the formation that same year of the nine-nation Southern African Development Coordination Conference (SADCC), dedicated to four goals, of which the first was a reduction of external dependence, especially on South Africa.

South Africa's leaders became convinced that the survival of the Republic as they knew it required an aggressive military and economic "total strategy" to counter what they perceived as a Soviet-engineered "total onslaught" ultimately aimed at subverting the Republic. Pretoria's "total strategy" took the form of a systematic "destabilization" campaign against neighboring countries known or believed to be providing bases or other support for the outlawed African National Congress or Namibia's SWAPO. The United Nations has estimated that the cost to the region of South Africa's destabilization policy was $60 billion for the period 1980–1988. In Mozambique alone, attacks by South African-backed rebels on such key economic targets as power lines, mining facilities, and transport routes reduced the value of exported goods from $281 million in 1980 to $76.6 million in 1985.

Beginning with the Nkomati Accord signed with the government of Mozambique in March 1984 and moving through ups and downs to the 1988 Angola-Cuba-South Africa accords that set in motion Namibia's transition to independence, Pretoria's regional policy has largely shifted from destabilization (which became increasingly unaffordable in economic terms and less justifiable in relation to Soviet actions) to bridge-building.

Political Prospects in South Africa

Although there are deep divisions among both blacks and whites in South Africa and the negotiation process faces many potential blocks, a point has been reached where all parties have too much to lose by abandoning the joint search for a workable postapartheid system of government. How long the process will take is another matter. Black leaders are under pressure to show results sooner rather than later, while the white leadership must deal with a constituency that would prefer fundamental changes later rather than sooner.

Under the present constitution, which accords blacks no vote, parliamentary elections are due by 1994. Given President F.W. de Klerk's parliamentary majority, it may be possible to postpone that date, but not indefinitely. Although negotiations between the government and the African National Congress (ANC) are moving slowly and have not yet directly engaged the constitutional issue, there is a growing body of opinion–black and white–that South

Africa will have a new multiracial constitution and some form of genuinely representative government by 1995.

In all likelihood, the government that emerges from the process now under way will be a coalition including the ANC as the majority party but having significant white participation. Should that be the case, there would be some parallels to the SWAPO-led government of today's Namibia. A key implication of such a development would be that coalition governments tend to eschew radical policies in favor of compromise and pragmatism, an approach that, realistically, South Africa will have little choice but to follow.

The Postapartheid Economic Challenges

Professor Servaas van der Berg of the University of Stellenbosch has estimated that the cost of introducing parity between the races in health, education, housing, and pensions could cost a future government as much as $17 billion per year over the next decade in addition to normal expenditures. Once parity is achieved, van der Berg says that between 18.8 and 21.6 percent of the gross domestic product would have to be spent on education alone. As the present population of over 30 million grows at a rate of between 2 and 3 percent a year, the economic costs will mount accordingly. The nature of coalition governments, along with these somber realities, will dictate pragmatic economic and social policies.

Although South Africa is the continent's most highly developed country, the economy has structural imbalances that will be difficult to overcome. Mining still accounts for nearly 70 percent of exports (with gold constituting approximately 40 percent), but declining revenues over the past several years indicate that gold may have lost its glitter. As the *Financial Times* (London) noted in June 1990, South Africa has in the last decade gone from being the world's lowest-cost producer to the highest. Labor costs have risen and much deeper excavation is required to extract the metal as the richest deposits are mined out. The capital needed to meet these costs is increasingly difficult to obtain, given the depressed state of South Africa's economy and the country's inability to borrow abroad as a consequence of its debt moratorium.

Lower productivity in the overall economy has resulted in structural unemployment of blacks, officially reported to be 17 percent but unofficially said to be more than twice that figure and growing. Of even greater concern, more than half of the black population is illiterate (owing in part to the disruption of education in the troubled townships in the 1980s), resulting in a paradox: the country is simultaneously experiencing massive unemployment and a shortage of professional and technical workers.

Although the economic situation appears daunting, it is not hopeless. The principal obstacle to growth is not the country's structural problems but apartheid. The Investor Responsibility Research Center (Washington, D.C.) estimates that the overall impact of diminishing foreign reserves, disinvestment, and the country's considerable efforts to avoid sanctions have cost the economy between $15 and $27 billion. The abolition of apartheid will bring an end to trade and investment sanctions (which have cost South Africa an estimated $3.2 billion), give South Africa access to capital markets, open the possibility of debt restructuring, enable the bureaucracy to shed much duplicative activity associated with apartheid, and permit access to bilateral and multilateral assistance from abroad.

Of these projected benefits, perhaps the most important would be access to capital markets. An internationally and domestically acceptable representative government and a perception of political stability would largely stem capital flight, bring an end to sanctions, halt corporate disinvestment, and permit the country to roll over its maturing loans. The potential impact on the economy is significant. By some calculations, financial sanctions have cost South Africa more than $14 billion over the past five years.

In a recent advertisement in the *Financial Times*, Chris Stals, governor of the South African Reserve Bank, suggested that if a future South Africa were to consider dismantling its present system of financial controls, lift its debt moratorium, eliminate the dual financial system, and end its restrictive fiscal and monetary policy, the country might become eligible for balance-of-payments support from the International Monetary Fund. Such eligibility would enhance prospects of securing additional commercial lending. Although South Africa's per capita income makes the country technically ineligible for World Bank support, Stals suggested that the costly challenge any postapartheid government would face in reducing the vast economic disparity between blacks and whites might lead the bank to make an exception.

Another postapartheid priority would be reorganization of the budget to do more for less. Elimination of the expensive homeland bureaucracies and a further trimming of military spending would free funds for more critical domestic needs. Although allocations to the six self-governing homelands increased by nearly 30 percent to $2.28 billion last year, Finance Minister Barend du Plessis has warned that their 1991–1992 budgets will be severely trimmed.

In the process of reassessing priorities, any pragmatic future government would be forced to look more closely at privatization for a single compelling reason: privatization of selected public assets could net the government between $80 and $200 billion. Finally, if market share could be recaptured – and there are indications that this is already happening in the case of coal and some agricultural products – South Africa would receive a much-needed windfall through increased trade with the international community. The European Community has already lifted its ban on new investments and opened an investment promotions office in Johannesburg.

Should South Africa succeed in ironing out its serious internal distortions, the country would be reasonably well positioned financially to pursue rational economic and social policies while providing a sound foundation for sustainable, export-oriented growth. Regional expert Stephen R. Lewis makes this point succinctly:

> The lowest 40 percent of the population in South Africa receives less than 10 percent of total income. If the economy could return to the annual growth rate in excess of 5 percent that it achieved in the 1950s, the income of the poorest 40 percent could double after only two or three years of economic growth, without any decline in incomes in any other part of the population, if growth is carefully directed. ("After Apartheid," *Washington Post*, February 18, 1990.)

SADCC in Transition

Although SADCC was established in 1980 as a regional economic organization, its primary purpose was first and foremost the political isolation of South Africa. With the demise of apartheid, the political justification for SADCC's original objectives will fall away, and more rational trade patterns can and will emerge. Member-states will have more freedom to act in their own national interests regarding South Africa, basing economic decisions on economic rather than political considerations. As a result, South Africa, Swaziland, Botswana, Lesotho, Namibia, and perhaps Mozambique could develop into a closely knit economic zone. A similar relationship already exists or is evolving within the context of the Southern African Customs Union comprising South Africa, Botswana, Lesotho, Swaziland, and Namibia (whose members trade freely among themselves and share a common pool of customs receipts). The more likely prospect, however, is that SADCC will eventually evolve into a regional trading bloc or common market along the lines of the European Economic Community (EEC).

If the devastating internal wars in Angola and Mozambique can be resolved, the way will be cleared for the daunting task of developing the significant economic potential of these countries. In the postapartheid era, a large part of the goods and services required for the reconstruction of Mozambique and Angola will be procured in South Africa, thereby giving a boost to the Republic's construction and manufacturing industries.

Looking beyond the Region

Although foreign investment is critical to growth in southern Africa, development capital will be difficult to attract in the immediate future. Eventually, however, growing economic integration of the region could attract outside interest in three-way deals linking outside investors, South Africa (with its infrastructure and expertise), and the neighboring countries. Such agreements would be likely to emerge first in the mining sector. At present, however, only Zimbabwe among the SADCC nations with significant mineral resources (Botswana, Zambia, Angola, and Namibia) has the investment, skills, and technology to exploit these resources fully.

Constructive economic developments within the region would have a positive impact throughout the continent. Two major Nigerian voices have already been heard on this point. Following an August 1990 visit to South Africa that included meetings with President de Klerk and a wide range of other individuals and groups, former head of state General Olusegun Obasanjo said it was time to start thinking of opening ties with Pretoria. In a newspaper interview, Nigeria's current president, General Ibrahim Babangida, said that he supported Obasanjo 100 percent and saw nothing wrong with normalizing relations with South Africa "if eventually the stumbling block, which is apartheid," is removed.

Commercial links between the two largest economies

of sub-Saharan Africa would have enormous implications. Nigeria's more than 100 million citizens are perhaps Africa's most voracious consumers, and a ready market for the agricultural and manufactured goods produced by South Africa. On the other hand, South Africa lacks petroleum, which Nigeria produces in abundance. Although Angola also has oil resources and is much closer to South Africa, the price of doing business in Nigeria's attractive market would probably be a reciprocal trade agreement (i.e., a deal to buy Nigerian oil). South African investors could also benefit from Nigeria's efforts to attract foreign investors through its debt-conversion strategy. Another noteworthy historical footnote is that many of Nigeria's leading entrepreneurs have long argued that the most effective way of ensuring black empowerment in South Africa would be to invest in the homelands and South Africa's various industries.

One of the reasons for postindependence Africa's economic decline is that there has been no country or region with sufficient economic strength to serve as a catalyst. With the emergence of a southern Africa free of the shackles of war and apartheid, Africa would finally have at its disposal the engine for growth that it so desperately needs.

Index

Academic Support Program (ASP), 101–2

Afrikaans language, 7, 8, 11, 55, 127, 145

African National Congress, 9, 25–26, 36, 37; armed struggle issue, 32, 39–41, 68–69; Black Consciousness movement, 30, 31, 32, 42; civilian-military wing relations, 39–41; constitution, 44; democracy, transition to, 31, 109, 117, 147–48, 149, 153–54; economic policy, 25, 138, 182–83; education, 93–94, 100; Freedom Charter, 31; generational issue, 38; internal *vs.* external movements, 41–47, 48; leadership, 37–39; nationalization issue, 182–83; organization, 28–29, 33–37, 41–43; South African Communist Party relationship, 46–47, 159; South African Defense Force, position, 79, 80, 81, 82, 83; symbolic identity, 29–33; unbanning, effect of, 28–29, 36; *see also* Negotiations, transition

African population: economic participation, 8; liberals, position on, 9; urbanization of, 15; white population, acceptance of, 12

Afrikaner republics, establishment of, 7

Afrikaner Volksfront (AVF), 167, 168, 172

Afrikaners, 6, 8, 138, 146

Air force, 71–72

Alternative Admissions Research Program (AARP), 103–4

Anglican Church, 5

Anglo American Corporation, 96

Angola, 19–20, 35, 62, 64, 66, 67, 68, 79, 80; economy, 186–88, 195, 196

Apartheid, 7–8, 13, 17, 23, 27, 94–95, 97, 121–22

Armed struggle issue, 32, 39–41, 68–69

Armscor (Armaments Development and Production Corporation of South Africa), 63, 70–72, 73

Ashley, Michael, 104

Askaris, 91

ISBN 0-275-95086-7

90000>

EAN

9 780275 950866

HARDCOVER BAR CODE